TRIALS

The progress in treating the most common cancer in children, acute lymphoblastic leukemia, has been described as a medical miracle and the greatest success story in the history of cancer. Indeed, Nobel Prizes have been awarded for its treatment discoveries. The progress is due to healthcare professionals and scientists around the world, many of whom had to overcome the pessimism and objection of colleagues and administrators. Bradley not only captures this story magnificently, but he also relates how the children themselves and their families contributed to the progress.

—ARCHIE BLEYER, MD,
world-renowned pediatric oncologist

In his new book, Trials, *Larry Bradley takes readers into one of the most unlikely, and painful, coincidences imaginable. Because the common denominator is cancer, it is a coincident fraught with a painful one-two punch that no family should have to experience. Though personally involved, Bradley doesn't let that get in the way of his storytelling. Instead, he helps us understand the insidiousness of the disease and the courage of those who fight it from not only a personal perspective but through exhaustive research with experts. The result is a book that, above all, reminds us of the power of something more powerful than even a disease: hope.*

—BOB WELCH,
author of *Saving My Enemy*

TRIALS

Two Cousins, Cancer, and the Doctors
Who Fought to Save Their Lives

LARRY BRADLEY

LUMINARE PRESS
WWW.LUMINAREPRESS.COM

Luminare Press
442 Charnelton St.
Eugene, OR 97401
www.luminarepress.com

LCCN: 2020922547
ISBN: 978-1-64388-530-8

To Aaron, the bravest boy I've ever known

And to our Candlelighters Angels:
Alley, Brandon, Holly, Ian, Jasmine, Jazmyn, Jesse, Lilli,
Mary, Stevie, Tess, Travis & Yvonne

TABLE OF CONTENTS

Introduction 1

—————————— **PART ONE** ——————————

Chapter 1
There's Something Wrong With His Blood 9

Chapter 2
One Bucket at a Time 19

Chapter 3
That's How Science Is 32

Chapter 4
With Children, It's Never Their Time 40

Chapter 5
Tougher Hills Than This 51

Chapter 6
That Gift of Childhood 56

Chapter 7
The Best Stuff Out of the Chute 70

Chapter 8
A Third Partner 76

Chapter 9
He Didn't Have a Lot of Time 83

Chapter 10
One Who Falls Through the Cracks 97

Chapter 11
Two Things About Heather 107

Chapter 12
An Experimental Thing 113

Chapter 13
The Valley of Darkness 123

Chapter 14
The Bad Thing Happened 130

Chapter 15
A Real Boy 143

Chapter 16
When I Wear My Mask 151

Chapter 17
I Don't Want to Die 161

Chapter 18
The Thought of a Miracle 168

Chapter 19
What Do We Do If This Doesn't Work? 175

Chapter 20
He's With Me 183

PART TWO

Chapter 21
Too Much Alike 213

Chapter 22
Your Best-Case Scenario 218

Chapter 23
You Scrape Off a Little Bit of Your Soul 229

Chapter 24
Spinning Out of Control 239

Chapter 25
Houston, We Have a Problem 250

Chapter 26
All Must Die, and So They Do 256

Chapter 27
His First Mountain 262

Chapter 28
What Were You Thinking? 272

Chapter 29
Let's Find Some Sticks 276

Chapter 30
Are You Willing to Be a Guinea Pig? 285

Chapter 31
He Doubled Back 293

Chapter 32
It Makes Us Stronger. 302

Chapter 33
Lightening Their Load 307

Chapter 34
There's No Crying in Baseball 312

Chapter 35
What Do You Think? 316

Chapter 36
That Mixture of Horror and Sympathy 319

Epilogue 324
Acknowledgments 328
Bibliography 330
About the Author 339

Children who die young are some of our greatest teachers. We are allowed to die when we have taught what we came to teach and when we have learned what we came to learn.

—Elisabeth Kubler-Ross

INTRODUCTION

When people hear the name Barbara Bush, they likely think of her husband, President George H. W. Bush; her son, President George W. Bush; or her youngest child, Jeb Bush, former Florida governor and presidential candidate. Fewer people know that young "Georgie" and "Jebbie," as they were known during their childhood, had a middle sister, Robin, born in 1950. Robin was three years old in 1953 when Barbara noticed her daughter appeared anemic and lacked her normal energy. Barbara took Robin to see her pediatrician, Dr. Dorothy Wyvell, who ordered blood tests and shared the results with the future president and first lady.

"Dorothy was not one to pull any punches," Mrs. Bush wrote in her 1994 memoir. "She told us Robin had leukemia. Neither of us had heard of it. She talked to us a little about red and white blood cells and told us as gently as possible that there was no cure. Her advice was to tell no one, go home, forget that Robin was sick, make her as comfortable as we could, love her, and let her gently slip away. She said this would happen very quickly, in several weeks.

"In those days, many people thought it was catching and did not let their children get near Robin. Cancer in general was only whispered about, and some people just couldn't cope with a dying child."

The Bushes disregarded Dr. Wyvell's advice to go home and accept the inevitable. They sought treatment through George's uncle, a physician at Memorial Sloan-Kettering in New York. "Uncle John also thought Robin had little chance to live," wrote Barbara, "but he thought we should by all means treat her and try to extend her life, just in case of a breakthrough."

Robin received the best treatment available, but she also experienced many of the terrible side effects associated with the therapy. She went into remission on several occasions, but quickly relapsed each time. Robin died in October, 1953, six months after her initial diagnosis.

Until the early 1970s, the only difference among children diagnosed with leukemia was the number of days, rarely more than double digits, between the date of their diagnosis and the day they died. Leukemia was the leading cause of death for children ages five to fourteen and it accounted for more than half of childhood cancer deaths. Doctors largely avoided treating childhood "victims" of leukemia. It was considered a career killer. The depressing thought of treating hopeless children and dealing with distraught parents was more than most doctors could bear.

One notable exception was Dr. Sidney Farber, chief pathologist at Children's Hospital in Boston in the 1940s and 1950s. Dr. Farber, widely considered to be the father of modern chemotherapy, used a synthetic drug called aminopterin to induce remission among leukemia patients for the first time. The drug was later replaced by an equally effective, but less toxic agent, methotrexate, which is used extensively today.

Dr. Farber's work drew many critics. Memorial Sloan Kettering Hospital in New York was at times referred to as a "human lab" because Dr. Farber and his associates caused enormous suffering as they experimented with new drugs on their young patients. Dr. Farber rejected those assertions and insisted that before any chemical could be administered to a child, it had to be studied intensively in the laboratory for toxicity.

"Perhaps the benefits of the next medical advance will come in time to help *their* child," he said. "Every child's life must be prolonged as far as possible, no matter how hopeless the outlook, because any day or week or month from somewhere in the world there may come a new drug which may be specific for his type of cancer."

The most dramatic advancement in pursuing a cure for childhood leukemia occurred when institutions nationwide embraced for the first time a radical new process in which they coordinated their efforts in a series of clinical trials, administering a common set of treatment protocols and pooling their results into a central database.

No other disease had ever been studied in such a comprehensive and centralized manner, and it took a remarkable level of cooperation to make it work. It became the prototype for how to study a disease and its treatment and it became a central pillar in building the concept of chemotherapy treatment as we know it today.

Parents gave informed consent for their children to participate in the trials, but they did so under the most stressful of circumstances. The toxic new drugs carried dreadful side effects, but most parents felt they had no other choice. No effective treatments existed and their children were dying.

The extent to which individual children benefited from the trials depended to a great degree on where they landed chronologically in the timeline of the trials. Children who were diagnosed earlier benefited less from the improved treatment options that grew from their participation, but they played a crucial role in contributing to the growing pool of scientific knowledge. By 1961, doctors were able to extend children's lives by a year or more, but the mortality rate remained near 100 percent.

In 1963, cancer biologist Dr. Emil J. Freireich began caring for children in the leukemia ward at the National Cancer Institute. His first order of business was to address his patients' bleeding. "Leukemia prevents blood from clotting," he said. "Children bled to death. The leukemia ward looked like a slaughterhouse. Blood covered the pillowcases, the floor, the walls. . . it was horrific." Dr. Freireich hypothesized that giving patients platelet transfusions would help their blood clot. The medical community rejected his hypothesis outright, but when he tried the transfusions, the patients' bleeding stopped immediately. Problem solved.

Dr. Freireich's most important contribution came from his suggestion that patients be given multiple chemo drugs simultaneously instead of sequentially. Contemporary treatment protocols called for patients to be given a series of drugs, each of which would achieve a short-term remission before the patient relapsed. Doctors repeated the process until their drug options were depleted. Then the patient died.

Dr. Freireich began a series of trials whereby patients were given up to four drugs simultaneously. The medical community protested. "They said I was unethical and inhumane," Dr. Freireich said, "and I would kill the children. Instead, ninety percent of them went into remission immediately. It was magical."

By 1970, the cumulative gains from the clinical trials meant that ninety percent of children achieved at least an initial remission. Potent drugs were often coupled with massive doses of radiation. Children experienced severe side effects, but many lived surprisingly normal lives for short periods of time. They lived at home, went to school, and played with others. Still, a cure remained elusive. Most eventually died. Scientists had to deal with what world-renowned pediatric oncologist Dr. Archie Bleyer called the "Doughboy" principle. The Pillsbury Doughboy, also called "Poppin Fresh," was an animated mascot used by the company for many years to promote its line of products. "The idea behind the doughboy," said Dr. Bleyer, "was when you pushed in his tummy, because he was made of dough, it would pop out somewhere else on his body." Like Poppin Fresh, when doctors achieved long-term remissions in a child's bone marrow, the patients inevitably relapsed in the central nervous system (CNS) or elsewhere. "The doughboy idea became very important to us in the treatment of leukemia," said Dr. Bleyer.

In 1970, Dr. Don Pinkel, the first director of St. Jude Children's Research Hospital, came up with the concept of "Total Therapy," which called for applying the standard amounts of high-dose chemotherapy to the child, accompanied by radiation to the brain and the spinal cord. With the radical new approach, a miracle was in the making. In 1973, Dr. Pinkel announced that childhood leukemia was no longer necessarily an incurable disease.

"For the first time," said Dr. Bleyer, "he showed that some patients survived—about fifteen to twenty percent. That was miraculous. Until that happened with kids with leukemia, the idea of curing cancer in anybody was not known."

Our story begins in 1976, when my two-year-old nephew, Aaron Forman, received his leukemia diagnosis. Aaron's odds of survival stood at less than thirty percent. Whether or not he lived, he would join thousands of other young trial participants who contributed to finding a cure. But from his parents' perspective, Aaron was neither a statistic nor someone to be studied and analyzed. He was Aaron, their precious two-year-old boy.

PART ONE

Chapter 1

THERE'S SOMETHING WRONG WITH HIS BLOOD

"**A**aron's not going to die, Marty. You have bad information." My brother-in-law, Keith, was telling me about the day his two-year-old son, Aaron, was diagnosed with acute leukemia. Keith's good friend and fellow junior college professor, Marty, had done some quick research at the campus library before visiting Aaron and his parents, Judy and Keith, at Mary Bridge Children's Hospital in Tacoma, Washington.

"Marty would get a question in his mind and he would research it," Keith told me. "He was visibly shaken and crying when he came to the hospital. He said, 'This is what's going to happen, Keith. They will give Aaron this drug and it will put him in remission and then he will relapse. And then they'll give him this other drug and he will go into remission again. And then he will relapse. Eventually he will die.'"

The information Marty had gleaned from the library was outdated—library resource books become stale the moment they are published—but it was the most current information available. These were pre-internet days, when a gallon of gas set you back fifty-three cents and you could mail a first-class letter for eight cents. Twenty years would pass before it became common practice for people to "google" their own symptoms and show up at the doctor's office with a self-diagnosis. Marty's prediction that Aaron would experience a series of remissions and relapses from chemotherapy drugs was not necessarily true. Nor was it a foregone conclusion that Aaron would die from his leukemia. Doctors were beginning to administer multiple chemotherapy drugs simultaneously rather than sequentially, and achieving remarkable results. A cure remained elusive, but nearly half the children diagnosed with leukemia at the time were alive three years later. About a third survived five years.

Judy and Keith showed little interest in research data as they sat in their toddler's hospital room. The young parents were struggling to regain their footing after their son had slipped, first gradually and then abruptly, into a health crisis neither parent could have anticipated.

Aaron, always a vibrant little boy, was born two years earlier, on Father's Day. Judy, a prodigious writer, recorded his birth statistics—six pounds-five ounces, and nineteen and a half inches long—in both his baby book and in her personal journal, along with the most trivial details about his first two years. She noted the types of food he ate, the time and duration of each nap, the moment he crawled and walked, who visited him and for how long, and each word or phrase he learned on a daily basis.

As the little boy with blue eyes and chestnut-brown hair approached his second birthday, Judy noted how he could count from one to three and from four to ten, "but not all ten together." Aaron exhibited the growing independence of a twenty-one-month-old boy (he knew the word "no"), but he still depended on his mother's milk for nourishment and comfort.

In March, 1976, Judy's journal entries about Aaron's physical and mental development began to share space with comments about his general health. "Sick, listless, feverish. Learned a lot today. Can say his name. Sounds like 'Owen'. No appetite, very hot." The twenty-eight-year-old mother wasn't overly concerned. All kids catch a bug now and then—fevers in toddlers are rarely signs of serious disease. Aaron's symptoms came and went throughout the spring. Judy remained unconcerned until the last week of March, when his ailments escalated. He became fussy, his gums were swollen, and his fever elevated to 104.

Judy and Keith decided to seek advice from Dr. Norton, Aaron's pediatrician. They made the twenty-minute drive to Tacoma, where the physician examined Aaron and sent him home with a prescription for antibiotics. Judy and Keith gave Aaron a cool bath in the kitchen sink before bedtime, confident his symptoms would soon subside.

When Aaron's condition did not improve within a couple of days, they went to see Dr. Norton again. He told them to be patient, that Aaron would get well in time. "Doctor Norton kept telling us that Aaron had the flu," Keith said. "He said, 'It's going around. Everyone's getting it. Don't worry. In a few days his fever will break and that will be the end of it.'"

Keith questioned the doctor's diagnosis. "Aaron's eyes were swollen and he had thick saliva dripping from his mouth. He was also very pale. But his appetite was stronger than ever and kids with the flu don't like to eat. Aaron's sitting at the table chowing down his cereal."

Several days later, Aaron's aches and pains disappeared, taking with them Judy's and Keith's concerns. It must have been the flu after all. Judy returned to being the optimistic chronicler of her little boy's life: "Aaron had a super day today…Very talkative…Helped with watering, played in the dirt!" All was good again.

For two weeks.

When Aaron's symptoms returned, they did so with the ferocity of a wounded animal. His fever rocketed back up to 104, he didn't like to be handled, and his eyelids were swollen.

For the third time, the family visited Dr. Norton. And for the third time the doctor sent them home without a diagnosis. On Tuesday, May 4, Judy returned from her evening yoga class to find Aaron's fever approaching 105. She called Dr. Norton in desperation. He told Judy to take Aaron to the emergency room at Mary Bridge Children's Hospital.

The trip from their home in Gig Harbor, across the Tacoma-Narrows Bridge to Tacoma General Hospital, reminded Judy of their sprint to the same hospital two years earlier when she was in labor. By the time they arrived, Aaron's eyes were swollen, he had thick saliva dripping from his mouth again, and he was very pale. The emergency room doctor gave Aaron a thorough exam and ordered x-rays, but he failed to come up with a diagnosis. He gave Aaron something to reduce his fever and sent the family home, again.

By the following morning, no one in the family had slept much in three days. They visited Dr. Norton twice over the next two days, only to receive the same verdict: "Nothing visible." By Wednesday, May 5, Aaron's fever was back up to 103. His eyes had lost their sparkle and he cried constantly. Finally, Doctor Norton suggested they admit Aaron to the hospital for a day or two so they could take a closer look and at least give the fledgling parents some rest.

Visiting clowns from the Shriner's Circus, accompanied by a photographer from the local paper, roamed the hospital's hallways that afternoon, but failed to draw Judy's attention as she completed the hospital admitting procedures, a routine that would soon become an integral part of their lives.

The hospital staff transported Aaron to the third floor, where they took several blood draws and prepared him for spinal tap, a procedure where Dr. Norton would extract fluid from Aaron's spinal column and analyze it for clues. Spinal fluid continually bathes the brain and the spinal column and works independently from the body's circulatory system. It can be a valuable source of diagnostic information.

The procedure can be challenging with toddlers because of the need to physically immobilize them. Older children can be bribed, coerced, or otherwise convinced to sit still long enough to complete the brief, but invasive medical procedure. Infant children, surprisingly, tend to squirm less than toddlers. Toddlers embody perpetual motion.

Keith accompanied Aaron and Dr. Norton to the exam room for the spinal tap while Judy stayed behind. She didn't want to hear his crying anymore, and she couldn't watch him endure more pain. Aaron lay on an exam table in the middle of a sterile room. Keith helped the nurse position Aaron into a quasi-fetal position from the front, helping to increase the space between his son's third and fourth vertebrae, where Doctor Norton, after numbing the area, inserted a needle into Aaron's spine and watched the enlightening liquid drip into a vial.

Keith gave a subdued report to Judy when he returned. He saw no benefit in reliving the details. "It went okay," he said. "We had to hold him down tightly, but they got the sample." Keith handed his crying son over to Judy. The redness around Aaron's eyes unsettled Judy and her eyes began to tear, but she wouldn't let herself cry. She set her jaw. It was a trait that would serve her well. Her internal strength was the trump card that would get them through this.

Nurses monitored Aaron's vital signs and extracted blood samples from his tiny veins throughout the day, to the point where he began to cry whenever a nurse entered his room. He called out "Bye-bye" and "Good boy" to his parents as if he was being punished. His normally vibrant blue eyes conveyed fear and fatigue.

Judy felt helpless. She couldn't get Aaron to sleep all day and the nurses wouldn't let her nurse him because he was on a clear liquids order. Without the ability to nurse, Judy and Aaron lost the link through which they shared much more than physical nourishment. Judy's frustration mounted as the day wore on. She was just getting Aaron quieted down when another nurse came to get him for a cooling bath. Aaron didn't like it at all. When they returned from the bath, two more nurses came in to draw more blood and give him a transfusion.

The nurses sidestepped Judy's questions about the need for so much blood. That afternoon, the nurses noticed some purple marks where the tourniquet had been for his blood draw. "Does he bruise easily?" they asked. Judy was unaware that excessive bruising could be a sign of leukemia due to a low platelet count in the blood. The nurses searched the rest of Aaron's body for more bruising, found none, and remained mum about any suspicions they might have had.

Aaron regained some color and perked up a bit after they gave him a half-pint of blood. He was hungry, but he still remained under a clear liquids order.

Dr. Norton came by that evening with some frightening news from Aaron's blood test. All elements of his blood (white cells, red cells, platelets, hemoglobin) were way below normal. He asked Judy and Keith if they knew of anything toxic Aaron could have gotten into. Negative.

"He said he'd like to consult with Dr. Origenes, a child blood specialist, who would run some tests, such as a bone marrow test," Judy wrote. Dr. Norton didn't mention that Dr. Origenes, who was traveling home from Toronto the next day, was the only pediatric oncologist in the Tacoma area. Keith and Judy dealt with their anxieties as best they could. Keith went downstairs to eat while Judy stayed in the room and wrote in her journal. When Keith returned to Aaron's room, Judy left the hospital and drove home to call her mother in Eugene, Oregon.

Judy's mom, and my future mother-in-law, Jeanne Armstrong, recalled the conversation. "Judy called me and said, 'Mom, Aaron's in the hospital. I don't know what it is, but there's something wrong with his blood.' I immediately said to myself, 'It's leukemia.' I don't know why, but I just knew it was leukemia." As a junior college teacher of early childhood development for many years, Jeanne had studied a lot about childhood diseases and their symptoms. She bought a ticket for the next flight to Seattle.

Keith and Judy spent most of that evening watching television in Aaron's hospital room. Keith channel-hopped from "The Waltons" to "Little House on the Prairie" and from "Ironside" to "Kojak" while Judy recorded the day's events in her journal. It was nearly midnight when Keith left to pick up Jeanne at Seattle's Sea-Tac Airport and return home for the night.

Judy spent the night in Aaron's room. She hadn't had a decent night's sleep in more than a week and desperately needed a diagnosis for her little boy's illness. Yet, she sensed this was going to be a long road, and she recognized the need to take care of herself. After Keith arrived with Jeanne the next morning, Judy walked around the corner to the Hob Nob Café for breakfast. The local landmark featured walls covered with large black and white photos of Tacoma's past. More importantly, it offered large portions of comfort food. If the food was insufficient, an interior door linked the café to the Side Door Lounge.

After breakfast, Judy walked through Wright Park, an urban oasis located directly across G Street from the hospital. The wide expanse of grass, mature trees, and water fountains was bordered by a nearly one-mile walking-running trail. Judy's mind was in good shape the rest of the day. She fought off thoughts of the future and tried to stay in the present as much as possible.

Drs. Norton and Origenes arrived shortly after Judy returned to Aaron's room. The first thing most people noticed about Dr. Origenes was his height, or lack thereof. The fifty-one-year-old doctor stood five feet-four inches, the average height of a Filipino man, but he carried himself as though he were taller. His black hair yielded to a hint of gray at the temples and tapered into his high forehead. His thinly framed glasses gave him a professorial quality. The white lab coat camouflaged his taste for fashion. Beneath his medical attire, he wore tailored slacks, a monogrammed white shirt, expensive cuff links, and his trademark bowtie.

The blood specialist shared the lab results with Judy and Keith. Aaron's blood showed nearly 100% lymphocytes, immature white cells that inhibit the production of healthy blood cells and characterize leukemia. They had to consider the likely possibility that Aaron had the disease.

Dr. Origenes, accompanied by Keith, took Aaron to a sterile procedure room to conduct a bone marrow exam, usually the final arbiter in diagnosing acute lymphocytic leukemia in children.

A nurse helped Dr. Origenes maneuver Aaron's body on the exam table so that his hip area was exposed and facing the doctor. The nurse cradled Aaron into nearly the same fetal position used for the spinal tap. She held him gently but firmly so there was zero chance Aaron could move. Keith spoke to Aaron in a calm manner in an effort to keep his son quiet and motionless.

The doctor used a specially shaped "Jamshidi" needle to remove the marrow sample. The needle is longer and thicker than most and has a special T-shaped handle that provides a firm grip. The shaft, designed to penetrate the dense, outer shell of the bone, includes a removable core that once withdrawn, leaves a hollow tube through which bone marrow can be suctioned.

Dr. Origenes applied steady pressure and used a slight twisting motion until the sharp tip of the needle made contact with the outer surface of Aaron's hipbone. A bone's surface is like a pine board—generally firm, but penetrable. The bones of young children are softer than those of adults, since bones gradually harden with age.

Dr. Origenes rotated the needle back and forth, applying gentle pressure until the needle broke through to the marrow cavity. He then withdrew the central part of the syringe and extracted the samples. He created specimen slides and sent them to the lab for analysis.

The results came back in less than an hour. Doctor Origenes spoke candidly to Keith and Judy, much like Dr. Wyvell had done with Barbara and George Bush twenty-one years earlier. "Aaron has leukemia," he said.

"No, he doesn't!" Judy argued. Then, in typical Judy fashion, she quickly went from denial, to acceptance, to optimism. "We were all very shocked and upset," she wrote, "but no one broke down." By the end of the day, Judy was putting together a plan to handle the crisis.

Friday, May 7, 1976, became the Judy and Keith's Pearl Harbor Day, their day "which will live in infamy." It was their "day of diagnosis," as parents who have children with cancer often refer to it.

Up to that point in Aaron's life, Judy had used Aaron's daily journal primarily to record his physical growth and his cognitive milestones. After his leukemia diagnosis, her notations focused on medical appointments, pill schedules, blood counts, and physical side effects. She wrote in the margins, on both sides of the page, and she used supplemental sheets when necessary.

She used the small space allotted for Saturday, May 8, to announce Aaron's discharge from the hospital. Once they had a diagnosis, the doctors were able to quickly stabilize his situation and he was released to go home, but only until the following day. On Sunday, they returned for their first visit Dr. Origenes' outpatient clinic to begin Aaron's chemotherapy injections. It was Mother's Day.

Chapter 2

ONE BUCKET AT A TIME

Eight years earlier…

Adventure was on the mind of twenty-year-old Judy Armstrong as she boarded a bus from El Paso, Texas, to Mexico City. She and her friend, Cindy Ott, had taken a short break from their junior year at the University of Oregon to move to Mexico for three months. They legitimized their escapade by enrolling for the quarter at the University of the Americas in Mexico City, but their true intent was to watch their friends compete at the 1968 Summer Olympic Games.

The XIX Olympiad, held in October that year to avoid Mexico's rainy season, would be remembered as much for the protest of US sprinters Tommie Smith and John Carlos as it would be for the impact the 7,350-foot altitude had on the athletes who competed.

Judy knew several of the runners personally so she felt comfortable moving among the athletes. Since anyone dressed in athletic clothing was presumed to be an Olympian, Judy and Cindy donned their running attire and ventured into the Olympic Village. She searched out Margaret Bailes, who won the gold medal in the 4 x 100 meter relay. "I had run some meets with her at the Oregon Track Club,"

Judy said, "so I knew her and I wanted to see if I could talk to her."

The two imposters moved to the track and field practice area, where less knowledgeable fans approached them and asked them for their autographs. They accommodated their new followers by switching last names and signing Judy Ott and Cindy Armstrong.

The two friends then joined a group of athletes for a bus tour of the Mexican countryside, chatting along the way with some racewalkers from Australia and Great Britain.

That was Judy. Full of life. Adventurous. Spontaneous. Courageous. Above all, energetic. According to her mom, Judy was always that way. "As a young child," Jeanne said, "it was nearly impossible to get Judy to shut down. She never wanted to go to sleep. If she liked what she was doing, she wanted to do it some more. That's her personality. She's was always high strung. She was always healthy and very active."

Judy's was not aimless energy. She also knew when to focus. At age six, her mom could leave her home alone with instructions to do the laundry. "I would tell her how to separate the laundry," Jeanne said. "Here's the soap and here's how you use the machine. She could do it, and would do it. She was extremely responsible."

Judy Eileen Armstrong, the oldest of Ed and Jeanne's five children, was born on May 20, 1948 in Portland, Oregon. She grew up in a stable, middle class household. Her father graduated from Oregon State University with degrees in civil and constructional engineering and opened his own business after moving the family 100 miles south of Portland to Eugene-Springfield. Her mom initially deferred her higher education to raise the children, but later returned to college to earn a bachelor's degree in home economics from Oregon State and a master's degree in Early Childhood Education from the University of Oregon.

When I met and married Judy's younger sister, Mary Lou, in 1980, I often teased my new bride about having grown up in "The Adventures of Ozzie and Harriet," an ABC sitcom that exemplified the middle-class values of the 1950s and 1960s. Judy's parents weren't overly religious, but they provided a strong spiritual foundation for their children by attending the local Presbyterian Church regularly. Their milkman, John, let himself in through a side door, replaced the milk, eggs, and cheese in the refrigerator as necessary, and often took a break to play their piano. The family gathered around a traditional, but chaotic dinner table each evening as the children vied for airtime to discuss their respective days.

I made the Ozzie and Harriet reference in humor, but it was hard not to envy the conventional lives they led. Still, the family had occasional spats. Judy was a good big sister to her siblings, but she recalled that Mary Lou, eight years her junior, could be a bother. "She was this pesky little sister. I used to hate it because she was always snooping into my things. I wouldn't say we were super close when I was at home, probably because of the difference in our ages."

As a teenager at Thurston High School, Judy fell in love with running as a result of watching the boys' track team after school. She and her girlfriends were initially interested in the boys, not the running, but the boys' coach, Bill Dellinger, a six-time American record holder, a world-record holder, and a three-time Olympian, had other ideas. He approached the girls one day and struck up a conversation.

"You girls must be very interested in running," he said.

"Oh, yes, we just love running!" they answered sarcastically.

"We are going to start a girls' track team," he told them, "So if you are going to be out here, you need to be running around the track."

Judy and her friends formed the first Thurston High School girls' track team. After she graduated from Thurston in 1966, she attended nearby University of Oregon, where her passion for running continued to grow.

The women's track team at Oregon wasn't an official team per se, but they took their running seriously. They were a loose-knit group of college coeds who ran together for camaraderie and fitness. When they entered competitions, they bought their own t-shirts and running shorts.

One benefit from Judy's running at Oregon was that she got to meet many of the male runners at the university. One of her friends introduced her to Keith Forman, a young man who had previously competed for the Ducks, and who had recently returned to Oregon for graduate studies after coming home from Vietnam. The friend suggested that Judy and Keith might make a good couple. Their mutual passion for running formed a bond between Judy and Keith, but their backgrounds suggested they had few other things in common.

Like Judy, Keith was born in Portland, Oregon, but that's where their childhood experiences diverged. Keith came into the world on February 24, 1941, nine months prior to the Japanese attack on Pearl Harbor. His father, John, joined the US navy and went to war shortly thereafter. Consequently, Keith has no father-son memories prior to age four, when his dad returned from the war.

Keith, the youngest of three children, had health struggles as a child. In first grade, he contracted scarlet fever. His older sister, Gay, who suffered from the same illness at the same time, recalled how they endured 104-degree temperatures for more than a week.

"In those days, the doctor came to our house. He took swabs from our throat, diagnosed us, and gave my mother medicine to keep our fever down. Both of us were really, really sick." The siblings' high temperatures, combined with a lack of regular dental care, resulted in permanent damage to their teeth.

"I suspect my father was not enthused about my arrival in the world," Keith said. "I doubt I was planned. I don't have fond memories of our relationship while growing up. He was pretty gruff and short-tempered. He was always reluctant to spend time with me."

Keith's mother, Marjorie, counterbalanced his father's absence from Keith's life. Keith referred to an Abraham Lincoln quote in describing his mother's contribution to his life: "All that I am, or hope to be, I owe to my angel mother."

"She wasn't well educated, but she shared a lot of wisdom with me," Keith said. "She found a way for me to think I could be successful in running and get a college degree. I suspect my dad didn't think I was going to amount to anything when I was young, and she worked hard to make me believe otherwise."

Keith's father worked long hours for the US Post Office as a mail carrier and then moonlighted from May to October operating the Fly-O'-Plane carnival-ride at Oaks Amusement Park. John also traveled with the carnival to different regional fairs. Even when their dad did something nice for them, they suspected an ulterior motive. "A lot of times," Gay said, "he would put us on the Fly-O'-Plane and leave us on there for extended periods. We liked it, but I think it was sort of a come-on to get other kids to pay for the ride."

Keith's parents divorced when he was in seventh grade. "I was much more comfortable when he left the house," Keith said. "It caused some financial stress, but I preferred that to the tension surrounding his presence." Keith only began to draw attention from his dad when he showed athletic prowess as a multi-sport athlete at Portland's Cleveland High School.

"He never paid me any attention my whole life until I started winning sports accolades in high school," Keith remembered, "He still didn't pay attention to me, but he had this scrapbook where he kept track of all my accomplishments in football and track. When his friends came to his house, he would show them all this stuff and say, 'Look at my kid. He did this and he did that.'"

In 1959, legendary University of Oregon coach Bill Bowerman recruited Keith to run for the Oregon Ducks. In his book *Bowerman and the Men of Oregon*, author Kenny Moore wrote that though Bowerman convinced Keith to come to Oregon, "Bowerman didn't see much promise in him." According to Moore, Keith was one of only three runners that Bowerman referred to as "bumblebees."

"Engineers can prove," Moore quoted Bowerman as saying, "that a bumblebee, with its heavy body and little bitty wings, can't fly. But nobody tells the bumblebee. And they fly just fine. Keith Forman's rump was too big. He was not a classic miler, but he didn't know that and I never told him and he ended up running just fine." On May 26, 1962, Keith became the fifth American to run a sub four-minute mile. He also became a world-record holder as part of the University of Oregon's 4 x 1-mile relay team. Bumblebee, indeed.

When Keith graduated from Oregon in 1964, he faced the same dilemma as other young men during that era.

"Back in those days," Keith said, "you got drafted if you weren't in college. I believed that if you made the Olympic Team, a senator or somebody would pull strings, and they wouldn't draft you until after the Olympics were over."

Keith's attempt to make the 1964 Olympic team fell short when he failed to qualify at a meet in Rutgers, New Jersey. Before returning home, he visited the New York World's Fair in Queens, where he ran into a guy who had run for arch-rival Oregon State University. The guy told Keith he had joined the Marine Corps right out of college, and he now ran on their track team.

"He told me, 'You ought to go into the Marine Corps. It's the greatest thing in the world. You go through boot camp and officer training school and the whole time you're in, you're going to run. This is the greatest thing and they just love runners in the Marine Corps.'" Keith went home and immediately joined the Marines.

"When I signed up, I had very little understanding of what was going on in Vietnam and that I could possibly get swept up in that." Keith compared his boot camp experience to the daily-doubles he went through before the start of high school football season.

"The main criteria for flunking out was physical stuff, guys who fall out on runs who couldn't keep up. That wasn't an issue with me. They were on your ass all the time, but I knew I could run any of them into the ground so I wasn't worried. I was good at dealing with that kind of pain. I didn't feel threatened by a DI telling me to do pushups."

Keith's vision of running for the Marines dissipated only three months into his enlistment when America launched its deep involvement in the Vietnam War. He spent the final ten months of his three-year military commitment as the platoon leader of a radio-relay operation in Vietnam. He was headquartered in Da Nang, but his job required him to travel throughout the northern section of South Vietnam. The closest he came to seeing combat was about a mile away. Every night he watched the tracers from firefights near his location, but the next day he would drive by the same area and it was peaceful.

One day, the pilot of a cargo plane agreed to give Keith a ride to another location, provided Keith helped him unload his cargo. "It was an Air America flight," Keith recalled, "and Air America was CIA. "The pilot said it was fertilizer, but this was the last country in the world that needed fertilizer. It was just this granular stuff in burlap sacks, like fertilizer might be. And it was kind of greasy on your hands."

Keith forgot about the incident until years later, when he learned of the cancers and other diseases contracted by soldiers who had been exposed to Agent Orange. As he searched for a cause for Aaron's leukemia, he wondered if his potential exposure to the herbicide could have been the culprit.

When Keith was discharged from the Marines in 1968, he returned to the University of Oregon to earn a degree in counseling. He continued running on a personal level, but he no longer competed collegiately. It was then that a friend introduced him to Judy.

The friend's hunch turned out to be right. Judy and Keith courted for a short time and on August 23, 1969, they got married. After their wedding, Judy and Keith completed their collegiate studies and moved to Tacoma, Washington, where Keith accepted a job as a teacher and a counselor at Fort Steilacoom Community College (now known as Pierce College).

Judy and Keith had been married four years when they purchased their first home on the outer edge of Gig Harbor, a small village located on the Olympic Peninsula directly across Puget Sound from Tacoma, Washington. Gig Harbor combined rural living with easy urban access.

To the west, the Olympic Mountains, within the Olympic National Park, insulated Gig Harbor from the Pacific Ocean. The Olympic Mountains, the wettest location in the contiguous forty-eight states, offer a luring environment to visit, but a disincentive to settle. Fewer than fifty miles to the southeast, 14,411-foot Mt. Rainier lords over the entire region and completes the 360-degree post card.

To access the mainland from the peninsula, Judy and Keith drove across the Tacoma-Narrows bridge. The span opened with much fanfare on July 1, 1940, and collapsed with just as much notoriety four months later when a gust of wind sent it crashing into the depths of Puget Sound. In its short life, the bridge earned the moniker "Galloping Gertie" from the way it whipped and sawed during high winds. The fact that people were surprised at the bridge's collapse was a surprise in itself.

Leonard Coatsworth, Editor of the Tacoma *News Tribune*, and the last person to drive his car on the span, described his experience. "Around me I could hear concrete cracking. The car itself began to slide from side to side on the roadway…the bridge was breaking up and my only hope was to get back to shore. My breath was coming in gasps; my knees were raw and bleeding…Towards the last, I risked rising to my feet and running a few yards at a time…Safely back at the toll plaza, I saw the bridge in its final collapse and saw my car plunge into the Narrows."

The span had been promoted as being the third-longest suspension bridge in the world behind San Francisco's Golden Gate Bridge and New York's George Washington

Bridge—a status it maintained for all of the 130 days it survived. Engineers eventually discovered the flaws in their design and a new bridge finally opened in 1950. It now stretches one mile and is the longest suspension bridge in the world.

The Formans' two-bedroom, 1,200-square-foot house sat about 100 feet off the roadway on the edge of a forest. The couple lived simply, but they never felt like they suffered financially. Self-described children of the sixties, they made a lot of their furniture from whatever materials they could gather. Keith tied four-by-four posts together with rope to form a frame for their living room sofa. Judy sewed fabric covers for the foam rubber cushions. An old rocking chair, given to Judy by Grandma Armstrong, sat adjacent to the sofa. An antique sewing cabinet, their nicest piece of furniture and another gift from Grandma, occupied the far corner of the dining room.

A low-profile single bed, covered by a decorative blanket, provided another sitting surface in the living room. Built-in bookshelves divided the living and dining areas and provided a home for Aaron's toys.

Judy often moved the family's only radio into the kitchen, where she listened to Seattle SuperSonics basketball games. During the rare times the family listened to music, the creamy voice of Johnny Mathis echoed from their reel-to-reel tape deck. They owned one black and white television.

The environment was perfect for raising a family. In 1974, they brought Aaron into the world. Judy and Keith loved the outdoors and they took Aaron outside at every opportunity. Their back yard provided an ideal outlet for their little boy's high energy. Aaron played in the yard, helped in the garden, and especially loved riding down the hill on the back of Keith's bike to Cromwell Beach, where father and son splashed in the saltwater and played on the rocky beaches typical of the area. Afterward, Aaron and "Papa," as Keith preferred to be called, retraced their path back up the hill toward home. Their regular bike rides epitomized their joyful existence.

Judy stepped away from her role as a fulltime teacher when Aaron was born. They lived on Keith's salary from the community college, where he split his time between teaching psychology and providing guidance to new and returning students about course options and financial-aid opportunities.

Judy was Aaron's primary caregiver, but Keith always took an active part in parenting, especially at bath time. "Even if he was working out in the garden," Judy said, "he wanted to be sure to be a part of that. It was a big deal for him to do stuff with Aaron and to be with Aaron."

Judy and Keith were ahead of their times in many ways. "We recycled everything," Judy said. "We saved plastic bags and we didn't use paper towels because it wasn't environmentally responsible. They composted their garbage to support Keith's garden, where they grew much of their food.

"The garden was Keith's deal," Judy said. "It wasn't just about the food. He loved to be outside. He enjoyed his time alone and the garden provided that."

The family enjoyed fresh beans, peas, lettuce, carrots, and tomatoes throughout the summer and fall. They collected native huckleberries from nearby fields and enjoyed raspberries from a vine Judy transplanted out of her grandma's garden. She canned or froze any excess food for the winter. Judy made all of Aaron's food from their garden bounty. He never ate canned or bottled baby food.

Judy made many of Aaron's clothes. Judy also made most of her own clothing—long dresses she described as "Bohemian style." She sewed in the master bedroom, where an old wooden door, suspended between two short filing cabinets at the foot of the bed, served as her sewing table.

No one would have described Keith as the quintessential "Marine's Marine." Judy described him as quiet and introspective. "Being a college counselor and teaching psychology type stuff," she said. "He was always interested in that. When Mom and Keith got together, they would have these long, drawn-out philosophical conversations, and I would just sit there rolling my eyes."

Keith enjoyed his time alone. Shortly after they moved to Gig Harbor, Keith decided to dig a basement beneath the house, by hand, so he could get away and have his own space. "I started about ten feet away from the house," Keith said, "and dug a ramp down to the foundation. I chipped away and sawed until I got through."

Keith dug and dug, putting up supports along the way. "I did a lot of it, but occasionally a friend would come over and say, 'What's all this about you digging a basement?' I'd make them do one wheelbarrow or something. All these friends would contribute a little bit."

Keith's reasoning for doing it?

"Part of it was that I got injured running. I couldn't run and I didn't know what to do with myself. I thought of the Chinese building a wall and I had the attitude of 'one bucket at a time.' If you just have patience and do a little bit here and there, and don't try to kill yourself trying to do it all at once, it will all get done."

When their lives collapsed, much like Galloping Gertie, Aaron's cancer blew in without so much as a light breeze to indicate a storm was coming their way. The surface beneath them crumbled as they struggled to find solid ground. Getting back on their feet would prove to be a challenge for some time.

To defeat Aaron's cancer, Judy and Keith would need to marshal their respective resources. Judy would need to summon her boundless energy, her solid family support, her spiritual strength, and her endurance.

Keith's "one bucket at a time" would serve him well in this struggle. Each day, he picked up a figurative shovel and dug what he could. Family members and friends pitched in with whatever tools were available. They provided childcare, transportation, meals, and emotional support. Their support and Keith's "one bucket at a time" approach would be crucial if Aaron was going to survive.

Chapter 3

THAT'S HOW SCIENCE IS

After a month of twice-weekly visits to the clinic, Judy was eager to receive some good news. Dr. Origenes had told them from the start that if they could get Aaron's cancer into remission within thirty days, he stood a much better chance at long-term recovery. It was day twenty-seven.

Immediately after his diagnosis, Aaron had been enrolled in a national clinical trial. Neither Judy nor Keith remembered speaking to Dr. Origenes about Aaron's participation in the trials, but like most parents with kids in a medical crisis, they automatically signed all the papers placed in front of them without reading the details; much like today when we automatically agree to the terms and conditions of a new "app" we're downloading to our smartphone without reading them.

Aaron's assignment to one of the "arms" of the most current trial was random and blind. Judy and Keith had no voice in the process and they would receive no feedback on the results. Aaron would be given the latest, most effective combination of chemotherapy and cranial radiation, along with any incremental modifications tied to the arm of the study to which he was delegated. None of the groups were given a placebo.

Dr. Origenes had given Judy and Keith a photocopy of Aaron's multi-phase treatment protocol at the time of his diagnosis. Judy familiarized herself with the details, noted them on a three-by-five card, and monitored them closely. Her diligence would prove to be crucial as she advocated for Aaron.

The first phase, called Induction, included the injection of high doses of chemotherapy drugs into Aaron's body. It was designed to achieve an initial remission of his leukemia, after which Aaron would move on to subsequent phases of his treatment.

The list of potential side effects from the drugs were too dreadful to contemplate: nausea, vomiting, mouth ulcers, hair loss, cramps, diarrhea, fever, chills, shortness of breath, bleeding gums, bloody stool or urine, skin rashes, swelling, and more. Long-term side effects included loss of motor skills, heart disease, cognitive dysfunction, autoimmune diseases, rheumatoid arthritis and secondary cancers. It's no wonder that chemotherapy has been referred to as "poisoning on a volunteer basis."

After nearly a month, Judy knew her way around the pediatric oncology clinic like she had been coming there for years. She knew the pharmacists on a first-name basis, and she had become fluent in the languages of leukemia and chemotherapy.

The atmosphere in the reception area resembled that of any other pediatrician's office. Some children read books. Others chased each other round the room like they were in the back yard. Not all the children looked sick. Some, further into their treatment schedules and experiencing fewer side effects, were indistinguishable from their healthy siblings. If not for their varying degrees of baldness and their puffy faces, many of the children would have been difficult to identify as cancer patients.

Most of Aaron's wavy, light brown hair was gone. Judy marveled at how quickly it had fallen out after he began his treatments. The few surviving follicles had turned into a wispy fuzz. Think cotton candy, but without the pink color.

Clinic visits lasted from two to four hours and always began with a technician, who took Aaron's vitals and did a "finger stick" to get a blood sample. Aaron surrendered to the painful poke about half the time without a whimper. Pain is a constant with children's cancer treatments. As one nurse said, "The key is to let them know the pain is coming, assure them there is an end, and reward them afterward for their sacrifice." Aaron's ability to experience pain and rebound quickly with a smile would become a hallmark of his life. No matter the length or intensity of the procedure, he nearly always found a smile within a short time.

The technician placed the blood sample on a slide and sent it to the lab right away to have it analyzed. The resulting "counts," combined with Aaron's physical data, would tell the nurses how to mix his chemo dosage for that day.

A horse theme dominated the exam room where Aaron received his injections. From the ceiling, a poster of a pony looked down on the exam table in the middle of the room and presumably gave comfort to children who chose to keep their eyes open during the procedures. A shelf filled with three-ringed binders hung over a large wooden desk against the far wall. Each binder was identified by a unique three-digit number and contained information on the various clinical trials, including the dosage and frequency of each drug. Nurses updated the binders as the clinical trials progressed, as often as each quarter, or as infrequently as each year.

The nurses referred to the manuals only if there had been a recent change. They knew as much about the protocols as the doctor. Any adjustments to a patient's drug dosage were due to the child's experiencing adverse side effects or to a drop in their blood counts. For example, if a child's immune system dropped below tolerable levels due to a low white cell count, the doctor might hold off on giving a specific chemo drug that day in order to allow the patient's counts to recover sufficiently.

A long Formica countertop stretched along one wall of the procedure room and provided a work surface for nurses to mix the appropriate dosage of toxic chemo drugs for each patient after their blood counts came back. Exhaust hoods with HEPA filters, used today to filter out poisonous fumes from the chemicals, were not commonplace in the 1970s.

Doctors and nurses took special precautions when giving injections of vincristine, the most common and the most caustic drug given to children in the clinic. In addition to the systemic side effects, the drug created severe burns if it was spilled either on or under the skin. Doctors ensured a strong connection between the needle and the vein by alternately pushing and pulling the plunger and watching the child's blood go into and out of the syringe. One doctor referred to it as "watching the worm go in and out." Most doctors preferred accessing a vein in the child's hand because a failure to establish a good connection would be apparent more quickly. One oncologist gave injections in a child's foot for three years because that was where he found the most accessible vein.

Once a connection was established, they flushed the line with a saline solution and watched for bumps on the back of child's hand that might indicate a missed connection with the vein. It was best to discover a weak connection with saline rather than vincristine.

One mother told of an incident where an intern spilled vincristine on the back of her child's hand. "The whole back of his hand turned black," she said. "The skin rotted off. It was awful. It was very painful. This was a six-year-old kid. My kid! It was early on in his treatment and I said, 'Okay that's it. We're not doing that anymore. You can learn on somebody else, but you are not going to learn on my child.'" A pediatric oncologist from that era occasionally sees some of his old patients who survived to be adults. He can tell which ones had leaky vincristine connections because today they have cigarette-type burns on the back of their hands.

After each of his scheduled vincristine injections, Aaron underwent a spinal tap, the same procedure he had undergone when being diagnosed. The procedure was painful, but usually went quickly and without incident due to the expertise of the nurses at the clinic. They couldn't physically hold down each child for every procedure so they had to establish a high level of trust with children before giving multiple injections. Aaron had been forcefully restrained for his first spinal tap a month earlier, but a gentle combination of support from Judy and the nurse usually achieved the same objective at the clinic without having to use physical force.

When Dr. Origenes came into the room with Aaron's blood counts, Judy received the news she had hoped for. "We made it!" he exclaimed. Aaron's leukemia had gone into remission just three days shy of the deadline. Judy breathed easier, if only for a moment. Someone once said, "When you are drowning, even a gulp of fresh air goes a long way."

On the way out of the procedure room, Aaron always got to dig into "The Red Box," a large container which sat in the corner and overflowed with toys—a small comfort for what he endured. Children usually entered the room with fear in their hearts, but always left the room with a toy in their hands.

Judy was grateful that the initial doses of chemotherapy during the Induction phase had done their job. But she was fully aware that remission wasn't a clean bill of health. Aaron's system still harbored millions of leukemic cells and there were numerous "sanctuary sites" in his body for them to hide.

Judy could now focus her mental energy on the next phase of his treatment, "Consolidation." Aaron would be taking 6-MP (6-mercaptopurine) tablets every day, methotrexate pills weekly, Deltasone (steroid) pills seven days per month, and he would receive a monthly injection of vincristine. He would continue to visit the clinic every two weeks for blood tests and a physical exam; undergo a bone marrow exam every three months; and he would take antibiotics as necessary to prevent a variety of bacterial infections. Other drugs and procedures would be added, depending on whether or not he experienced any of the myriad side effects associated with the initial battery of chemical concoctions. Dr. Origenes would guide them along their journey.

Aaron and his family were fortunate to have Dr. Maurice Origenes as their oncologist. He had worked in the trenches in the 1950s, when much of the groundbreaking work was done to find effective treatments for acute lymphocytic leukemia. He had operated his own pediatric oncology clinic in Tacoma for nine years when he met the Forman family, and he had worked as an investigator for the Children's Cancer Study Group within the National Cancer Institute for twice that long. He knew all the protocols and stayed current on all the latest clinical trials.

His wife, Pat, who worked full-time as his office manager at the clinic, said Dr. Origenes loved working as a pediatrician, but he was foremost a researcher. He poured over scientific journals late into the night and he often brought a scientific journal to the dinner table. "He ate his dinner with a book by his side," she said. "When people left the table, it was 'open the journal!'"

Pat shared how her husband had suffered emotionally early in his career when he worked to develop new drugs to save young cancer patients. "He told me more than once that he hoped he was doing more good than harm. A lot of the time the doctors didn't know how the kids were going to react to the new drugs. It was often very, very painful.

"He told me many stories about becoming close to the patients and the families. Most of the children died. But the thing is, that's how science is. You try this and you refine it, and you take what you have learned from it and you advance it over time."

Dr. Origenes' used his height as an advantage in working with his young patients. "He was short," Pat said, "and since he was more their size, the kids weren't looking up at this giant of a person. He was very gentle with the kids," said Pat, "but if he had to do a bone marrow, he did it, no matter what. It's like there were two sides. 'I am this doctor who cares about you; I'm trying to do everything I can for you. In order to do that, I am going to have to do some things that you're not going to like. And I'm not going to hesitate to do those things.'

"He had to do things his way," she said. "He was very adamant about that. He worked with his families as closely as possible, but when push came to shove it had to be his way. I think it is so easy to be misunderstood when the anxiety level is so high."

Dr. Origenes' insistence that patients and parents always do things his way would eventually lead to difficulties in his relationship with Aaron's parents. But that would come many years later. When the Forman family first met Dr. Origenes, the consensus among patients, families, and the general community was that he was the doctor you wanted on your team.

In a newspaper article published two weeks prior to Aaron's diagnosis, Dr. Origenes referred to leukemia as the "Olympic event of childhood cancer," and noted that forty-five percent of his childhood cancer "victims" were leukemia patients. "Since it so common," he said, "it is also the disease we have made the most progress with."

The writer described Dr. Origenes' role in the ongoing clinical trials and the experimental nature of his work at the clinic. "Origenes carries on clinical research in which new investigative drugs are tested on cancer patients, with their parent's approval." The article focused primarily on the incremental gains achieved as a result of the trials, but didn't probe into the physical and emotional trials endured by patients, their families, and medical professionals during the clinical process.

During the interview, Doctor Origenes made one statement that, while seemingly inconsequential at the time, would turn out to be prophetic. "One special problem in dealing with childhood cancer," Dr. Origenes said, "is that a chronic illness is a big home breaker."

Chapter 4

WITH CHILDREN, IT'S NEVER THEIR TIME

N o horses decorated the walls of the radiation chamber. No children's books or red toy boxes. The windowless room was simple and serious. Six-foot-thick concrete walls protected the outside world from two massive cobalt radiation machines located on opposite sides of a centrally located treatment table. The technicians had already programmed the prescribed amount of radiation into the machines, based on precise directions from the radiotherapist. The techs set up the exposure field to cover Aaron's whole brain and then maneuvered a lead block in each cobalt machine in such a way as to block Aaron's eyes from being exposed. It was crucial to protect his eyes, especially the retinas, to prevent cataracts from forming.

A technician used a special carfusion dye to draw dark purple lines on each side of Aaron's face to target the area to be exposed. The lines provided a radiological roadmap that outlined his brain on both sides of his head. The marks began at the outer edge of Aaron's eyebrows, like the lines of a thick, purple eyebrow pencil, and continued their slight downward curve until they reached his temple. At that point, they turned at a right angle down to his cheekbones, and then made another ninety-degree turn toward the back of his head, halting at mid-ear. The permanence of the dye would allow the original drawings to be used daily for the duration of Aaron's radiation treatments.

Administering radiation to both the right and the left sides of Aaron's brain simultaneously assured he would receive fairly uniform doses throughout his brain. If they had treated from only one side, the radiation would have been more intense on the contact side and would have dropped off gradually as it worked its way through to the other side of his brain. It was crude by today's standards, but it was the system they had.

An anesthesiologist prepared Aaron by giving him an injection of ketamine, a general anesthesia. This was the step that Aaron, Judy, and Keith hated most. The drug ensured that Aaron would stay unconscious for the entire procedure, but the shot was very painful. By the fifth day, Aaron began crying as soon as he saw the anesthesiologist. "Papa! Papa!" he would cry. "Good boy! Good boy."

Aaron's reaction was consistent with research that shows toddlers undergoing medical treatments often view the procedures as punishment. Regardless of Aaron's physical pain and his parents' emotional trauma, Judy and Keith had limited options.

Physicians have expressed their surprise at learning of ketamine's use as a general anesthesia for children in the 1970s. Ketamine, developed in 1962, was first given to American soldiers as a wartime anesthesia in Vietnam. Today, it is used widely in veterinary medicine and as a battlefield sedative in developing nations. During the past several years, it has also been prescribed by some doctors to treat severe depression, although it can have chronic and debilitating side effects. As of this writing, the drug has not received approval by the Food and Drug Administration for that purpose.

Aaron began his radiation treatments on June 6, 1976, ten days shy of his second birthday. Aaron's protocol dictated that his radiation be spread over the sixteen consecutive daily sessions. Had he been a few years older, the use of general anesthesia might not have been necessary. "All patients weren't sedated," a radiotherapist told me. "We would probably treat any child who could lay still, say ages five or six upward, without sedation. You could treat little infants without sedation because you could put them on a little papoose board with a little bit of tape and they can't move. But toddlers, there is no way."

Aaron was sedated and transferred from a gurney, on his back, to the treatment table. The technician placed a soft sponge beneath Aaron's head. He checked Aaron's breathing, guided a tracheal tube down his windpipe to ensure continued airflow, and then stood by. They made final adjustments to the position of Aaron's head so the crosshairs from the cobalt machines aligned with the dark purple roadmaps.

The final step was to tape the toddler's head to the table. The tech quickly tore two three-foot sections from a roll of white tape, laid them out across the table above Aaron's head, and pressed the adhesive sides together. He placed the center of the tape over Aaron's forehead, stretched out the tape until it was taut, and attached the ends to the either side of the table. Aaron's head could not move during the radiation procedure. The anesthesiologist was the last one out of the room.

Aaron lay alone and unconscious, his head tied to a metal table, ready for the gamma rays to deluge his brain.

The giant yellow image of Big Bird on the front of his shirt underscored the insanity of the whole process. The red light above the door began flashing when the tech hit the go button. He set the exposure time to two minutes. The anesthesiologist watched the black and white video monitor from outside the room and made sure Aaron's chest was moving up and down. The buzzing sound from the radiation room indicated that the rays were doing their job. When the noise ceased and the door was unlatched, the anesthesiologist was always the first one through. It was nerve-wracking to leave a sedated two-year-old boy alone in a radiation room without any sort of breathing monitor. They removed the tape from Aaron's forehead, transferred him back to the gurney, and transported him directly to the fourth-floor recovery room. It would be several hours before he regained consciousness and rejoined his parents.

Even after Aaron reawakened, he remained listless and without an appetite for the rest of the day. He would recover by the next morning, in time to return to the radiology department and repeat the same procedure. The process took its toll on the whole family, and after a week of frustration, they were in search of other alternatives. Judy mentioned their troubles to her friend, Janet.

"I don't know why the anesthesiologist thinks the ketamine is better," Judy told her, "but he obviously prefers that over the gas." Janet mentioned that her neighbor was an anesthesiologist and she promised to talk to him. The next day, as the family walked into the radiation department, a different anesthesiologist approached them. He introduced himself as Dr. Klaus Siebold, but he insisted that Judy and Keith call him "Klaus."

"My neighbor, Janet, whom I believe you know, has discussed your situation with me and I believe I may be able to help you." The doctor spoke with a pronounced German accent. He wore blue scrubs, as if he had just come from surgery. His matching surgical cap covered most of his dark brown hair and made him look taller than his 5'11" height. Dr. Klaus Seibold was known as a bit of a maverick by his peers. His anesthesia methods sometimes put him at odds with the prevailing practices in Tacoma. The forty-one-year-old doctor had strong views on the use of ketamine, which got him off to a good start with Judy and Keith.

"I knew that ketamine was an accepted method of sedation," Dr. Siebold told me years later, "but I never liked it. Not in children, except for very exceptional indications. It involved a painful injection. I always felt strongly to cause as little pain in children as possible. Also, ketamine has unpleasant side effects—mainly really unpleasant nightmares. It is a psycho-active drug, closely related to PCP."

There was also the issue of keeping the child deeply sedated for so long. "If you have a child who comes in every day for three weeks, and you give him a long-acting sedative every time, then the child is sleepy all day. He doesn't eat, he will lose weight, and it is not healthy.

"The only instances when I used it were with severely mentally impaired children who were unmanageable," he said. "We would sneak up from behind, give the injection and then wait ten minutes. There was no other way of doing it. You couldn't do it from the front because they would fight."

Instead of ketamine, Dr. Siebold used either halothane or nitrous oxide with a vaporizer to put the child to sleep— much like a dentist would do. To gain his young patients' cooperation, he attempted to bond with them and, when possible, he used sleight of hand tricks. He often came to an appointment with a surgical glove, occasionally painted, and blew it up in front of the young child. He gave the inflated glove to the parent to divert the child's attention and free up both his hands.

Once the child was distracted, Dr. Siebold worked his way behind the child and gently reached around to place his cupped hand just under the child's chin. With his other hand, still from behind, he held a gas-emitting mask over the top of the child's forehead. The gas fumes, being heavier than air, floated invisibly down over the child's face and were redirected by the doctor's cupped hand into the child's nose and mouth. Mission accomplished.

Some of Dr. Siebold's colleagues considered his use of gas to be unsafe. They preferred the use of Ketamine primarily because a deeply sedated patient was less likely to move during the radiation process. This was particularly important with toddlers. His critics felt strongly that Dr. Siebold's approach of using lighter sedation increased the odds that the child would awaken and move during the radiation session.

It was standard operating procedure to intubate a patient with a tracheal tube during major procedures. This ensured that the patient's airway remained clear. Dr. Seibold did not generally intubate his pediatric patients when using his preferred procedure. Some of his associates considered it unacceptable to leave a sedated child alone in a room for two minutes without sufficient intubation or breathing monitors.

Klaus acknowledged the logic behind his detractors' criticisms. "That is the crucial part," he told me, "and that is where the controversy came in. For the radiation, you have to leave them alone. I would have to put the child asleep and I would have to make sure, number one, that the child stays asleep and doesn't move during the treatment, which is only one or two minutes. The child had to be absolutely still. Number two, that the child is breathing, and that it was safe to leave the child for those two minutes when nobody could be in the room with the child. In those days, we didn't even have monitors (on the patient's body). No portable monitors, no wireless monitors. We could not even monitor the heartbeat. It was felt at the time that if you put somebody to sleep with Ketamine, it was preferable to gas, ether, or nitrous oxide. Some people felt that you had to put a tube down the windpipe to make sure the airway is open. It was standard procedure during surgery.

"But if you do this repeatedly to a child, you can get some swelling of the windpipe and you can get something very serious, like croup. And you can get serious impairment of the air passages. I elected not to intubate the child. I had to make sure the child was asleep and didn't move. Also, I would turn the child on his stomach and watch them for a minute or two to make sure he's breathing.

"When everybody was ready, we would dash out of the room, do the treatment, and after two minutes, I would be the first to dash in, make sure the child is breathing, and give him some oxygen to wake him up."

One of the biggest advantages to this approach was that Aaron no longer had to spend hours in the recovery room after the procedure. "I don't think we ever had to take him to the recovery room," Dr. Siebold remembered. "Because the recovery was so short, the standards were not as strict. The normal rules were that everyone had to go to the recovery room. My objective was, 'Is the child safe to go home?'"

Aaron's attitude toward his radiation treatments changed overnight. After all, he was asleep during the radiation, and he had no deep awareness of its underlying purpose or what the radiation might be doing to his body. To Aaron, it was about the sedation and how they administered it. Klaus took over Aaron's anesthesia responsibilities and from that day forward, on seeing Klaus come through the door, Aaron reached out with open arms and said," Gas! Gas!"

"You know," Dr. Siebold said, "when you have to hurt a child for three weeks, every day, it's hard on you, too. Even with the mask, if the child doesn't want it, it haunts you." That haunting feeling was universal among radiotherapists and technicians who administered the radiation treatments. "I was happy when my practice quit treating children," one therapist told me. "It was the one group that I felt bad for. Occasionally, I would wake up in the middle of the night and wonder if I was doing everything right. Not only was it the children, but it was their families. If you treat somebody who is seventy years old with lung cancer, even though the family may miss them and there is a lot of emotion, you sort of say, 'Good ole Joe has lived a good life. Plus, we told him years ago to quit smoking ten packs of cigarettes a day.' People are more likely to say, 'Okay, it was their time.' With children, it is never their time."

When Aaron was being treated for his leukemia, nearly all of the protocols called for cranial radiation. Sound reasoning underpinned the decision to add cranial radiation to the clinical trials in the early to mid-1970s. Six years before Aaron was diagnosed, ninety percent of childhood leukemia patients achieved initial remission. But in spite of the lengthy remissions, resistant leukemic cells often migrated to the central nervous system (CNS), found sanctuary in the meninges (the lining of the brain), and eventually caused a relapse in the bone marrow. The anti-leukemia drugs could not pass through the blood-brain barrier except in concentrations too low to be effective.

One of the pioneers who suggested using radiation to address the high rate of relapse was Dr. Don Pinkel, the first director of St. Jude Children's Hospital. He and other researchers were discouraged that, despite all of the success in achieving lengthy remissions, nearly 85 percent of the children still died. If a child relapsed in the short term, the cancer most likely reappeared in the bone marrow. However, the longer a child stayed in remission, the more likely the remission would be in the central nervous system.

Doctors tried injecting methotrexate into the patients' spinal fluid, but sufficient quantities in high enough concentrations failed to reach the brain. Physicians became convinced they needed to give sufficient radiation to the brain itself to supplement the methotrexate injections in the spinal fluid.

"They didn't want to use large amounts of radiation on a growing child's brain," said Dr. Archie Bleyer, "so they started small—and they had no response at all. They bumped it up until they finally hit the right dose. The relapse rate dropped from about fifty percent to about ten percent. The problem was that they began to associate it with learning problems and growth problems, to younger children in particular."

One Tacoma radiotherapist reflected back on the damage done to some of the children he treated under the clinical trials during the 1970s. "I can think of one child we treated. I saw the little kid six months later and we ruined his brain. You know, you just kind of think, my God. He would basically be a ward of his parents his whole life. He was such a smart little kid and you kind of feel like a failure when that happens. Even though you go, 'By God, we didn't realize.'"

As Pat Origenes said, "That's how science is."

Doctors continued to focus on the task at hand, finding a cure for leukemia. When they designed the radiation protocols specifically, and the clinical trials in general, they were certainly concerned about each child's life, but they brought a global perspective to their work. They could not accurately predict the potential long-term effects of irradiating children's brains, but they didn't let their lack of knowledge keep them from moving forward. For every question they answered, another one surfaced. The primary question posed by parents like Keith and Judy was, "Can you save my child?"

⎯⎯⎯

JUDY AND KEITH HAD NO WAY OF KNOWING AT THE TIME that the radiation being flooded over Aaron's brain would ultimately be discovered to do more harm than good. In the book *The Cure of Childhood Leukemia*, Dr. Don Pinkel from St. Jude reflected on hurting children in the name of moving scientific knowledge forward in search of a cure. "These sorts of things tear you up inside. . . Yet I'd rather face these problems and make progress for the children than not move ahead. We are constantly learning, and that can make it better for the next patient, possibly even a matter of life and death. It was a great satisfaction to find…that the powerful radiation treatments were indeed bringing about more cures."

In the end, the doctors and the parents answered many of the questions in much the same way: "We're doing the best that we can."

Chapter 5

TOUGHER HILLS THAN THIS

"It was a beautiful day for running," according to the Sunday Tacoma *News-Tribune*. Nearly 1,800 competitors gathered at the old Point Defiance Boathouse for the fourth annual "Sound to Narrows" race. The runners included a seventy-two-year-old man from Zurich; a five-year-old boy, running the race for his second consecutive year; a middle-aged fellow who ran in slippers; a group of chanting GIs in combat boots; a college freshman who ran the course facing backwards; a Congressional Medal of Honor winner; and a young mother who had just learned that her two-year-old son's cancer was in remission.

Judy pinned her racing number to the front of her pink shirt. She had worn her favorite color so Keith and Aaron could pick her out of the crowd. She tied her long, blonde hair into a ponytail; then she stretched her calves and her quads one more time. She handed her sweatpants to Keith, who put them in the diaper bag.

"Wish me luck," she said. "Aaron, I'll look for you at the finish line." She kissed her son on the cheek, gave a final hug to Keith, and headed toward the boathouse for the beginning of the race. Keith and Aaron waved to her until she disappeared into the crowd.

Returning to normal for Judy meant getting back into her running routine. Running was more than exercise for the twenty-eight-year-old mother. It gave her piece of mind. It was her equilibrium.

Judy was regarded as one of the elite female runners in the greater Tacoma area. She usually ran toward the head of the pack. The *News-Tribune* had celebrated her victory three years earlier when she finished the inaugural race nearly five minutes ahead of the second-place female runner. Keith and Judy had also placed first in the couples division that year. The size of her photo on the sports page equaled that of Secretariat, who won the Triple Crown the same day.

Ironically, Keith sometimes took a back seat to Judy's local celebrity status as a runner. Three years earlier, after Judy's photo had been splashed all over the sports page, Keith introduced himself to a local physician, who asked Keith if he was related to the famous runner Judy Forman. Despite being the only world-record holder in the family, he took it good-naturedly, as Keith would do.

Judy's competitive nature normally drove her performance, but on this day, she also ran to escape the doctors' offices and the medical procedures, and to get away from a singular focus on Aaron's cancer—for an hour at least. Judy was intensely focused on Aaron's troubles, but she would never become consumed by them. She somehow intuited early on that she needed to maintain her own mental health if she was going to be able to take care of Aaron. She realized she couldn't spend one hundred percent of her time taking care of a sick child. Running gave her time to clear her head and keep things in perspective.

A guy with an air horn described the course to the runners just prior to starting the race: "There's a hill," he said. "Then there's another hill, and some more uphill and then it finishes going up a hill!" Judy was well aware of the obstacles along the tree-shaded, 7.6-mile course. The first one, "The Monster," was a long, steep incline that earned its name because it demoralized and devoured any runners who weren't prepared—and some that were. Judy's stamina waned as she ascended the slope. She had been unable to maintain her regular training schedule since Aaron's diagnosis. In better times, she would have outlasted many of the people who bypassed her this year.

The next climb was never too far away as she ran through Point Defiance Park. Each hill required Judy to dig a little deeper and to come up with a new source of motivation. All athletes have sources of strength they draw upon when facing obstacles. Inspirational techniques are crucial in a competitive race. Thoughts of her 1973 victory gave her strength. Each hill brought a new challenge. Judy took them on one at a time, and converted each to a personal victory.

Judy reached the tip of the peninsula, where openings in the trees offered beautiful views of Puget Sound and the Narrows Bridge. She allowed herself only a brief glance across the Sound toward Gig Harbor. She was about half-way home.

The "Nisqually Backstretch," a level section that ran along the bottom of the peninsula, gave Judy a chance to gather her remaining strength. The most challenging part of the course awaited, ahead and around the corner. She passed old Fort Nisqually without noticing it. The sun hit her in the face when she exited the park. She followed Mildred Street around the bend and prepared to run downhill into "The Dip," or as one writer named it, the "Hellish Vassault Canyon."

The nearly vertical drop lasted for one tenth of a mile before rising just as abruptly. Judy's knees ached as she reached the bottom and began climbing. Sweat flowed down her forehead and into her eyes. She let them burn as she drove her arms to stay in stride. She escaped the "The Dip" with a burst of energy, and when she turned left at North 51st Street, she knew she had only a mile and a half to go. It wouldn't be easy. Two blocks later she turned right, and there it was. Vassault Hill.

The straight one-mile climb awaited, eager to devour its weakened prey. The flashing yellow light at the top of the hill taunted Judy and the other runners. Judy knew only one way to the top and to the finish line. She lowered her head and kept churning her arms and legs until she reached the crest of the hill. She rounded the final corner and sprinted the final 100 yards to the finish. Keith and Aaron waved to her as she crossed the line in fifty-eight minutes—four and a half minutes slower than her 1973 time, but she felt like a champion. She picked up one of the cold orange drinks and walked over to where Keith and Aaron stood side by side. They were easy to find, since they had followed Dr. Origenes' orders to stay away from the crowd. Aaron had just achieved remission two days prior and his immune system was still compromised from the ongoing chemo treatments.

"We made it, Aaron," she said.

It was her first competition since Aaron's diagnosis. In future years, Aaron's struggle became a source of inspiration and an integral part of her toughness when Judy entered road races. She would often talk to Aaron during a race. "Come on, Aaron," she would say. "We've climbed tougher hills than this. We can do this together."

How many hills had Aaron conquered already? He had learned to take the constant finger sticks with minimal tears; he had suffered through multiple bone marrow exams and spinal taps while his parents held him down; he repeatedly summoned the courage to hold out his hand so the nurses could begin yet another IV; and at the end of each procedure he always found a smile.

Aaron's race had just begun, and steeper hills would always lie in wait. Once conquered, they would lead to yet steeper challenges. Aaron had gained remission, but he faced new drug concoctions and he had yet to finish his radiation regimen. His life's race would turn out to be an ultra-marathon, much longer than the 7.6-mile Sound to Narrows course. But the same approach would see them through. They would lower their heads keep churning their arms and legs until they conquered the final hill.

Chapter 6

THAT GIFT OF CHILDHOOD

The family did their best to return to their normal lives. Keith rejoined the carpool to the community college with Marty and his other colleagues. Ironically, his job called for him to counsel people who had significant family issues that drew them away from their educational and career pursuits.

Judy maintained her role as Aaron's primary caregiver and plugged back into her active social network. She reconnected with her associates at the YMCA, where she taught a fitness class; she restored contact with friends in her babysitting co-op; and she resumed her schedule with the "Bridge Girls," several close friends who provided a social life and became her primary support group.

Each of the four members of the "Bridge Girls"—Judy, Nancy, Billie, and Phyllis—had spouses who worked at the college with Keith. They rotated among each other's homes every two weeks, first during the day, and then in the evenings after their kids started to get older. It seemed like at least one of them had a child each year until they eventually had nine children among them. They called them the "Bridge Kids."

Nancy, who lived with her husband (and Keith's friend) Marty just up the street from the Judy and Keith, recalled her shock when she learned of Aaron's leukemia. "I remember feeling panicked because I had a one-year-old. It was an overwhelming sorrow. I hadn't heard of anyone who had leukemia. It was this word that you heard and it was always bad. I was twenty-five years old and I didn't know what it all meant. It was just so scary."

Judy and Aaron made regular visits to the clinic for his scheduled chemo treatments and bone marrow exams. She faithfully logged his daily and weekly pill consumption. Between his medical procedures, Aaron played in the park, ran around the house, and behaved much like any other two-year-old. Their lives had changed, but the family couldn't stop living; they had to keep moving forward.

A simple bike ride to the beach no longer held the same attraction for Aaron after he lost his strength. "We started to do it after he got sick," Keith said, "but he wasn't feeling well enough to really enjoy it. He no longer wanted to go." Disappointed, but resilient, Keith found other ways to stay engaged with Aaron and remain a positive force by his son's side.

Some dads find it nearly impossible to adjust to cancer's intrusion. The mother of another boy diagnosed with leukemia at the same time shared her experience when her husband learned of his son's cancer. "I have a wonderful picture of my son just before he got sick," she said. "He was such a carefree kid. Someone took a picture of him on a swing with his shirttail untucked, old shoes with strings hanging, hair flying all over the place, this enormous grin on his face. It was one of my favorite pictures of him. My husband made me put it away." The father struggled coming to terms with his new world. "He just had a hard time dealing with it," she said. "He just didn't want to be reminded of what our son had been like prior because he totally changed. I don't think he went out and played again the way he used to. It was just too hard."

We all react differently when our dreams are shattered. The father's reaction is understandable, at least initially. Reason is often washed away by the ebb and flow of emotional waves. The story of his son's life had not unfolded as he anticipated and being helpless to turn back the page, he chose to close the book. Perhaps his reaction sent an unspoken message to his son that he would never be the same in his father's eyes, that he was somehow damaged goods—a fate that may have been worse than the cancer itself.

Judy and Keith struggled to understand how their son had been struck with such a horrible disease. Judy had experienced an uneventful pregnancy. Aaron ate organic foods and lived in a healthy environment. Neither parent smoked, drank excessively, or had an extensive history of cancer in their families.

Many parents, lacking an obvious villain, blame themselves for their child's illness without any reason to do so. Their most important responsibility is to watch over the safety of their child. When their child receives a cancer diagnosis, they assume they must have done something to put their child in jeopardy. It is more common among mothers than it is fathers, according to pediatric oncologists.

"All mothers have guilt," a physician told me. "It must have been something they did during their pregnancy or it was something else they did. One of the things I tell parents is that we have looked at this. We have computers so we can categorize all these kids. We take them from around the country and we try to see what things they have in common. We've looked at the father's occupation, your exposures, what you did during pregnancy, what medications you took, and we have never found anything. We know that lung cancer is related to cigarettes and we know that breast cancer is related to genetics.

"I know that you are looking for what you did wrong. It's just not true. We have never found anything that the mothers did wrong that caused their child's cancer. I am convinced that even years later the maternal guilt will still be there. It's a mom thing. I think that dads don't have nearly the problem with that that the mothers do, but everything that happens to a kid is mom's fault."

Keith harbored his own suspicions about the cause of Aaron's leukemia. He remembered a large dirt pile left in front of their house after utility workers sprayed weed killer along the road. Aaron played in the soil while Keith dug up the dirt for use in the back yard. A sepia-toned photo from the time shows Aaron sitting in a hole, surrounded by the potential hazard. Could incidental exposure to contaminated soil have been the cause of his leukemia? What about Keith's Air America experience in Viet Nam? Did Keith suffer cellular damage from Agent Orange and then pass along his vulnerability to his son?

Answers to such questions rarely reveal themselves and further frustrate an already maddening predicament. Judy and Keith eventually did what most parents do in their situation. They focused their energy on helping Aaron get better.

Many things had changed in the Formans' lives since Aaron's diagnosis, though on the surface much of it appeared the same. They returned home from the hospital to find their house as they had left it. Their furniture was still in place. Pictures and mirrors hung as before. Judy's sewing table awaited her next project. Toys, clothing, food, towels, and books—all in place, but with their relevance diminished.

Judy modified Aaron's baby book to reflect his new world. She used a blue ballpoint pen to change the heading of a page previously entitled "Contagious and Infectious Diseases," presumably designed to record Aaron's first fever, a head cold, or, God forbid, something more sinister like the measles. She crossed out the heading and wrote "Hospital Stays."

Aaron's cancer never affected Judy's commitment to being the best mother she could be. Prior to his illness, she cut out an article written by a Harvard professor, who stated that the brightest, happiest, most charming children spent their earliest years with their mother. The mother is "the single most important factor," he wrote, and "she has a greater influence over a child's experiences than anyone else." She kept it in Aaron's baby book for quick reference.

Aaron acted much like any other tempestuous two-year-old, laughing one minute and crying the next. Judy couldn't always tell whether his mood swings were caused by the onset of the "terrible twos" or by the high doses of corticosteroid pills he ingested. Alternately known as Deltasone, prednisone, or just "steroids," they played a key role in his initial treatment. Aaron experienced all their common side effects: facial swelling, ravenous hunger, and hyperactivity.

His immune system recovered to the point where he could attend birthday parties and play with other children—if Judy could keep him away from the food. A photo from one of his first outings shows Aaron, still wearing his ID wristband from his most recent hospital visit, surveying a coffee table filled with hors d'oeuvres. He is stuffing a chunk of cheese into his swollen cheeks with his left hand as he readies the next bite with his right. The edge of the coffee table fits neatly just below his waistline and supports his extended belly. Aaron continues to eat while the other children in the photo play in the background.

Aaron's growing vocabulary took on a medical dimension, as did his playtime routines. Dr. Siebold gave his young patient a surgical hat and mask, and Aaron wore them around the house in his new make-believe role as a doctor, giving injections to his parents and his playmates from his new toy medical kit.

Judy, Keith, and Aaron celebrated Aaron's final radiation treatment on July 1, three days prior to America commemorating its bicentennial anniversary. Both American political parties conducted their presidential nominating conventions that summer, building toward a Jimmy Carter-Gerald Ford showdown in November. The family purchased a new color television that summer so they could better enjoy the Montreal Summer Olympic Games. During the track and field events, Keith extended a baseball bat in the living room while Aaron hurdled it, pretending to be world record holder, Edwin Moses.

Judy attended her ten-year high school reunion in August. Two weeks later, she left Aaron at home with Keith and escaped to San Francisco with her mother and two younger sisters, Mary Lou and Lisa. Judy's relationship with Mary Lou, now twenty years old, was developing into more of an adult friendship. They shared a love of running—Mary Lou had followed in Judy's footsteps as a runner for the University of Oregon women's track team—and their San Francisco trip allowed them to jog together through San Francisco's Golden Gate Park. As they ran, Judy updated Mary Lou on the traumatic effects of Aaron's illness on her family. After the sisters returned, Mary Lou told her mother, Jeanne, "I could never go through what Judy is going through." Her mom's prophetic response was, "You could if you had to."

During a clinic visit in early September, a nurse mentioned to Dr. Origenes that Aaron's walk seemed a bit funny. Judy added that Aaron had seemed tired and didn't have much of an appetite. When Dr. Origenes asked Aaron to walk down the hall, the toddler fell to the floor. The doctor checked the results of Aaron's latest bone marrow exam, examined his treatment history, and discovered that Aaron had failed to begin a steady dose of Deltasone as scheduled nearly two months earlier. The experience undermined Judy's faith in Dr. Origenes and she discovered the importance of being an advocate for Aaron at all times. On several occasions in the future, Judy again discovered errors in the way Aaron's treatments were being administered. Each time, she brought it to the doctor's attention and vowed to be even more diligent in her efforts to protect her son.

By late September, the family's lives had returned to near normal. Aaron had regained most of his strength. His parents began tracking his improved "potty" behaviors rather than focusing solely on his drug intake. Judy and Keith resumed their running routines, one of their primary stress relievers and one of the few things within their control. They continued to see Aaron's fight as a long race—one that could be tackled one stride at a time. Feeling confident that things were going in the right direction, they went ahead with plans to have another child.

Judy became pregnant immediately and by late year, they were receiving good news on all fronts. The physical side effects of Aaron's chemo treatments continued to loosen their grip on him. His puffy face deflated to its normal size and his hair grew back, a darker shade of brown and a little less curly. Cancer patients often experience changes to the color, coarseness, or waviness of their hair when it returns from exile. Aaron's fight wasn't over by a long shot—his chemotherapy would continue for another four years—but it consisted mostly of taking his dose of daily and weekly pills, at home in the kitchen. The visits to the clinic for bone marrow exams and vincristine injections continued, but they were reduced from twice a week to once a month.

On May 26, 1977, three weeks shy of Aaron's third birthday, his sister, Heather, came into the world. The arrival of a healthy baby brought an infusion of positive energy. Judy inaugurated a new baby book and began a separate journal to document Heather's developments. It had been just twelve months since Aaron's cancer diagnosis and the change in emotions since the prior year could not have been more striking. The previous May, Aaron's diagnosis had produced shock, anxiety, and fear. Twelve months later, the miracle of new life created an atmosphere of wonder, gratitude, and amazement.

It's hard to say in the long run which sibling would have a greater impact on the other's life. Heather loved her brother and would ultimately welcome an opportunity to save his life. Aaron's love for his sister, though heartfelt, was often concealed by his resentment. As they grew older, Heather would become the primary target of Aaron's spiteful behavior, making her wonder at times why she loved him as much as she did.

Judy and Keith introduced Heather to running almost immediately, just as they had done with Aaron. Their daughter had barely been home for two weeks when they took her to her first Sound to Narrows race—only this time it was Keith's turn to run while Judy watched the children. She put Aaron in a stroller, loaded Heather in a front pack, and boarded the shuttle bus to Point Defiance.

The day of the race marked the first anniversary of Aaron's initial remission and Keith celebrated the occasion with one of his best efforts. The local paper reflected back on Keith's running pedigree as it described his performance that day: "Keith Forman, who now has grey in his beard but still has steel in his legs, won the 30-39 age division—fifteen years after he ran a 3:58.3 mile for the University of Oregon."

These were good days for the Forman family. The healthy arrival of Heather and Aaron's ongoing recovery from his leukemia allowed the family once again to begin thinking of the future.

Another development in Aaron's world, less personal but nearly as impactful, occurred just twenty-four hours prior to Heather's birth, when George Lucas's space adventure *Star Wars* appeared in theatres for the first time. The movie arrived at the perfect time for Aaron to incorporate the movie's main characters as members of his cancer-fighting team. Han Solo and Luke Skywalker fought side-by-side with Aaron for years as he tried to defeat the "dark side" of his leukemia. Judy bought *Star Wars* sheets and pillow cases for Aaron's bed, he had *Star Wars* PJs, and he regularly wore *Star Wars* clothing. Pretend battles against Darth Vader and his dark forces dominated Aaron's make-believe world. As Aaron got older and gained a better understanding of the real battle he faced, he began to replace the dark forces of leukemia as substitutes for the evil antagonists in the movie. He incorporated this strategy into his make-believe battles, and he used the *Millennium Falcon's* victories as inspiration for his colorful artwork when his drawing talents emerged.

Aaron entered the Berry Patch pre-school on schedule in the fall of 1978 at age four. The worst of his leukemia symptoms and treatments appeared to be behind him. The Berry Patch, a pre-kindergarten school located inside an old, remodeled horse barn, gave Aaron an opportunity to interact with twenty other children his age three times per week. Marion Ekberg, Aaron's teacher and the co-owner of the school, remembered Aaron as "this chirpy, happy little guy. I knew he was coming in as a leukemia child, and I remember being stunned the first time I saw him because he was just as normal as normal could be. If you didn't know he was sick, you wouldn't have picked him out in a crowd. He fit in with everybody else."

Judy remained mindful of the more subtle effects of the drugs still coursing through his veins. His regular chemo still caused nausea. She suspected some of the drugs and the cranial radiation Aaron had received a year earlier may have affected his motor skills and his cognitive development. She took steps to optimize Aaron's chances for success.

"My strongest memory," said Marion, "was not only her courage, but her insistence that he have the most normal childhood that we could possibly provide for him. She wanted him to have that gift of childhood, that experience every other child has in pre-school. We were to treat him exactly how we treated everyone else, with the exception of course that when the other kids got sick, he wouldn't come to school because he couldn't be exposed to all those germs." Most children stayed home when *they* were sick. Aaron stayed home when anyone was sick.

Marion established a special bond with Judy, who impressed the teacher as much as Aaron did. "I was stunned at how brave she was and how she handled everything. She was a good friend as well. She not only was a great parent, but she was easy to like and to get to know."

Aaron generally held his own with the other kids. Keith witnessed his son's stamina during an evening event for fathers and their children. "Those boys were like hellions. They would just come charging by and then go climb a tree. I winced every time a group of them came by. I was like, someone is going to get killed here. Aaron was right in the middle of it."

Neither Keith nor Judy should have been surprised at Aaron's ability to run with the pack. Keith was a world-class athlete who had run US Marines into the ground during basic training. Judy's running accomplishments commanded respect in their own right. Neither parent had any intention of pushing Aaron to be a runner, but Keith acknowledged a time when he gave it just a moment's thought.

"We were at a run at Point Defiance and they had a little running thing for kids. I don't know how far it was, but there was a hill. Aaron was running up the hill with a friend and he said to the other kid, 'You have to put your head down and keep going.' Aaron did very well, and I thought maybe he's got some genes." Aaron's cancer and treatment regimen preempted any potential running career before he got out of the starting blocks, but it's clear he learned how to persevere at a very early age.

Aaron enjoyed success at the Berry Patch. Before long, he was approaching the end of his chemotherapy treatments and the time to begin kindergarten. Marion requested a meeting with Judy and Keith. She had become concerned after teachers noticed some behavioral and learning issues with Aaron. She knew the parents carried a heavy load, and she wasn't sure how to begin the conversation.

She asked Judy if any of Aaron's chemotherapy drugs could have affected his learning capacity or his behavior. He had a great imagination, but he often stayed in that imaginary world. He didn't respond as expected to games, songs, or stories. He would much rather play.

Marion also explained that Aaron had become a little pushy one day, resulting in a "timeout." During the quiet time, his teachers noticed he just looked out the window. He didn't verbalize much. Aaron was scheduled to enter kindergarten in the fall and Marion wondered if they had considered holding him back for a year. She was concerned that kindergarten would stifle Aaron's imagination. Maybe it would be better to just let him play—enjoy him as he is. "Frankly," she told Judy and Keith, "we are having a hard time getting him to pick up his toys, or complete a task."

Judy and Keith had noticed the same behaviors at home. Marion had sent home a *Star Wars* game and Aaron wouldn't play by the rules. Judy asked him to move his game piece and he didn't understand. Instead, he ran to get a paper and pencil so he could draw what was happening in the game. Drawing would become a strong area of interest for Aaron throughout his life. He initially used his artistic skills as a basic means of expression, but he eventually developed his talents and used them to create superheroes on the page who would assist him in his fight against cancer.

Judy and Keith talked briefly about holding Aaron back for a year, but in spite of his parents' and teachers' concerns, Aaron enrolled in Mrs. Wilbert's kindergarten in fall of 1980. He was six years old.

I met Aaron at about this time, when I became engaged to Judy's sister, Mary Lou. I didn't know much about Aaron and his family at first, since Mary Lou and I lived five hours south of Gig Harbor, in Eugene, Oregon. Prior to our wedding in November of that year, I spent very little time with the Forman family, and I relied primarily on Mary Lou for information about Judy and her family.

Mary Lou informed me that her six-year-old nephew, Aaron, would be one of the two ring-bearers in our wedding. She also mentioned in passing that Aaron had had leukemia as a small child. I knew leukemia to be a serious illness, but I didn't equate it with cancer. I had no idea he had just completed his treatments the previous year.

Aaron showed no signs of illness. He had been in remission since he began treatment nearly four years earlier. I empathized with the family for their having gone through a bad experience, but since the mystery disease was no longer a threat, I didn't give it much further thought. Looking back, it's clear that Aaron's illness remained on the minds of Judy, Keith, and anyone else who shared the horrible experience, but as the newcomer to the family, my response to learning of his past illness was minimal. Chemotherapy and radiation never made it into the conversation. As far as I knew his leukemia days were ancient history.

On Thanksgiving weekend in 1980, Mary Lou and I got married. Our wedding and the surrounding activities provided my first opportunity to spend significant time with Judy and her family. Judy served as Mary Lou's matron of honor; Heather, now three, was our flower girl; and Aaron shared responsibilities with my three-year-old nephew, Brad, as one of two ringbearers.

During the ceremony, Aaron looked and played the perfect part. But anyone who knew both families and who looked closely at the ringbearers might have noticed that Aaron stood only two inches taller than my nephew, Brad, who was three and a half years his junior. Children grow at different rates, of course, and it is only with the benefit of hindsight that we could see early indications of the long-term physical effects of Aaron's treatments.

Our wedding celebration materialized into a joyous weekend. Aaron's leukemia was behind him and it appeared the Formans' lives had returned to normal. However, cracks in a foundation are not always visible on the surface. While spending the better part of four years focusing nearly all their energy on taking care of their sick boy, Judy and Keith had left little time and energy to feed their relationship. As Mary Lou and I began our lives together, Judy and Keith were contemplating whether their marriage would survive.

Chapter 7

THE BEST STUFF OUT OF THE CHUTE

March 11, 1981, began like any other Wednesday. Judy dropped three-year-old Heather at a friend's birthday party and took Aaron, now six-and-a-half, to see Dr. Origenes for his quarterly checkup. No more chemo injections or bone marrow exams, thank you very much; just a scheduled follow-up visit routinely prescribed for all children who completed leukemia treatment to ensure they remained in remission, and to report their status to the Children's Cancer Study Group as part of their ongoing clinical trials. Though Aaron's family had celebrated the end of his chemo treatments a little more than a year earlier, researchers continued to track the progress of Aaron and other children to gather long-term data on side effects and potentially guide them regarding changes in future treatment protocols.

Aaron skipped Mrs. Wilbert's kindergarten class that day to see Dr. Origenes. He loved kindergarten and he especially loved Mrs. Wilbert. His teacher personified the schoolmarms from the early twentieth century—prim and proper, strict and structured. She had begun her teaching career in Tacoma, but was recruited to Gig Harbor to design their new kindergarten program. She resisted at first, but made the change after one of her Tacoma students squeezed her pet hamster to death.

Judy's journal entry that evening omitted the parts of Aaron's exam that checked out normally. "When the doctor came to the testicle check, he noticed right away the hard swelling in the right one. Said it appeared to be fluid, but with Aaron's history, had to consider it a tumor until proven otherwise." Doctor Origenes referred Aaron to Mary Bridge for an immediate biopsy. On the way to the car, in a rare role reversal, Judy became tearful and told Aaron she was scared for him. She told him it was okay for him to cry, but he didn't.

Keith met them at the hospital, where they went through the familiar admission procedures. They made arrangements for a friend to pick up Heather from the birthday party and stay at a friend's house until matters quieted. Aaron checked into his hospital room, where he lay quietly on the bed until the anesthesiologist came in to introduce himself. It had been several years since Aaron had received anesthesia, but he needed no introduction to the gas mask.

The medical attendants rolled Aaron into the operating room while Judy and Keith found a place to wait. Finally, their names were called and they met the doctor at the operating room door. "Dr. Origenes gave us the bad news. They found leukemia."

The parents granted the doctor's request to remove Aaron's right testicle. "We both walked away in shock—both crying," wrote Judy. "Spent the next hour pretty much in shock—some crying, some talking, a lot of silence. Finally got the message he was in recovery room. The spinal fluid looked clear. Bone marrow exam was borderline. Not a complete relapse, but not perfect either."

Aaron insisted on attending his kindergarten class the day following his surgery. He refused to miss "class picture day." Judy's mom, Jeanne, ever-present during a crisis, recalled Aaron's resilience. "It was really cute because his crotch was hurting like hell. He had an ice pack on it all the time, but he wanted to go kindergarten. These kids went outside and he hobbled out there with them. He did whatever he could do and he stayed through the whole session. I was just cringing on his behalf." Aaron was merely heeding his own advice: "You have to put your head down and keep going."

Aaron stood in the back row for the class photo that day, dressed in a crewneck, long-sleeved gray sweater with a long chain necklace. His characteristic broad smile gave no hint of the physical pain he felt as he posed for the photo. His thick, brown locks belied the many times he had lost and re-grown his hair.

Aaron's relapse presented several alternatives, none of them good. At a minimum, he faced another multi-year chemotherapy regimen, beginning with the same Induction phase he had experienced as a two-year-old. Dr. Origenes contacted the Children's Cancer Study Group at St. Jude Hospital to learn the latest protocols for childhood cancer patients who had experienced a relapse in the central nervous system (CNS) after completing their initial four-year treatment protocol.

At the time, doctors considered Aaron's relapse to be "only" a testicular relapse, thought to be less severe than having a full-blown relapse in the bone marrow. Consequently, the doctors considered giving Aaron a lighter treatment than he might otherwise receive.

"We thought it was easier to treat," said Dr. Archie Bleyer. We didn't know too much about it at the time, but we've since learned there is a real testes barrier, too—just like the blood brain barrier." Scientists at the time knew of the existence of a blood-brain barrier, an impenetrable wall between the blood stream and the central nervous system, that prevented medications from passing from one to the other. As a result, leukemic cells sought refuge in the CNS after being eliminated from the bloodstream. Doctors knew less about the existence of a similar barrier between the testes and the bloodstream that allowed leukemic cells to seek refuge in the testes.

"It's not quite as strong a barrier, but it's real," said Dr. Bleyer. "We would radiate the testes, get rid of the cancer, and put it back into remission. Within weeks or months, the leukemia would come back in the blood, in the marrow. It got there either because the leukemic cells in the testes went back to the bone marrow, or when we irradiated or removed the testes, it was already back to the bone marrow. It could move from one place to another. That's what leukemia does. It can go back out the barrier and if you ignore the rest of the body, inevitably it would come back. It was the doughboy problem."

Today, a testicular relapse is considered to be as serious as a relapse in the bone marrow and is treated accordingly. Doctors are much more likely to recommend a transplant immediately after the first relapse for patients like Aaron. Patients who relapsed had already received the best treatment available and it made no sense in most cases to defer a transplant. Once again, Aaron's timing was off by just a few years.

The fact that Aaron had already completed his first treatment episode was cause for optimism. Patients who relapsed while still receiving chemo drugs during their initial treatment experienced lower odds of long-term survival.

Doctor Origenes briefly discussed the possibility of a bone marrow transplant, but transplants remained in experimental stages during the early to mid-seventies. Doctors at Seattle's Fred Hutchinson Cancer Center, commonly known as "The Hutch," generally preferred to exhaust all chemotherapy options before putting a child through a transplant. However, children like Aaron, who had relapsed one or more times, faced declining odds of survival. Even had they gone ahead with the transplant at the time, Aaron's odds of survival with a transplant were less than thirty percent.

Aaron's doctors ultimately advised against a bone marrow transplant in favor of an enhanced chemotherapy protocol similar to the one he endured as a two-year-old, minus the radiation treatments. Clinical trials were beginning to show significant loss of cognitive function for children who had received radiation as part of their treatment. They had given the best-known treatment to Aaron when he was initially diagnosed as a two-year-old, but that had been nearly five years earlier. Ongoing trials had led to incremental changes in the frequency and intensity of drug doses and significantly reduced the use of radiation.

Had Aaron been diagnosed ten years later, doctors would most likely have suggested an immediate bone marrow transplant. Dr. Larry Fickenscher, a Eugene pediatric oncologist for more than three decades, explained: "We gave you the best stuff out of the chute. We didn't save any 'good stuff' for later. If you don't do well the first time, you better go to the transplant because you're just going to beat your marrow up and beat yourself up. You're going to get a bunch of resistant cell strains that won't help anybody."

Dr. Archie Bleyer agreed, noting that it was fruitless to do a transplant after a child had experienced multiple relapses. "In those days, if we waited that long—five or six relapses—they all died. Even if we got them back into remission temporarily, they didn't live. That was a universal outcome. Because they transplanted patients at different times—some after the first relapse, some the second relapse, some the third, fourth, or fifth—they could look back and see who survived. It was almost always the ones after their first or second remission that survived.

"It was not only a health decision," said Dr. Bleyer. "It was a business decision. We stopped doing the ones that didn't work. The Hutch said, 'We're just wasting resources and hurting our own results.' Not only is it not going to work for that family; it's not going to work for the Hutch. You get bad results. You're in competition with other centers. The Hutch received the Nobel Prize for their work with transplants, but you're still in competition."

Drs. Fickenscher and Bleyer spoke with the benefit of hindsight, an advantage unavailable to Aaron's doctors. The knowledge came too late to benefit Aaron.

Hearing your child has relapsed with cancer carries with it the same range of emotions—hurt, denial, fear, anger—as the initial diagnosis. Aaron and his family had survived four years of pills and injections; toxic chemo drugs with their painful side effects; the mental torment; and the marital stress, only to be told they had to start all over again.

Chapter 8

A THIRD PARTNER

A child's cancer diagnosis puts an enormous stress on the strongest of marriages, and it will break the back of a weak one. Parents often go through what amounts to a grieving process, where they watch their hopes and dreams for their child's future diminish or die. Moments normally reserved for intimacy between spouses disappear. Most times, one parent gives up a job, creating financial stress at a time when enormous medical bills are mounting. In some cases, couples manage to pull together and work as a team. Others fight individually against a common threat and manage to keep their relationship together. In many instances the marriage doesn't survive.

Research studies are inconclusive in determining whether or not parents of children with cancer or other serious illnesses experience a higher rate of divorce. The pediatric oncologists I interviewed acknowledged the lack of firm data, but they said there was significant anecdotal evidence to indicate a child's health could be a determining factor in the success of their parents' marriage.

"It is not that unusual," one pediatric oncologist told me, "for a kid going through chemotherapy and have the parents split up because it puts so much stress on them. If they're not on good terms when they start, just imagine the amount of stress they go through. And then you get this blame thing. 'Well, if you would have done this, or if you wouldn't have done that.' I had a young lady with leukemia who had just finished up therapy and as soon as she finished up, the parents split up. I don't know what it was like before, but you kind of see what happens as they go through the stress and it gets to them.

"You have people who are remarried who are fine and you have people who are married and who by the end of it are not fine. I've had families come in who are very dysfunctional and the kids end up being cared for by grandparents. The parents were having troubles before, and this is something they can't handle so they leave. But I don't think it is any different for kids with leukemia than it is for kids with cystic fibrosis, or Down syndrome or any of the chronic illnesses."

Broken families are not necessarily a precursor to dysfunction. "I also have a youngster now who had leukemia," the doctor continued. "She has two separate sets of parents—both parents are remarried. One time she comes in with one, and the next time she comes in with the other. They can sit in a room and have talks together and that works very well."

We've all heard of parents who stayed together "for the sake of the kids," only to break up after the kids have grown. If you were ever going to stay together for the kids, wouldn't you do it when your child has a potentially fatal disease? From that perspective, one might argue that having a child with cancer should be a factor in keeping the marriage together.

Neither Judy nor Keith pointed to Aaron's leukemia as a primary reason for the failure of their marriage. "At the most," Keith said, "it was the straw that broke the camel's back." Keith suggested that they both explore their own social activities as their marriage came to a conclusion. Judy initially balked at the idea, but when Keith persisted, she joined a group of men and women who ran together each Monday evening. The group enjoyed occasional potlucks and generally maintained an active social circle.

During one of the gatherings, Judy met Doug Erwin, a recreational runner and president of State Mutual Savings Bank, a local financial institution. Doug was separated, living alone, and in the process of a divorce from his first wife.

The subject of Aaron's cancer came up during one of their first conversations, the night before the group ran the Seaside Marathon. Doug overheard a comment about someone who had cancer, and he said something to the effect that people generally don't survive the disease. His comment drew Judy into the conversation. "No, that's not true," she told him. "My son had leukemia. He had it when he was two. He's six now and he is doing fine." Doug rarely offered opinions on unfamiliar matters and he later chastised himself as being a "dummy" for wading into the deep end of an unfamiliar pool.

Two weeks later, Doug stopped by his bank early on a Saturday morning and saw Judy coming from the hospital. When they met later that morning with the rest of their running group, he asked her why she had been there. "She told me that Aaron relapsed and I said, 'Oh, god. I'm sorry.' We talked about it and I felt just terrible for her because I thought, 'What an awful way to live, to have your child ill like that.' But she said, 'You know, I'm going to do the very best I can for Aaron, but we've all got to live, too.'"

Doug's and Judy's friendship warmed. They increasingly broke away from the pack and ran together. Keith had encouraged Judy to seek out relationships with other men so he supported the development. But the final result may not have been what he had in mind. Before long, Doug told Judy he would like to have a little more than just a friendship. Judy felt the same, but neither she nor Doug liked the lifestyle of being married and finding companionship elsewhere.

"It's not a good way to live your life, I tell you. It's not." She searched out a friend for consultation, who told her, "You know, you've been through so much, you deserve to be happy and to be with someone you really enjoy being with." Judy took her friend's advice and decided she needed to make a change.

At one point in their whirlwind courtship, Judy and Doug delved into a deeper discussion about Aaron's leukemia. Doug had become more aware of Aaron's long-term possibilities, and that the little boy might have a short life.

"Are you sure you know what you're getting yourself into?" she asked him.

"I'm not sure that I do," he replied, "but I do know I can handle whatever comes along."

Anyone who knew Doug would have agreed. His goal-oriented approach to life served him well. He often expressed his pride that he had worked his way to the top of the business ladder without ever having attended college. His was the kind of native intelligence that drove him to do the *New York Times* crossword daily. Doug would have done well has a contestant on *Jeopardy!*

He saw it as part of his calling to help others get as much out of their potential as possible. "I've always been a person of high expectations," he said. "Every person who has ever worked for me would say, 'Boy, he expects a lot out of you.' But they always said it in the context that they enjoyed it. I'm not going to expect something from you that you can't do."

Judy's friends liked both Keith and Doug, but the only common characteristics they saw between the two men was their love of running and their love for Judy and her children. Both Keith and Doug thrived on competition, but in different ways. Keith enjoyed running competitively while Doug was competitive about everything. "The competitive part of my personality is probably the biggest," Doug said. "All my life, if somebody told me, 'You can't do that,' my response would be, 'Don't tell me I can't do that. I'm going to show you, Charlie!'" His competitive drive, coupled with discipline and determination, would prove to be tremendous assets in assisting Aaron in his battle against leukemia.

Judy's friends described Keith as being "laid-back, free-spirited, and mellow." Aaron's sister, Heather, called her Papa "super, super laid back" and added the word "granola" for emphasis.

Doug enjoyed a reputation for being kind and generous, but also for being socially conscious. Following his separation from his first wife, his image awareness became more acute and indirectly led to his passion for running. Accustomed to going home to his wife and two children at the end of a work day, the found himself a bit out of sorts. "I thought to myself, 'I have to do something at the end of the day and one thing I prided myself on is that in the three years (following his separation), I never set foot in a bar, other than with somebody. I said I am not going to be one of these guys who hangs out in bars looking for women. I thought that was the saddest thing you could do."

Doug refused to eat dinner alone in a restaurant. "That was another of my little hang-ups. I'd be tired at the end of the day. It would be six o'clock or six thirty and all I wanted to do is go to bed, so I would stop somewhere to get something to eat. I would take it home because I didn't want to be the guy where people said, 'Oh, look at poor Doug Erwin over there, sitting by himself eating dinner.' I'd go home and eat dinner, and I'd still be tired so I would shower and say, 'I'm just gonna crash.'"

Doug searched for an alternative to the dormant lifestyle and, at age forty, he discovered running. He ran every day after work. His fourteen-year-old son, Pat, who ran competitively in middle school at the time, sometimes joined him for a run at Point Defiance Park.

Aaron's leukemia treatments didn't wait for the romantic entanglements to unwind. He completed his kindergarten year while taking frequent absences to receive injections of vincristine, undergo bone marrow aspirations, and take large quantities of pills as they worked to achieve remission with his leukemia once again. His hair fell out again and his face puffed up as a result of the steroids.

Through their marital transition, Judy and Keith never wavered from their commitment to achieve the best possible outcome for Aaron. They both remained directly involved in his care and welcomed Doug as a third partner—effectively a third parent—in that effort.

Keith and Judy filed for divorce in June, 1981. By the end of the year, nine months after Aaron's relapse and two months after finalizing her divorce from Keith, Judy Forman became Judy Erwin. "I got divorced and remarried in such a very short time," Judy said. "It has worked out for all of us, but I certainly wouldn't recommend doing it that way, so quickly and everything." Doug and Judy deferred their honeymoon until the following April, when they ran the Boston Marathon together.

Mary Lou and I received the news of Aaron's relapse and his parents' faltering marriage at nearly the same time. Only then did I begin to grasp the seriousness of Aaron's condition. I had been in the family for less than a year, and it simply wasn't yet part of my world. We hadn't spoken much about Aaron's leukemia, and it was ancient history as far as I knew. But Mary Lou's tearful response and her family's emotional reactions told a different story. Mary Lou and I had no children of our own at the time, but I couldn't imagine the pain of having a six-year-old son with cancer.

The sudden change in Judy's nuclear family introduced a layer of complexity into our lives. As the newest family member, I had seen Judy, Keith, and their kids fewer than half a dozen times, mainly at our wedding less than a year earlier. Everyone in the family loved Keith. Most of us were as surprised at their divorce as we were with Aaron's relapse. To digest both at once required some time. Our family photo album from 1981 best illustrated the upheaval. In April, our Easter pictures included smiling images of Keith and Judy Forman with their two healthy children. By Christmas, we were looking at picture postcards of the Doug and Judy Erwin family.

Chapter 9

HE DIDN'T HAVE A LOT OF TIME

"Okay," Aaron said. "You put yours on the far track this time. Then we have to get back up in the tree." Aaron listened for the high-pitched vibration from the rails that warned of approaching trains. The locomotives didn't always blow their whistle before they came racing around the bend. Their stealthy approach made the penny exercise much more dangerous. Several times Aaron had been caught off guard before Michael taught him to listen for the soft tingling sound. It wasn't foolproof. Aaron didn't always hear it, but when he did it gave him about a seven- or eight-second head start to reach the protection of the huge black walnut tree before the train blew by. Michael set two coins on the far set of tracks, retreated past Aaron, and slid back down the rocky slope. Aaron placed his penny on the near rail just as it started to sing.

"Hurry up, Aaron! It's coming!" Michael had just reached the tree. He swung his legs over the bottom branch, pulled himself up, and reached for the next limb. He needed to leave the lower perch open for Aaron. Each boy had laid claim to a perch to avoid chaos at the last moment. Aaron saw the train emerging from the turn, about half a mile to the north, which gave them about thirty seconds. His feet stumbled over the rails as he turned to run. He regained his balance, ran to the edge of the platform, and followed Michael's path down the gravel incline. By the time he reached the tree trunk, the ground vibrations and the blast of the train's horn announced time was up.

"Get behind the tree!" Michael yelled as he curled his nine-year-old body against the trunk and covered his head with his hands. Aaron dropped to his knees and wedged himself between the back of the tree trunk and the adjacent picket fence just as the train thundered by. A blast of wind pruned the weaker limbs from the tree and sent a cloud of debris over Aaron's head. Michael remained in a ball and gripped his branch with both hands as the tree trunk vibrated against his torso. After the longest seven seconds of his life, Aaron raised his head and peaked around the trunk. The train vanished as quickly as it had appeared, its horn fading in the distance. The shivering sound that had forecast its approach now whispered of its departure.

Michael descended and joined Aaron at the base of the tree. "Wow, that was close," Michael said. "Do you think they saw you?" Michael's grandparents lived in the house closest to the tree and the boys worried more about being seen by adults than they did about being killed by a train. "I don't think so," Aaron said. "Come on. Let's go find the pennies!"

In legal terms, the railroad tracks by Aaron's house would have been considered an "attractive nuisance." To local residents, their daily interactions with the trains were unavoidable, and sometimes deadly. The strip of houses along the water's edge of Puget Sound had been built on the downhill side of the tracks in the thirties and forties, long after the two parallel sets of rails were in place. The waterfront homeowners parked their automobiles in a small private lot at the top of the hill and followed an asphalt footpath down to a pedestrian walkway, which crossed the tracks. Bold signs cautioned people to look both ways and warned of "fast frequent trains on both tracks."

More than one person had died who failed to heed the warnings. Two teenagers were killed as they walked down the middle of the tracks wearing headphones, unaware of the train approaching them from behind. In yet another tragedy, a neighbor had lost his life after waiting patiently to cross the pedestrian walkway as a noisy train traveled from his right to his left on the far tracks. Certain the entire train had passed, he stepped out and began to cross, only to be hit by a train on the near tracks coming from the opposite direction. This was perfect environment for Aaron and Michael to challenge fate.

Michael Prince, today a forty-four-year-old attorney with children of his own, cringes when he looks back. "We were always on the tracks and climbing the trees next to them. That sidewalk was so close to the trains that you could almost touch them as they came by. Sometimes you might be walking across the tracks and a train would come around the corner and you'd have to hurry to make it. If it was close, you might have to jump over a fence into someone else's yard. When that sucker came screaming by, it was more than a thrill; it seriously scared you.

"A couple of times we weren't very smart and we played chicken with the train," Michael said, "where we would stand in the middle of the tracks and see how long we could stand it before we had to jump off. Don't ask me why we did that—real stupid. I did that once or twice until I realized it was a real dumb thing to do.

By the time Aaron began taunting trains, he and his family had been settled into Doug's house for several years. It was less than a twenty-minute drive from their old home in Gig Harbor to their new life on Sunset Beach. Doug's house rested at the water's edge of Puget Sound in the small Tacoma suburb of University Place. One neighbor called it "affordable waterfront living."

The home was built in 1942, two years after Galloping Gertie collapsed. It remained one of the few vertical log homes in the area. Its internal walls and kitchen cupboards, built with knotty pine, gave it the feel of a mountain hideaway. The first-floor layout featured an open living-dining space, a small kitchen, one and a half baths, and the master bedroom. The bookshelves and the mantle above the living room fireplace contained a mixture of hardback bestsellers and Doug's collection of antique nutcrackers and piggy banks.

A large concrete porch with a fireplace and hot tub provided as much functional living space outside as the house had inside. A three-foot-tall concrete retaining wall protected the porch from winter's high tides and raging storms. Six giant window panes in the living room offered a panoramic view from Fox Island to the south to Galloping Gertie to the north.

A steep, narrow stairwell led from the living room to a small landing on the second floor, where a seven-by nine-foot alcove at the top of the stairs, made even smaller by low walls and angled ceilings, served as Heather's room. A small window on the east side of the room gave Heather a view of the fruit trees in the small back yard and the railroad tracks on the other side of the white picket fence.

Aaron's bedroom, directly across the landing, shared the same slanted ceiling, but it was three times the size of Heather's. A small west-facing window in Aaron's room offered the best view in the house, an encompassing view of Puget Sound. A continuous parade of leisure craft circumvented tugboats pulling gravel barges and cargo vessels navigating south to the Port of Olympia. On rare occasions, the family caught a glimpse of a US naval submarines, conducting drills just below the water's surface.

A small yard at the rear of the house sank nearly two feet below sea level; it would have been underwater for much of the winter without protection from the concrete bulkheads on either side of the house. High tides and fierce winds still hurled occasional waves over the bulkhead. After one storm, Doug found two young sea otters swimming in his flooded backyard.

During summer months, the beach stretched 100 feet from the front bulkhead of the porch to the water's edge. Local residents played in the sand and launched rowboats and rafts into the Sound. A subsequent owner of the house once caught a fifteen-pound salmon as he stood just outside the living room.

The move by Judy and her children to Doug's house turned out to be much more than a change in geography. They generally experienced an economic upgrade across the board as a result of Judy's marriage to Doug. Judy and Keith had never felt impoverished, but Doug lived in a different world. For Judy and the kids to live in the world of a bank president, things needed to change.

Prior to their marriage, Doug considered Judy's wardrobe to be insufficient for the social activities of a bank president's wife. With Doug's input, Judy upgraded her wardrobe as soon as they were married. Doug became agitated when he saw the clothes Aaron and Heather wore. He simply stated, "These kids need new clothes," and proceeded to upgrade their attire, as well. Doug grew to love both children. He treated Aaron and Heather like they were his own from the moment he and Judy were married. He very much wanted Judy and the kids to share in his economic success, but there was always a social awareness factor, too.

Before he married Judy, Doug's exposure to Aaron and Heather had been brief. He remembered his first experience with them in public when he met Judy and the children for lunch at local restaurant.

"This was going to be a test," he remembered. "I had seen them before, but not really. They were totally undisciplined. I still remember both of them sitting in the restaurant with olives on their fingers, and I said to myself, 'I don't think I can handle this.' They were pretty much out of control. I told Judy, 'I don't think that is appropriate in a restaurant.'" Doug felt strongly that the children's behavior reflected on him and he would have been embarrassed had one of his friends or clients entered the restaurant while the kids were wearing olives.

When Judy married Doug, Aaron and Heather gained two new siblings in Doug's children from his first marriage. Pat, aged seventeen, welcomed his dad's new family with open arms. He left for college shortly after the marriage, but he became closer to Judy and her children each time he came home for a visit. Kelley, eighteen months older, not only welcomed Judy, Aaron, and Heather, but she became particularly close to Aaron over the years.

"It was a little different because of the age difference," Kelley said. "It became more maternal than sisterly." During the frequent times she would housesit or babysit, she sat on the beach and sifted through the rocks with Aaron and Heather to find shells. Other times, she and Aaron would just snuggle on the couch. "He would come sit next to me and just cuddle right up," Kelley said. "He had that warmth about him. Whoever was there, he wanted to be close to them."

While Judy, Doug, and the children adjusted to their new lives, Keith continued on with his. He approached the divorce and his children's new living situation in his trademark low-key manner. His older sister, Gay, described him best. "Keith has always been the nice, easy going guy that he is today," she said. "If we ever had a disagreement as children, I was the one who started it. We might argue back and forth for a little bit and then he would just walk away and say, 'Okay. Whatever you say.' He never wanted to argue."

Aaron and Heather went to Keith's place every other weekend, and he spent Wednesday evenings with them, too. The arrangement worked well most of the time. Keith remained very committed to his children and always took an active part in their lives. Doug and Judy committed themselves to ensuring Aaron and Heather maintained regular contact with their Papa. The three parents worked out any disagreements quickly, due primarily to Doug's assertive personality and Keith's accommodating approach to any differences of opinion. This dynamic became consequential when decisions had to be made regarding Aaron's treatment and choice of doctors.

"When there were issues that had to be dealt with," Keith said, "one of the things I told myself is that a big flare-up among the three of us is the last thing Aaron needed. None of our disagreements ever got to the point where it needed to be that. I admire Doug for that and I have often thought that having Doug there made it easier because there were three of us to carry the load." Judy's unbridled commitment and organizational prowess provided the team dynamic that Aaron needed.

The "load" Keith referred to was Aaron's new chemotherapy regimen. It began while Judy and Keith were still married, and continued with their change in marital status. Now seven years old, Aaron was once again in the thick of his chemo regimen. The new clinical trials used most of the same drugs he had received during his first battle against cancer, but in different combinations and in heavier doses.

Eight months after his relapse, Aaron was able to join Mrs. Nokes' first grade class at Sunset Elementary School—just in time to be included in the class picture. The group photo provided a good snapshot of his overall health. Aaron's hair had yet to grow back completely and his cheeks held less color than usual. He wore his trademark horizontally striped polo shirt. His smirk said he knew something funny and couldn't wait to reveal it.

Aaron did well academically in spite of missing half the school year. On his report card, Mrs. Nokes noted, "Aaron read nineteen books this quarter, the most of the whole class. He received 100 on every spelling test. What a nice boy he is! I'm glad he moved here!"

Aaron showed few outward signs he was still undergoing chemo treatments. He still went to the clinic, where Dr. Origenes continued to inject vincristine into his veins and conduct painful bone marrow aspirations, but he approached his visits to Mary Bridge as if they were pit stops in a race against time. He never wanted to be referred to as a cancer patient and he lived every moment to its fullest.

"From early on," Keith said, "it's like he knew he didn't have a lot of time to have as much fun as we wanted, so he'd better get as much as he could while he was here."

Cindy, one of his nurses, described his attitude: "Aaron was the type of kid who would come in, get his treatment, and then ask when he could go to the movie or just plug back in and be a normal kid. He liked his life as a kid. Aaron was really resilient and he never let the treatments get him down. He had an incredible need to survive."

His courageous approach to chemotherapy treatments resulted at least partially from the disciplined approach of his parents. "A very strong part of our belief system," Doug said, "was that Aaron was going to have to go through some very tough things, so he's got to be tough. Judy never coddled Aaron. We always treated him like a normal boy. There was a lot of damage done to his body so there were things he couldn't do physically. But he was never given special treatment. You know, if you've got a sick child and you treat him like a sick child, that's what you get."

Aaron's second round of treatment was much like the first round. After he achieved remission with his cancer, he took most of his chemo in pill form—methotrexate, 6-MP, and prednisone. By all appearances, his daily pill consumption could well have been vitamins or daily supplements. Aaron's hair eventually regrew to a point where it went unnoticed by his friends.

When Aaron and his buddies tired of cheating death on the rails, they migrated to the beach on the other side of Aaron's house, where they acted out the latest *Star Wars* scenarios. They transformed kelp into whips and converted driftwood into light sabers as they took on Darth Vader and the Dark Side. *The Empire Strikes Back* and *The Return of the*

Jedi had hit the theaters in 1980 and 1983, respectively, and Aaron never strayed too far from the *Star Wars* universe. His toy shelves overflowed with *Star Wars* figurines. Aaron combined his burgeoning drawing talents with his knowledge of *Star Wars* to depict epic battles between good and bad. The Dark Side in Aaron's drawings represented the resilient and deadly leukemic cells in his body. He labeled them as "bad cells" or "cancer cells." The always-triumphant good guys incorporated the aerial fighting skills of Luke Skywalker and Han Solo as they crushed the leukemic cells in battle after battle.

Aaron sometimes steered his fantasy world away from *Star Wars* to mimic the antics of Hulk Hogan and King Kong Dundee in the World Wrestling Federation (WWF). He and his friend, Eric Freitag, acted out the wrestling moves of WWF superstars until 2:00 a.m. at Papa's house. The boys jumped off the couch and body-slammed stuffed animals they had placed around the living room. Aaron lived his life as it unfolded. Perhaps that is why his friends rarely noticed his illness. Eric remembered him as just being one of the guys.

"I knew he had leukemia, but I don't think I knew he had cancer," he said. "They never said he could die, or he may die. Just that he was sick. It wasn't something that I ever thought about him not surviving, because kids don't think of those things, I guess.

"When we were playing on the beach and running around, he would do everything with the same level of energy that a healthy child would muster up. I don't ever remember his being sickly, even when he was sick. If he came with a mask or without any hair, I don't remember him having any lack of energy or lack of ability to be a kid."

In spite of Aaron's efforts to live a normal life, steady reminders tethered him to reality. "I do remember one of my birthday parties," Eric said, "where my mom made all the other boys wear a mask so that Aaron could attend. Everyone was cool about it."

Chemotherapy drugs continued to take a gradual toll on his body. His fourth-grade class photo clearly shows his smaller stature compared to other boys his age. His deteriorating strength and stamina eventually began to affect his relationship with Heather, now a strong and healthy eight-year-old. The three parents learned that taking care of a chronically ill child gets complicated when there are healthy siblings under the same roof.

"Aaron didn't treat Heather very well at all," Keith said. "Every chance he got, Aaron would be mean to her." Aaron's behavior toward Heather worsened as the years of chemotherapy took their toll on his skeletal and muscular systems. "I remember one time there was a horizontal ladder on a jungle gym that kids could swing across," Keith said. "Aaron tried to go across and he couldn't even hold himself up before he fell. Heather was three years younger. She got on it and swung across it like she was a monkey. You could tell he was burned up at that. I think his issue with her was that she could do all these things that had been taken away from him."

Aaron became possessive of his toys, especially when it came to Heather. Han, Luke, Princess Leia, and the Millennium Falcon provided a backdrop for his continuing battle against tyranny. Because they represented the parts of Aaron's life that cancer couldn't take away, he wasn't going to let Heather have them. Any attempt on her part to touch his "things" resulted in a tirade on his part.

Less often, Aaron lashed out at his mom. Judy tended to be more patient with him, and attributed his outbursts to his understandable frustrations. Doug also understood Aaron's grievances, but he put stop to improper behavior immediately. "When you are in a situation like Aaron's," Doug said, "you tend to lash out at the person you love the most and the person you are the closest to because you know they won't reject you. That's the person you jump on."

The times Judy wanted to lash out, it wasn't at Aaron, but at Dr. Origenes. She recalled one time when the doctor gave Aaron the wrong dose of medicine. "Aaron was getting ready to go off treatment, and the doctor gave him a bigger dose of a drug than he was supposed to receive. Aaron lost his hair again. The doctor didn't think it was that big of a deal, but it was to Aaron." Incidents like this diminished Judy's faith in the system and prompted her to monitor Aaron's treatments even more closely.

The family's life at University Place gradually settled into somewhat of a normal routine. Judy and Doug continued to run—during one year they ran five different marathons. Keith kept up his running schedule and continued to teach at the community college, Judy met regularly with the Bridge Ladies, and Doug continued to advance in his banking career.

Any child with cancer goes through an occasional crisis, and Aaron went through more than his share. As he was wrapping up his fourth-grade year and nearing the end of his second chemo regimen, he contracted chicken pox, a huge threat since his immune system was compromised as a result of his chemotherapy treatments. Judy was well aware of the threat, so when some itchy bumps appeared on his scalp, she called Dr. Origenes. He referred Aaron to Mary

Bridge, where they admitted him right away. By age nine, Aaron had been in and out of Mary Bridge so many times that he had gained a certain comfort level in the environment. So much so that Judy was able to tuck him in and return home to her own bed by 1:00 a.m.

Aaron's condition worsened to the point where bumps covered his body and he had a fever of 104. Judy, Doug, and Keith rotated shifts to stay with Aaron throughout each day and then left him alone at night. Six-year-old Heather visited Aaron mid-week, with a predictable result. "He didn't want to see her at all," Judy wrote. Heather continued to be the target of Aaron's wrath and resentment, but she was affected in other ways, too. She became accustomed to being dropped off at neighbors' homes on short notice, or having other moms pick her up from school unexpectedly whenever a crisis arose regarding Aaron. She took it in stride most of the time. After all, Aaron had been fighting cancer off and on since before Heather was born.

Aaron survived chicken pox and returned to Sunset Elementary to close out his fourth-grade year. His teacher took the opportunity to bring some concerns to Judy's attention. She noted that Aaron was happy and well adjusted, but he was slow to complete his work and was easily distracted, comments similar to what his pre-school teacher had said five years earlier. Nevertheless, Aaron completed fourth grade on schedule—at nearly the same time he finished his second chemotherapy regimen. His last day of treatment officially fell on June 14, 1984, two days shy of his tenth birthday.

As Aaron completed his cancer treatments, Mary Lou and I passed the three-and-a-half-year mark in our marriage. Aaron visited us that summer and we treated him as the healthy ten-year-old boy he appeared to be. We enjoyed his visits because he was always so happy and cheerful. We took him to the movies and to feed the ducks at the park. He spent hours riding an old mare that we boarded in a five-acre pasture behind our house.

Judy's concerns about Aaron's leukemia faded away as he entered fifth grade on schedule in fall of 1984. Aaron survived scholastically, but he would never really catch up to his classmates. He always resisted Judy's attempts to get him to complete his homework. He preferred to create colorful drawings.

In early 1985, Doug, Judy, Aaron, and Heather sat for a family portrait. Aaron had done so well, and for so long, that Judy had begun to minimize the extent of Aaron's suffering from his treatments. "He really had a pretty easy time for those first five years," she wrote in her journal. "And then after that testicular relapse in 1981, I wasn't really too worried, because it was just testicular—it wasn't that big of a deal." Aaron's illness was the last thing on her mind.

Chapter 10

ONE WHO FALLS
THROUGH THE CRACKS

JUNE 5, 1985

"Dear Mom and Dad,

My hands are a bit shaky as I'm writing this, but I must put my worries and fears into words or I think I may go crazy. I'm waiting to see the doctor about Aaron. I'm very scared—I want to scream and cry, but I can't around Aaron. I need to be brave."

The crisis had started a couple of days earlier when Aaron's jaw became swollen and he began running a high fever. Judy called Dr. Origenes only to discover he was out of town for several days. Dr. Rivera, the on-call family physician, took some blood, diagnosed it as some sort of infection, gave Aaron antibiotics, and asked him to come back the next day.

Not wanting to wait, Judy called Dr. Cook, Aaron's dentist, on the way home. "He checked him over," Judy wrote. "He took some x-rays and found a tender area around his jawbone." The dentist promised to check with some other doctors to help determine a diagnosis. Then Dr. Rivera's office called and asked Judy to bring Aaron in again that afternoon. Judy asked the nurse about the results of Aaron's blood test. "She said she couldn't give that information to me over the phone, but said that's why the doctor wants to see us. I'm sure I immediately turned white. The news she gave me was very bad in my mind. Something is wrong with his blood." The same words she had used to describe Aaron's condition to her mom nine years earlier.

Judy cleaned house while she waited for their two o'clock appointment. She put clothes away, took a long shower, and cried when Aaron wasn't around. Then she recorded her thoughts in her journal while Aaron sat beside her and focused on his upcoming eleventh birthday party.

"About an hour ago," she wrote, "he pointed out some tiny spots on his skin—arms, legs, feet, torso. He's never had spots like that before and the sight of them sent chills down my spine." Judy was unaware the tiny spots on Aaron's skin were petechiae—small, round, red spots that appear on the skin as a result of bleeding. They are painless and often show up with leukemia patients when their production of platelets has been disrupted by the overproduction of leukemic cells.

"I don't want to think about what they might mean, but yet I can't stop myself. The thought of another relapse is just almost too horrible to imagine, but I think it may have happened. He's sitting here by me filling out invitations to his birthday party and that fills me with more sadness. I wonder if he'll be well enough to have one."

Doug was playing golf, unaware of the doctors' consultations or the spots. Cell phones didn't exist at that time. To contact him, Judy called Doug's son, Pat, and asked him to find his dad on the golf course. Then, Judy called Keith.

"I couldn't tell him about the spots. I didn't want to break down completely."

Keith met Judy at the doctor's office and by two o'clock the parents' worst fears were realized. "He's had a flare-up of his leukemia," the doctor told them. Aaron's blood had forty-five percent blasts, or leukemic cells. His red cells were low and the petechiae indicated a low platelet count.

Judy and Aaron had a pretty quiet ride home. Judy cried and spoke to Aaron about being a fighter again. Aaron drew his hand into a fist and said he felt like he wanted to hit someone. Aaron had been initially diagnosed at age two. He had relapsed the first time at age six-and-a-half. Being told his cancer had returned at age eleven felt different to Judy.

She wondered what was in store for them the next few months. She was frightened, but determined to fight like they had in the past. She had just turned thirty-seven a couple of weeks earlier. She had been fighting this battle for nine years, but remained as determined as ever to beat the cancer and save her son's life. She drew courage from the words her Grandpa Armstrong wrote to her in a letter after he heard of Aaron's latest relapse: "Don't despair. Just get mad and pour it on! If you beat it once, you can do it again!"

She knew it would be rough, but she resolved herself to keeping the family together—"I cannot neglect Heather and Doug to care for Aaron. That's not good for anyone."

Dr. Origenes called. He told them that in his absence another hematologist, Dr. Dan Niebrugge, would start chemo right away. Aaron would also need to start radiation to reduce the swelling in his jaw. Just before he got off the phone, Dr. Origenes made a comment that Judy and Doug never forgot. "Aaron's one who falls through the cracks," he said. It's unclear which "cracks" he was referring to. Perhaps he was talking about Aaron's repeated relapses, or the unfortunate timing of his setbacks as they related to the ongoing clinical trials. His remark wasn't well received. Judy broke down into tears on the phone.

She called her mom the next day, but she couldn't talk without sobbing. She knew Aaron could hear her from the living room, but she couldn't hold back any longer. She glanced in to see him hitting his two fists together. Once again, Jeanne immediately left Eugene for University Place.

Aaron's spirits rose when Judy told him it was time to go see Dr. Niebrugge. They talked on the way over about the importance of maintaining a fighting spirit and a positive attitude.

"Dr. Dan" Niebrugge admitted Aaron to Mary Bridge the same day he relapsed. Aaron's counts were not dangerously low, but the doctor needed to get some liquids into him, do a spinal tap, and begin Aaron's chemo treatments. Aaron settled into his third-floor room at Mary Bridge as if he was returning to a familiar hotel, one where he knew the personnel, where the service was excellent, but one in which he'd hoped never to return.

Dr. Niebrugge learned of Aaron's passion for *Star Wars* and brought a newly purchased VHS tape of the movie for Aaron to watch. All three parents warmed up to Dr. Dan quickly. "He was easy to talk to," Judy wrote. "He talked to Doug, Keith, Mom and me for a long time. He talked to us about the prognosis. Said it was good that Aaron didn't relapse while on drugs. Better chances when off a year. He said that Aaron's hospital stay might be as long as a month or as short as a few days, depending on how he is doing. Aaron heard a lot of the conversation and seemed to be taking it all in, but kept very quiet about it. We felt more

Larry Bradley

informed than we had in ten years!"

Dr. Dan came back later in the day to do chest x-rays and several other tests to ensure Aaron's heart was strong enough to take some of the newer, stronger chemotherapy drugs.

Judy left the hospital for a couple of hours in the afternoon to pick up Heather at school. She tried to explain to her daughter what was happening, but Heather became upset, not because her brother's cancer had returned or that he needed to be hospitalized again. "She just didn't like watching Aaron receive all the attention and gifts," wrote Judy. Who could blame her? In spite of her parents' best efforts, circumstances often dictated that they focus on Aaron first.

Dr. Dan talked to the three parents about the possibility of a bone marrow transplant, but none of them wanted to do it. In 1985, transplants were still not commonplace. They opted instead to incorporate some new drugs to fight the clone of resistant leukemic cells. They would address the matter of a transplant later, if necessary.

Immediately after Dr. Dan stepped in for Dr. Origenes, the three parents discussed switching doctors permanently. They all liked Dr. Origenes very much. He had treated Aaron for nearly nine years and he had seen them through some very tough situations. But Doug felt especially strong about changing doctors. He remained incensed by Dr. Origenes' comment about Aaron being one who "falls through the cracks."

Additionally, in many moments of crisis for Aaron, Dr. Origenes had been out of town attending conferences of one sort or another. He was in demand to make presentations, he traveled internationally to fulfill his obligations to his church, and his career had developed to the point where he enjoyed giving back, whether it be to the Boy Scouts or with the Catholic Church.

The three parents concluded that Dr. Niebrugge was a good fit for the family and a better match for Aaron. They decided that it would be easier for Doug to talk to Dr. Origenes. "Those things are never as bad as you think they are going to be," said Doug. "He was disappointed, but I think that he had kind of run the course with Aaron in his own mind. It went as well as it could."

Dr. Origenes took the message personally, according to his wife, Pat. "That rarely happened to Maurice. He adored Aaron and it broke his heart, honestly. I don't know, maybe it was just a mis-impression. But I think it is one of those things that happen in your life that you never really come to terms with. I don't think he ever got over it, to tell you the truth."

Dr. Dan Niebrugge had arrived in Tacoma in much the same way that Dr. Origenes had twenty years earlier—at the request of some local pediatricians who wanted an oncologist on their staff. He was recruited as somewhat of a defensive move on behalf of a local pediatric clinic. Without a pediatric oncologist of their own on staff, they faced a choice of either sending newly diagnosed childhood cancer patients thirty miles north to Seattle or referring them to Dr. Origenes, Tacoma's only pediatric oncologist.

If they referred their young patients to Seattle, their families had to endure frequent round trips and potential delays in the event of a crisis. If they referred the children to Dr. Origenes, the families often switched the healthcare for their other children to Dr. Origenes for the sake convenience, resulting in a significant loss of revenue for the referring clinic. They brought on Dr. Niebrugge to work part time in regular pediatrics and part time as an oncologist in order to maintain their client base.

A Midwesterner by birth, Dr. Niebrugge was the second oldest of thirteen children. He attended medical school at Southern Illinois University, completed his residency at the University of Missouri and then completed a fellowship in hematology-oncology at Children's Hospital in Seattle. Part of his fellowship included a rotation at the Fred Hutchinson Cancer Research Center so he was up to date on all the latest clinical trials and treatment protocols.

Dr. Dan had barely turned thirty when he joined the clinic in Tacoma. He worried that his patients and their parents may not take him seriously, so to present the image of a knowledgeable and experienced oncologist, he cut his long hair down to a short pony tail and he grew a well-trimmed beard.

Regardless of his appearance, any concerns about his lack of knowledge would have been unfounded. "The only way I could keep current with things was to be part of the clinical studies," said Dr. Dan. "Everything came down through the national studies. You would find things out long before they became published, and you couldn't get access to the data unless you were part of that group. It's a closed study and you can't just look it up unless you are involved and go to the meetings."

Dr. Dan marveled at the difference between how researchers tackled adult cancers as compared to the methodology used to study children's cancer. "With adults, they didn't start doing these nationwide studies until much later because people figured they had enough adult oncology that everybody could do their own studies. When I was going through oncology training, I would go to these adult tumor boards and they would be discussing the same thing every time. Because there was no national consensus, everybody did it their own way. In pediatrics, if you went to New York and you ask, "How do we treat a child with this type of leukemia?" it would be the same thing as you did in Seattle, San Francisco, or St. Louis. Everyone was on the same page."

Thirty-five years after he treated Aaron, Dr. Dan showed no indication that dealing with leukemic children had worn him down emotionally. He knew the disease's history and the hopelessness it used to represent. "I was lucky because I got into this in 1980. If you look at 1960, we had no treatment for almost any of these things, and by 1980 there was dramatic change. I still remember a number of kids that I took care of for years and who eventually died."

Dr. Dan and the three parents agreed to give the latest chemotherapy regimen a chance to get Aaron's cancer into remission again before considering more drastic solutions like a bone marrow transplant. They began the induction phase of treatment for a third time. By August, 1985, Aaron's cancer went into remission again. The family steeled themselves for another long journey. They had been through it twice before and Judy had confidence that they could do it again.

Aaron joined his classmates on the first day of sixth grade at Sunset Elementary School. Heather started in fourth grade at the same school. Judy volunteered in both her children's classrooms and occasionally worked there as a substitute teacher. Her running routine rarely faltered, and she continued to meet regularly with the Bridge Ladies, hosting them in her home when her turn came around. She incorporated Aaron's treatments into her busy schedule, visiting the clinic twice a week for Aaron's chemo injections. She continued to take the long view. Her experience told her things would be tough at first and then ease up as his treatments became more routine. She looked forward to the time they would no longer need to go to the clinic, when they could return once again to taking pills at home.

She had received good news on Aaron's academic performance on report card day. He and Heather were even getting along. Maybe it was because everything was going so smoothly that the news on November 11th hit her so hard.

It was during a routine quarterly visit to the clinic that events turned for the worse. Dr. Dan initially told them that Aaron got a good blood report. Everything seemed fine. The drugs were doing their job. Then the doctor extracted a sample of Aaron's bone marrow from his hip. Unlike past relapses, when Aaron's testicles or jaw were swollen, when he ran a fever, or when petechiae appeared on his skin, this time the cancer gave Judy no warning.

"The news today was extra hard to handle. Aaron was looking better than ever and he was in great spirits. Dr. Niebrugge called us into the next room to give us the bad news. Relapsing when on chemo is not good, but we are not giving up yet. At the same time, we need to face the hard facts, that Aaron's chances are not good."

The next step would likely be a bone marrow transplant. According to Dr. Dan, Aaron's chances of long-term survival stood at only thirty percent, even with a transplant. Doctors didn't like to perform a transplant if the patient was not in remission, so their immediate goal would be to get Aaron's cancer into remission once again. Dr. Dan drove north the next day to the Fred Hutchinson Cancer Research Center in Seattle to determine their next moves.

This situation created more of a "life and death" mood

than Aaron's prior relapses, but the parents' responses remained somewhat predictable. Judy asked lots of questions, took thorough notes, and processed her emotions by recording them in her journal. Keith internalized much of the information, took an active role in Aaron's care, and wondered to himself how far they should go in their efforts to save his son's life. Doug injected an element of defiance into the equation. He refused to accept the low survival odds. He believed Aaron could make it if they all maintained the right level of optimism and toughness.

The next morning, Aaron got out of bed in great spirits and walked up the hill to school as if nothing had happened the day before. Judy told him the most important thing was to remember to be happy. "I can't help it," Aaron responded. "I can't keep a straight face. I have to smile." Then he broke into a huge grin.

Their highest priorities were to get Aaron's cancer back into remission and to find a donor to match his marrow. They initiated their search the following day, beginning with immediate family members, who offered a twenty-five percent chance of success. The odds were lower than they would have liked, but much better than having to search through a national donor base. Without a donor, Aaron had no chance of survival at all. "We'll be testing Keith's, Heather's, and my blood this week for a match," Judy noted. "We will just take each day as it comes and keep Aaron happy."

They sat back, waited, and prayed for positive results.

Chapter 11

TWO THINGS ABOUT HEATHER

"**N**ews to raise goose bumps! Heather is a match!" Judy struggled to contain herself when the word came from Dr. Niebrugge on the day before Thanksgiving, 1985. She decided to keep a lid on the information until she got the full story from doctors in Seattle the following week. She told only Doug, Keith, Heather, and Aaron. Heather, the sister who had often been the target of Aaron's contempt, was now in a position to save his life. Aaron remained true to character when he received the news. "He said he wished it wasn't Heather that matched," said Judy. Later, after he'd had a chance to ponder it further, he asked, "After Heather's marrow is inside of me, will I like the things she likes?"

Heather got a kick out of Aaron's concern. She loved her older brother and she didn't hesitate a moment before agreeing to donate her marrow. She had only two questions: "Will it hurt?" and "Would she finally be able to pick a toy out of the red box in the doctor's office after it was over?"

"Two things about Heather," Keith said. "One, she got left alone a lot. Something would happen to Aaron and all of us would rush to him, take him to the hospital, and be all tied up. Heather might be at school and she would get a message to go to Shannon's house tonight or something like that. The other thing is that Aaron was jealous of her health and he didn't treat her very well at all. Every chance he got he would be mean to her."

Heather had never known a childhood when her brother wasn't sick. His leukemia diagnosis joined the family a year before she did. She had grown up with no other siblings against whom to compare Aaron's behavior, and she had no previous life to use as a comparative baseline.

Aaron hadn't always been abusive to Heather. They had played together happily as small children in Gig Harbor prior to the divorce. A photo from their very early child-hood shows a bald-headed Aaron examining his younger sister with a stethoscope as they played doctor. This was before Aaron became aware of his own health shortcomings compared not just to Heather, but to other children. His behavior toward Heather began to deteriorate shortly after their move to University Place and just after his first relapse.

Aaron and Heather shared a toy shelf at the top of the stairs between their rooms. "Aaron would occasionally allow me to play with a few of his *Star Wars* characters," Heather remembered. "As long as it was R2D2 or C3PO—or Princess Leia, because she was a girl." Under no circum-stances would Aaron allow her to touch the Storm Troopers, Darth Vader, or Luke Skywalker.

Heather's interest in playing with Aaron and his friends stopped when it came to playing chicken on the railroad tracks. She cursed the engines from her upstairs bedroom window forty yards from the tracks. They disrupted her radio shows, which she produced by intermixing her own voice on a tape recorder between songs from a local radio station. Each time she came close to having a finished product, a train rumbled by and necessitated a do-over.

Heather enjoyed an extensive collection of stuffed animals and Cabbage Patch dolls. She chose a Black astronaut Barbie Doll and two Black Cabbage Patch dolls as playmates. "I don't know if this was just the beginning of my 'I have to be different than anyone else' stage of my life," she said, "or part of my personality, but everything had to be different." Her Black dolls provided an early lesson on bigotry and racism. "My uncle's friend used to be a redneck, jerk of a guy. He said he wanted to bleach her because she was Black." She found that offensive, even as a young girl.

In a high school paper entitled "Memories Never Die," Heather reflected on her experiences living with a sibling that had cancer. "I was often left behind. I would stay with friends or neighbors. Sometimes I felt like an older child shoved away because of the arrival of a new baby."

Many of the emotions experienced by siblings of cancer patients—loneliness, fear, anxiety, and uncertainty—mirror those of their parents and are often expressed through anger. When a sibling is diagnosed with cancer, the normal rules of living often go out the window. In Heather's case, a sudden turn of events with Aaron demanded her parents' immediate attention and allowed only enough time to make a phone call to a neighbor or another parent to have Heather picked up at school and whisked away indefinitely.

The more frequently these circumstances occurred, the more likely it was for Heather to resent Aaron for relegating her to playing second fiddle. An eight-year-old couldn't be expected to understand the larger issues surrounding her brother's cancer diagnosis. To her, it merely meant that she spent less time with her parents and fewer nights sleeping in her own bed.

Each time Aaron's cancer took a turn for the worse, Judy's parents arrived from Oregon and the phone started ringing. The first thing everyone wanted to know was "How is Aaron?" The conversation eventually turned to Heather's status, but most of the special trips and surprises—Seattle Mariners games, WWF wrestling matches, and even gifts from the Boston Red Sox—were reserved for Aaron.

Judy, Doug, and Keith placed a high priority on Heather's needs, but in reality, Aaron's cancer often controlled their schedule and demanded their attention immediately. The best they could do was to promise themselves they would make things right with Heather as soon as possible.

Aaron softened his approach to his little sister during family vacations, when she and Aaron played pillow games in the back seat of the car. He often told her he loved her during some of his lowest times, but he quickly rescinded his comments when he felt better. Her parents told her that Aaron loved her deep down in his heart, so she referred to those special moments as Aaron's "bottom feelings."

One of the rare perks Heather received from being the sibling of a cancer patient was attending Camp Goodtimes, a summer camp sponsored by the American Cancer Society for children with cancer and their siblings. The camp offered a safe place for children with cancer to participate in normal childhood activities under the protective umbrella of doctors and nurses who volunteered their time. Children with diminished physical skills from their cancer or their treatments played dodgeball, rode horses, went fishing, climbed rock walls, and generally acted like healthy kids at summer camp.

The camp population of about 150 children included those with bald heads, leg braces, crutches, and wheelchairs.

Free from the over-protective, sometimes paranoid nature of their parents, they stretched their capabilities to the limit, knowing that the medical staff was there if necessary. Many of the children were past the crisis stage of their disease, making it difficult to differentiate between the patients and their siblings.

Heather was as much a VIP as Aaron at Camp Goodtimes. The counselors knew that the needs of cancer siblings were often subordinated to those of their sick brother or sister so they went to great lengths to make Heather and the other siblings feel as special as the cancer kids.

Heather remembers it as one of the best times of her childhood. "That was my life. I was a summer camp kid and my summer camp happened to be the American Cancer Society's Camp Goodtimes. I went every summer. When Aaron was healthy enough to go, he had his group of counselors and campers his age, and I had my age kids. We would see each other, but we wouldn't really hang out."

Heather searched out friends year after year for a reunion celebration. Some kept in contact throughout the year. A sad reality-check each year occurred as campers attempted to reconnect with friends from the past, only to discover their friends' lives had been cut short by the disease. The entire camp population gathered for a special ceremony to commemorate those who had died.

The good feelings from camp lasted for a long time after Heather and Aaron returned from camp and created a truce between the two siblings. But the ups and downs of Aaron's cancer eventually awakened his resentments toward Heather.

During one such resurgence, Grandma Jeanne thought it would be fun for her granddaughter to have a heather plant. She and Heather dug a hole outside the back door of the log house and planted it. Aaron went out there several days later and peed on it. The plant died.

On rare occasions, Aaron could show his sister a softer side. "During one of his times at the hospital," Jeanne remembered, "he was delirious—he had been in a coma. When he recovered from the coma, he handed a blue ball to Heather. He said, 'Here, Heather, I really love you.' She told me later, 'You know what? He can never take that back. He said it, and I heard it, and he can never take that back.' That was really a gift for her. He did love her. But she represented to him what he didn't have."

Chapter 12

AN EXPERIMENTAL THING

Within hours of hanging up the phone, Judy began doubting what Dr. Dan had said about Heather being a match. The confirmation came in a letter to Dr. Dan from Dr. Paul Martin at Fred Hutchinson. The letter condensed Aaron's cancer history and his odds of survival onto one page:

Dear Dr. Niebrugge:

I saw your patient, Aaron Forman, in consultation regarding the possibility of allogeneic bone marrow transplantation for treatment of acute lymphoblastic leukemia. As summarized in your note, Aaron was initially diagnosed with leukemia at age 2 and relapsed at ages 6½, 10½, and 11½ and is currently therefore in third relapse. Since diagnosis his longest period off chemotherapy has been 14 months between the ages of 9 and 10. At the time of his original induction he received prophylactic cranial irradiation (2,400 rads to level of C2). His first relapse occurred both in the bone marrow and testes whereas the second and third relapses have occurred in the bone marrow only. He has never had CNS involvement. A recent family tissue typing demonstrates that the patient and his sister, Heather, are HLA identical, MLC nonreactive siblings.

I discussed with Aaron's mother, father and stepfather the rationale and prospects for allogeneic bone marrow transplantation. We agreed that there was little or no hope of cure with conventional therapy and I estimated the chances of cure with allogeneic bone marrow transplantation to be approximately 30%. I emphasized that approximately 30% of patients die with complications within the first 100 days after transplantation and that with ALL a high proportion of patients have relapse of their disease after transplantation. I understand that the patient will be returning to Seattle in the week of January 6th to begin the pre-transplant evaluation in our Outpatient Department. In the meantime, I understand that he will be receiving chemotherapy attempting to achieve a fourth remission. If his disease proves refractory it may be possible to arrange an earlier date for transplantation. If we can be of further assistance please do not hesitate to contact the transplant coordinator.

Sincerely yours,
Paul Martin, M.D.
Associate Professor of Medicine, UW

Dr. Niebrugge began administering heavy doses of chemotherapy drugs to Aaron right away. The odds of a successful transplant increased significantly if they could get Aaron's cancer into remission one more time prior to his tentatively scheduled transplant on January 24, about six weeks away. Aaron needed to be ready to move when one of the limited number of rooms at The Hutch became available.

The family maintained a spirit of hope and gratitude through Christmas, Aaron's favorite holiday. But Aaron's transplant shadowed every holiday moment. A short weekend holiday trip for Heather and Keith to Longview, a one-hour drive away, carried an inordinate amount of risk and anxiety. She was Aaron's lifeline.

By January 9, two weeks before Aaron's scheduled transplant, his cancer was once again in remission. To prepare for the transplant operation, doctors surgically implanted a "Hickman Line" into Aaron's chest. The "Hickman" was a special intravenous catheter used to administer chemotherapy drugs and draw blood over an extended period without having to repeatedly stick patients with a needle. Doctors made a small incision in Aaron's upper chest and fed a silicone tube into a specific blood vessel until it reached the entrance to Aaron's heart. The special catheter was named for the man who developed it, The Hutch's own Dr. Robert Hickman. The modest physician reportedly said at the time, "They had to call it something. They named it after me because they didn't think it would work."

Judy, Doug, and Keith all received training on how to flush the Hickman line with an anticoagulant to keep blood clots from blocking the line. They were also shown how to keep the exit site clean. An infection could be deadly to Aaron once the radiation and chemo drugs eliminated his immune system prior to the transplant.

On January 14, Aaron was in the living room putting together a new space ship with Legos when the Hutch called to let them know a room was available. Aaron needed to check in as soon as possible. Judy had just returned from walking Heather to school after she missed the bus once again. As usual, Heather protested about always having to go to school while Aaron stayed home and played video games.

The family had prepared in all the conventional ways— bags packed, sitters for Heather, and work arrangements for Keith and Doug. To ensure their psychological readiness, a social worker at The Hutch had interviewed each member of the family and included her report in Aaron's medical file. "Parents speak openly to patient and donor regarding treatment," she wrote in her report. "Express concern over emotional needs. Father especially concerned regarding Aaron and Heather's relationship. States Aaron has been sick so long that he seems to be resentful of Heather's health."

The psychologist noted that both children "especially enjoy drawing" and she suggested they each continue to explore their feelings in that manner. She concluded the family was as prepared as possible for what lie ahead. "Pleasant, intelligent family with good understanding of disease and treatment. Have had multiple experiences with hospitalization and chemo. Very supportive of each other and aware of stresses."

The Hutch was a thirty-minute drive north from Tacoma, just up the hill from the Interstate 5 freeway in the Cascade Neighborhood of Seattle. The area was known as "Pill Hill" because of the numerous major healthcare facilities located nearby.

The Fred Hutchinson Cancer Center was established in 1965 by a Seattle surgeon, Dr. William Hutchinson, in honor of his brother, Fred "Hutch" Hutchinson, a professional baseball player and manager in the 1950s and 1960s.

Hutch was fiercely competitive and in 1961 he led the Cincinnati Reds to the World Series. Two years later he was diagnosed with lung cancer and passed away in November, 1964, at age 45.

The bone marrow transplant work being done at the Hutch by Dr. E. Donnall Thomas in the late 1960s and early 1970s was considered radical. Dr. Thomas and his team of researchers had achieved a worldwide reputation as the leader in the field, but his procedures were still experimental in nature. In the ten-year period from 1958-1968, 203 bone marrow grafts were completed and only three patients survived. Some members of the medical community were convinced that bone marrow transplants would never work. They suggested that "they shouldn't go on as an experimental thing."

Most investigators abandoned the field and rejected the idea that bone marrow transplants could ever become a valuable asset to clinical medicine. The relatively few researchers who remained came from all over the world to learn from Dr. Thomas as he brought patients to near death by giving them massive doses of radiation and toxic drugs, and then rescuing them at the very last moment.

At the time of Aaron's transplant, doctors at The Hutch had completed about 3,000 bone marrow transplants, but long-term survival rates were still low. Four years later, Dr. Thomas's pioneering work would earn him the 1990 "Nobel Prize in Physiology or Medicine."

Doug, the quintessential mind-over-matter guy, refused to accept the thirty percent survival rate for Aaron, saying, "We're not going to deal with thirty percent. Aaron is going to be part of the thirty percent that has 100% chance of survival." Aaron absorbed Doug's confident, defiant attitude.

After Aaron heard Judy and Doug discussing the long-term survival odds, he summoned a confident voice and said, 'I'll survive."

As part of another ongoing clinical trial, Judy opted to place Aaron randomly into one of four study groups to evaluate ways to prevent infection. Aaron was assigned to one of eight Laminar Air Flow (LAF) rooms on the North side of the second floor. One of the largest threats to a patient's life was the post-transplant threat of infection. Prior to the operation, the patient's entire immune system was destroyed. In order to maintain a sterile environment, LAF rooms were designed with a thick, transparent plastic curtain that divided the room horizontally down the middle. The patient lived behind the curtain at all times, except when leaving the room for radiation therapy. A constant positive airflow pushed any airborne pathogens away from the patient's portion of the room through a narrow gap between the end of the curtain and the wall. The small gap also allowed medical personnel to enter and exit the isolated chamber, but only if they first donned a full complement of sterile clothing—a mask, hat, gloves, booties, and a smock. LAF patients ate sterile food and were given additional antibiotics, commonly referred to as "LAF drugs," that other transplant patients didn't receive.

The sterile portion of the LAF rooms contained a hospital bed, a commode, and a tiny closet. The end of the bed nearly matched up with the end of the plastic curtain that divided the room so there was very little room to move about. A stationary bicycle next to the bed encouraged patients to exercise. Thick plastic "sleeves," like long, plastic, oversized gloves, allowed visitors to reach into the sterile part of the room and make insulated contact with the patient. The sleeve also worked in the opposite direction. It allowed the patient to reach out to family and visitors outside the curtain without skin-to-skin contact.

"When the Hutch started doing these transplants in the seventies," Dr. Dan said, "one of the biggest reasons for failure was infection. It is because your white cells are gone. The idea was that if you can keep all the germs off, the patient will get through it okay. In the end, you could guarantee only one thing—you can keep people from visiting because it was such a rigmarole to come in. They put in all these sterile things and it just kept people from visiting. I think we probably created a fair amount of psychoses with these things. They thought it was going to make a big difference, but when they did the study, it didn't make any difference.

"The way you get infections is by touch. Germs aren't riding the wind, per se. They have to be in contact, so it really comes from hand washing. They've done these studies looking at residents and doctors and how many times they wash their hands. That is where most of it comes from. Most of the laminar airflow is all gone away."

Dr. Dan described the psychological damage done to patients who were assigned to LAF rooms. "It drove people crazy. I felt really bad about the kids and the adults in those rooms because it really isolated them from life. It is terrible because almost nobody would come and visit because it was too difficult. Can you imagine? They would spend a month in those things, where your only contact would be with people who were willing to get dressed up in all this stuff and the only thing you could see is their eyes."

Michael Rubin, a successful transplant patient from that era, shared his experience behind the plastic curtain. "Anytime somebody wanted to come into your room they would have to stand in your doorway on a sterile field, gown up, cover booties and everything, and then come inside. As a patient, you have to take additional medication to sterilize your gut and put on certain creams and ointments to sterilize your skin. Everything that you took into your room had to be autoclaved. Magazines, whatever. To wash your hair, when you had hair, which fell out around day five, you had to actually sit in a chair right at the opening. A nurse would put on a sterile gown and gloves and stand just inside the sterile field. She would reach in and take sterile water and wash my hair. I guess they did it right in the doorway because it was easier to clean up."

Rubin terminated his participation in the LAF trials prematurely. "I told them I couldn't take it anymore. I also think there is a lot to say about the state of mind and the immune system. They turned off the machine and they turned the curtain to the side. They put me on what's called reverse isolation, where everybody who comes into your room washes their hands and puts on a surgical mask. I felt a lot better after that."

The LAF rooms had their own consent form that warned of bad-tasting sterile food, and the risk of skin rash, convulsions, irreversible hearing loss, and renal impairment. The last sentence read, "There may be other risks that we don't know about." Judy couldn't imagine what they could possibly be. She would learn soon enough.

The other authorization forms Judy signed prior to Aaron's admission affirmed the gravity of their situation. In addition to the normal side effects of chemo—infection, nausea, vomiting, and hair loss, the forms warned of new potential side effects due to total body irradiation and the transplant drugs: sterility, complete loss of immunity, and failure of the heart, kidney, lung, brain, and liver. And, of course, Aaron could die. The forms no longer referred to doctors as doctors. They were called investigators.

Both Aaron and Heather signed consent forms, too. I thought it odd that the Hutch would have two minor children sign legal consent forms for a life and death matter. Dr. Jean Sanders, who oversaw the transplant program at The Hutch for more than three decades, explained that the consent forms, while not legally binding, were a way of gaining the child's commitment. "First of all," she said, "a child has to understand what is going to happen to them. I don't care if you are six or sixty-six; you talk to the child. The parent gives permission, but the child has to be cooperative. They have to take the medications and they have to do the things we ask them to do whether they want to or not. It is not a choice.

"They all know they have leukemia. Once you are in, you can't say, 'Hey I don't like this medicine—I am going to go home. A transplant has therapeutic benefit for the minor child. They aren't required by law to sign the consent, but if they want to, they can, along with their parents. I am going to talk to that child and tell them in language they can understand what we are going to ask them to do to get rid of their leukemia."

In some cases, the parents' sense of panic or level of denial is so high that the message doesn't make it through. A friend of mine whose son underwent a successful transplant told of a young mother who came to her for solace after her baby died following her transplant. "All she could say to me over and over again was, 'They didn't tell me she could die.'" My friend wondered, "Did she sign the same release form I did? Because every sentence, every paragraph said this could result in death."

Aaron lightened the mood as he applied his loopy signature to the bottom of each page. When he saw the word "subject" he said, "I'm the predicate!" When he saw Heather signing, he said, "Heather just signed up for the marines!"

The forms were peppered with words like antigens, cytomegalovirus, and hyperalimentation. With his signature, Aaron authorized the removal of blood and skin samples and he gave his consent to participate in post-transplant studies. He attested that the medical risks had been explained to him and that he had been given ample opportunity to discuss them with his doctors. Nevertheless, he was prepared to proceed. Aaron signed the forms and prepared for the longest 100 days of his life.

Chapter 13

THE VALLEY OF DARKNESS

T he atmosphere on the transplant floor was surprisingly cheerful given that a third of the patients would die within three months. "What else are you going to do?" asked Pat Groff, a transplant nurse at The Hutch in the 1980s. "You can't really live thinking that you are going to die at any time. If you live like that, you are going to hasten it. You just take each day as it comes.

"You have to remember that when you got a transplant, you got a chance to survive. You had to walk through the valley of darkness to get there, but you have a chance. Whereas, those people who did not have a chance to get a transplant were going to die because their disease was going to get them. So, it was actually a very hopeful place.

"We laughed all the time. When you work with a family and a patient for ten hours a day, five days in a row, you share your life with them. We would even bring in treats for them. We all remember patients much better from those days than we do from later days because we became very bonded with them."

The view from each of the second-floor LAF rooms was limited to nearby buildings or the street below. A chaplain's office, a small pharmacy, and bath/shower rooms lined the interior walls of the hallway. A kitchen provided a gathering place for the families. A large, centrally located nurses' station served as command central.

Two giant, gridded erase boards hung on the wall within the nurses' station. Prior to the Health Insurance Portability and Affordability Act (HIPAA), patients' confidential medical information could be displayed as openly as a community calendar. "We had columns with names of the patients, their age, and their disease," said Nurse Pat. "Underneath it we had the doctors name and the nurse's name for the shift. We listed what we were supposed to do for each patient that day. If there was a certain lab test, a bone marrow, or chest ex-ray, it was up there. It would also have the day the patient was on, like day twenty-two, or day fifty."

Patients and their families paid close attention to the information on the board. The "days since transplant" number indicated whether a patient's new marrow had begun functioning within the expected two-week period. The number also tracked the patient's progress toward the one-hundred-day mark, when the patient could go home, provided there were no complications. The second important number was the white cell count. Each patient's immune system had been destroyed in the transplant process. A white cell count of 500 or more indicated the new marrow was doing its job in creating a new immune system.

Aaron joined his family for dinner at McDonalds before returning to his room to bathe, gown up, and enter the LAF room for the first time. He spoke pleasantly to the nurses and was sold on his room when he found out he'd have cable TV. Aaron settled in by working on his drawings. In one colored pencil drawing entitled "Building up the Bone Marrow," he depicted healthy white cells parachuting out of a jet plane and providing replenishment to a line of hollow bones below.

Andrea York, another of Aaron's nurses, reviewed with Judy and Aaron all the sprays, powders, and ointments associated with his LAF procedures. She helped Aaron get ready for bed while the family said good night and returned home to University Place. Aaron spent his first night at The Hutch without adult company. For this eleven-year-old boy, it was another night in another hospital.

The pre-transplant process began the following morning. It didn't take long for the LAF drugs to take a harsh toll on Aaron. His stomach rejected the drugs so quickly that Aaron began timing the process. He considered it a success if the drugs stayed down ten seconds or more.

Aaron's full-body radiation protocol included twice-daily sessions for forty-five minutes each over a seven-day period. Shortly after Aaron checked in, Dr. Rainer Storb, a German-born physician and one of the founding scientists at The Hutch, gave an interview to the ABC News television show *20-20*, in which he explained the massive doses of radiation.

"We are essentially exposing him to about two and a half times the lethal dose of radiation at the outset," said the doctor. "That is sufficient, we hope, to kill off the tumor cells in most cases."

"Why doesn't it kill him?" the correspondent asked the doctor.

"Because we have a rescue procedure at hand—the donor marrow. If patients don't have a bone marrow donor, they would die of infections or bleeding. Since we have a bone marrow donor, then we can give that marrow back after the treatment. Within a matter of two or three weeks it will start functioning and provide him with those important cells on which his life depends." The challenge would be to keep Aaron alive for two to three weeks until Heather's marrow had a chance to work.

It had been ten years since Aaron first received radiation as a two-year-old. Unlike the first time, when they radiated only his brain, this time they flooded his entire body. The radiation treatments began on January 18, or day "minus six." When his nurse, Andrea, came behind his plastic curtain and asked him to gown up for his first radiation treatment, Aaron had no way of knowing this moment would be the best he would feel for at least five months.

"He gowned up without complaint," Judy wrote. "He marched to the elevator and into the radiation room. Doug got tears in his eyes as we left him there." The parents usually accompanied Aaron on the elevator ride down to the basement, but they were discouraged from going beyond that point. Doug became uncomfortable and usually avoided the procedure. For Judy, it depended on the day and her mental frame of mind. Keith nearly always accompanied Aaron if permitted by the medical staff.

"I liked to be with him," Keith said. During one radioactive procedure, Keith insisted on being by Aaron's side. "They put all this stuff on me, this lead apron kind of gown, to go in. It just didn't seem right to take a little kid and shove him into one of those machines that make a lot of noise and then have him be in there all alone. I always wanted to be as close to him as I could."

On occasion, Keith's presence made the medical staff uncomfortable. "I don't think they liked me being there very well. Maybe they weren't comfortable about what they were doing, you know, irradiating people and killing them, essentially. As I was sitting there, they said, 'you know, you ought to move back because that door leaks a little bit.'"

A nurse always accompanied Aaron up to the point of entering the radiation chamber. "We would take them down," said Nurse Pat. "A physicist monitored the amount of radiation coming out and a tech turned it on and off. It was a lead-lined room with concrete walls about two feet thick. It was a huge room, probably forty by twenty feet. And relatively tall ceilings. It had a small ante-room, which had some radiation monitors in there.

"We waited in a big foyer on the outside. Cameras could see them so that if they threw up, you would stop the radiation and you would go in and medicate them or clean them up or whatever needed to be done. We had to stay down there while they were there. I just would sit there and read a magazine while they were being radiated.

"Inside the room, there were these two things, they were called pigs, on either side of the room. They were kind of like really big Benjamin Franklin stoves. The radiation emanated out from these pigs and the patient would be in the center."

The technicians rotated Aaron's body from side to side and onto to his back so the radiation would be administered evenly throughout his body. The effects were immediate. "When we left the radiation room," Keith remembered, "and we were walking back to the elevator, he felt weak or dizzy. He reached out and grabbed my hand and my arm to help steady himself.

"It wasn't like him. He wasn't touchy-feely at all." Keith said. "He didn't like massages and backrubs and that sort of thing. I don't know if his skin was easily irritated, or exactly what it was, but he didn't like it. There was a time he would get cramps in his feet from something and I offered to rub his feet, but he wouldn't let me do it."

The doctors supplemented the LAF drugs and the radiation with high doses of cyclophosphamide, or Cytoxan, as part of his "conditioning regimen." The side effects of the drug resembled those from the radiation: nausea, loss of appetite, and diarrhea.

The wide variety of anti-nausea drugs available to cancer patients today had not been developed thirty years ago. In 1986, Benadryl remained the only medical relief available to curb the constant nausea of cancer patients. The resulting drowsiness from Benadryl meant that Aaron was torn constantly between sleeping or vomiting.

Aaron lost his appetite and experienced regular bouts of diarrhea as the radiation sessions accumulated. He continued to take the LAF drugs, which made things even worse. Judy tracked Aaron's blood counts as the combined effects of the radiation and chemo killed his healthy cells along with his cancer cells. Aaron's mood plummeted alongside his blood counts, but rebounded as he rediscovered his fighting spirit.

The day before the transplant, the doctors introduced one more drug to Aaron's system, cyclosporine. The new drug would serve as a prophylactic to graft vs. host disease, a common and deadly consequence of a transplant, when the patient's body rejects the cells from the donor.

Heather's pre-op routine paled in comparison to Aaron's. The day before the transplant, she checked in next door at Swedish Hospital, where her marrow would be extracted. She would have a one-day stay in the hospital and, assuming everything went as planned, she would be back in school the following day. On the way to Swedish prior to checking in, she wanted to visit Aaron one more time.

When she arrived at Aaron's room, Aaron had been vomiting up his LAF drugs all day. The Cytoxan made him feel "hot" and the doctors had just about finished the procedure of killing off the life force within him. It was a tough time for him to be cheerful. Heather stayed briefly before going over to Swedish to check in.

The evening before the operation, Aaron watched the *Cosby Show* on television as he ate his last dinner before his transplant. He enjoyed a meal of popcorn and 7-UP…and immediately threw it up.

Chapter 14

THE BAD THING HAPPENED

Performing a bone marrow transplant is similar to doing a large paint job in that you spend a lot more time doing the prep work and follow-up than you do on the actual job itself. After Aaron suffered through days of full-body radiation and received massive doses of Cytoxan, the actual procedure of receiving Heather's marrow was somewhat anticlimactic.

"The transplant was mildly surprising," said Doug. "It really wasn't any different than taking a transfusion. I went into Aaron's room and it's just going into his arm. I expected it to be more of an event than it was. Instead, it wasn't much different than getting a pint of blood."

"Aaron didn't seem to think much of it," Judy noted. "At least that we know about." He worked on a drawing while he waited for Heather's bone marrow to arrive from Swedish Hospital next door. His artwork depicted healthy blue cells destroying the red-colored leukemic cells as they attempted to flee.

As mundane as the day may have seemed to Doug and Aaron, it was the biggest day in eight-year-old Heather's life. Eight years later, she recounted the experience. "I was the only one who could maybe cure him and take away his pain. I knew the doctors were going to stick me with a bunch of needles to take out my bone marrow. I remember lying in the bed while being wheeled down a long brightly lit, but still eerie hallway. My mom was on one side and doctors were on the other. I clutched a small stuffed dog that my favorite neighbor had given me for being so courageous. My whole body was shaking. I clearly remember fading out." Heather's most prominent memory was lying face-down on the operating table while wearing an open-backed surgical gown. "I was really embarrassed," she said, "because I knew they could see my butt."

Judy stayed until they took Heather into the operating room. Then, she returned to Aaron's room at The Hutch. Doctors bored twelve holes in Heather's pelvic bone with specially designed, wide-bore needles and removed several pints of Heather's spongy marrow. The procedure took less than an hour.

It was imperative they begin the process of restoring Aaron's marrow right away. Nurse Pat described the urgency in starting the transfusion. "It would be walked over and given as soon as it hit the floor. You'd give it in usually two bags of what looked like red blood cells, like a transfusion. Two people checked to be sure. 'Is it the right donor? Is the right blood type? Is today the day to give it? Yes, Yes, Yes.'"

Aaron worked on his drawings and watched TV the rest of the day while the marrow dripped from the bags into his veins. Heather spent an hour in her room recovering from her procedure and then asked to visit Aaron. "I knew it was a good thing that I did, so I wanted to watch me being put into him. I was wheeled through the tunnel from Swedish Hospital to Aaron's room at The Hutch, where I watched it happen. Shortly after receiving my marrow his cheeks flushed with a red glow."

Heather's visit produced a predictable outcome. "She was very cheerful," wrote Judy, "but Aaron ignored her at first. She watched her marrow go into him and it seemed sad he wouldn't talk to her." Heather had donated her marrow to save her brother's life, but she continued to be the target of his resentment. At eight years of age, she may have assumed Aaron's behavior was typical of all older brothers. How would she have known what was normal or abnormal?

After being rejected by Aaron, Heather asked her mom to wheel her down the hall to visit Brianna and April, two little girls going through the transplant process. Heather had befriended them earlier and she had been of valuable assistance to "Bri's" parents in getting their resistant child to take her pills. Both girls loved visiting with Heather and she thoroughly enjoyed the attention. After Heather returned to Aaron's room, he was much nicer to her, having received a stern lecture from Judy in Heather's absence.

The successful transfer of Heather's marrow to Aaron was just one more step in a lengthy process. As painful as the radiation and chemotherapy had been for Aaron prior to the marrow transfer, his biggest battles and most of his suffering lie ahead.

His greatest threat and a frequent cause of death to patients following a bone marrow transplant was Graft Versus Host Disease (GvHD), a situation where the donor's marrow identifies the recipient's body as a threat and attacks it aggressively. The disease manifests itself by attacking the patient's skin, eyes, lungs or other organs. It is as painful as it is deadly.

Aaron also suffered from an agonizing condition called mucositis. The radiation prior to the transplant caused ulcerous mouth sores that made it difficult if not impossible for the him to eat, drink, swallow, or speak. "The mucositis you get from the radiation and the initial chemo gets very serious," Nurse Andrea explained. "It is really thick and it is awful to get out. They are rinsing with salt water all day long and spitting. It is right after the transplant when you don't have enough white cells to fight it. It gets worse until your counts come in. When your pain peaked, you knew you were over the hump. That usually meant that you were grafted.

"All the transplant patients had terrible mouths so helping them with their mouth care was a big thing. They had big buckets so they could just gargle and rinse and spit. Everything was too painful. Their platelets were so low, they couldn't brush their teeth because they would bleed. If they didn't get it out and they swallowed it, it wouldn't digest so they would throw up, which is also really unpleasant. You could do that two to three times a day.

"They couldn't eat for at least a couple of weeks so we had IV's hanging on them with foods and whatever antibiotics we had. We worked a lot with managing their pain and getting them to try to take medications. Everybody needed blood frequently because they would be bleeding so much. A cold sore would turn into a sore that would go over their face and their chin and down their throat. It was really gruesome."

Andrea had been a transplant nurse for five years when she was assigned to Aaron's care. Prior to her tenure at The Hutch, she had been a nurse in the burn unit ICU at Harbor View Hospital in Seattle. "That's why my ex-husband thought I was the one with the problem," she said. "Who in their right mind would take care of burn patients and then cancer patients?"

How did she keep from burning out in such a high-stress environment and such a low patient survival rate? "It's a self-weeding business," she told me. "Those who can't do it anymore stop doing it and those who love it can't get away from it. Dr. Thomas always said that his secret weapons were his nurses. The day he won the Nobel prize, he gave every one of us a hug. He said, 'This doesn't belong to me, this belongs to all of you because you are the ones who got these patients through it.'

"Of course, it belongs to him, but his attitude toward us as nurses has always been collegial. It was never from the top down because we were taking care of the patients eight hours a day. The docs came in, did their rounds, and we would say, 'When you did this, this is what happened to the patient. Maybe this would work better next time.' There was always room for innovation and always room for change."

The patient load was distributed according to the degree of difficulty and the sickness of the patient. The LAF rooms were distributed evenly among the eight or ten nurses on a shift because it was more cumbersome to work through the curtains. Each nurse might have one LAF room and one other room.

Gowning up to take care of a patient behind the curtain was quite a process. It was common practice to ask for coverage from another nurse if you were going behind the curtain. Judy often gowned up and joined Aaron behind the LAF curtain to assist with his mouth treatments when the nurses weren't there. Outside of the curtain, mechanical equipment pumped medications to Aaron through a thirty-foot tube, the entire length of which had to be replaced every twenty-four hours.

After his daily bath, Aaron applied a series of LAF powders to every moist part of his body. "It was a combination of three different anti-microbial and anti-fungal powders," nurse Andrea said. It was believed that it would help minimize their chances for infection."

Every morning, the attending physician of the month, the pharmacist, the social worker, the chaplain—everybody from the team—made their rounds. They got a report from the nightshift nurse and then walked the perimeter of the floor to see each of the twenty patients. "They would go in the room and discuss the patient's or family's issues or concerns for the day," explained Andrea.

A lab person showed up about 10 a.m. each day with the blood counts of every patient. The test results, handwritten on one sheet of paper, were posted on the bulletin board of the family room. "All the families would anticipate around 9:45 that the numbers would be posted soon," said Andrea. "They might be in their rooms and say, 'I'm going down to take a look at the numbers to see if they have posted them yet.'"

Judy joined other family members each day as the numbers came in. Everybody could see which patients were getting blood and platelets. Patients and families shared their counts and cheered each other on. The sheet spoke volumes about who was making it and who wasn't. It was a survival tally.

"There are different types of white blood cells," explained Andrea. "There are bands and polys. The neutrophils are a combination of both and they are the infection fighters. Once they got up to 500, you could stop the antibiotics."

Aaron's stay in the LAF room effectively insulated him from most bacteria and viruses. Fresh fruits, vegetables, plants, and cut flowers were prohibited, since they carry fungi and bacteria that pose a risk for infection. Visitors and hospital personnel vigilantly washed their hands with antiseptic soap before entering his room. Anyone who went behind the curtain was required to wear a gown, gloves and a mask. Consequently, few visitors ventured behind the curtain, including Keith and Doug. Judy was the only parent to go behind the curtain on a regular basis.

Two days after Aaron's transplant, his friend Eric Freitag joined him to watch Super Bowl XX between the Chicago Bears and the New England Patriots. Eric watched the game through the plastic sheet that separated the two friends. Normally, both boys were Seattle Seahawks fans, but like most Americans, they became fans of the 1985-86 Chicago Bears, at least for a short time. Coach Mike Ditka's Bears defeated the New England Patriots 46-10, in a game that was remembered as much for the characters on the team as for the game itself. The Bears were loaded with talent, but the player who received the most attention was the 300-pound defensive tackle, William "Refrigerator" Perry, who was occasionally inserted as an unstoppable running back.

Eric brought a teddy bear to Heather, who happened to be visiting Aaron at the same time. When Aaron realized the stuffed animal was for Heather, he reached through sleeves in the plastic screen and choked it. Heather missed Aaron's antics because she had left the room and was hobbling down the hall, suffering from the "Hutch Shuffle," a painful walk experienced by marrow donors from the multiple punctures in their pelvic bones.

On Tuesday, January 28, four days after Aaron's transplant and two days following the Super Bowl, Judy listened to the radio while traveling up Interstate-5 from University Place to The Hutch. It was 8:39 a.m. when she learned that the Space Shuttle Challenger crashed into the Atlantic, taking the lives of all seven crew members, including social studies teacher and astronaut Christa McAuliffe. Much of America witnessed the launch and nearly the entire country heard about the disaster within the hour.

Three days later, President Ronald Reagan spoke at a memorial service and gave tribute to the fallen heroes. "Sometimes," he said, "when we reach for the stars, we fall short. But we must pick ourselves up again and press on despite the pain." The Forman-Erwin clan picked themselves up and pressed on despite their pain. Hopefully, after so many failed launches, this mission would succeed.

Aaron continued to depict epic battles between good and evil cells. The good cells carried hand-held weapons that projected solid streams of blue liquid at the red, or bad cells. Each red cell exploded on impact when flushed by the triumphant blue liquid.

Keith and Judy set up a system where at least one of them spent each night in Aaron's room during his posttransplant period. A chair in the room folded into a small bed. Not the most comfortable accommodations, but it sufficed. Under that arrangement, Keith could maintain his job while Judy managed her household in University place and spent as much time as she could with Heather.

During this time, Mary Lou and I drove to Seattle with our three-and-a-half-year-old son, Matt, to visit Aaron. Judy was behind the LAF curtain, dressed in her sterile attire, when we arrived. Aaron's eyes lit up when we walked into the room. We brought a *Garfield* book as a gift, which a nurse whisked away to be sterilized before Aaron could receive it. Mary Lou helped Matt reach his hands through the plastic sleeves to touch his cousin.

From behind the plastic curtain, Aaron appeared to be on display. It felt intrusive to look at him, though I was certain he was glad we were there. He didn't look like the old Aaron. He sat up in bed, his face red and bloated, surrounded by myriad machines, cables, and plastic tubing, while Judy and a nurse, masked and gowned to the max, attended to his needs.

We didn't hear them during out visit, but the Hutch's dog labs were located just above Aaron's room on the third floor. At night their howls could be heard when it was feeding time. They served as a reminder that the patients were also research subjects. "They were all dogs going through transplants," said Nurse Andrea. "That's how we got to the humans. Nobody was allowed on those floors so I really don't know much about it. I try not to think about it because I am a dog lover."

More dogs die of cancer than any other disease. The Hutch has partnered for many years with the American Kennel Club and other cancer researchers to explore treatments that might be beneficial for both dogs and humans.

Dr. Jean Sanders, who oversaw the transplant operations at the Fred Hutchinson Cancer Center for more than thirty-seven years, explained why the use of dogs was so important in their clinical research. "We transplanted dogs and demonstrated the basic principles of transplantation to see if you can transfer those principles directly to man."

Dr. Sanders spoke with an air of detachment when discussing her canine subjects, a skill that she honed by working with both her canine and her human patients for more than four decades. "In order to survive you don't become best friends with the families. Or at least I didn't. If you hamper yourself and become best friends with all your patients, you can't be objective. You absolutely have to be the best you can be for your patients and that does not include becoming emotionally involved. It doesn't mean you are unkind; you just don't get emotionally involved. Big difference."

The first three weeks following his transplant turned into a blur of painful experiences for Aaron. He developed GvHD so the nurses kept him on a steady morphine drip. The pain from GvHD was so intense and so common among transplant patients that, according the Andrea, "All of the nurses who took care of those patients vowed that we would never have a transplant. It was so grueling."

Conversely, Nurse Pat considered it a special time. "The families supported each other tremendously. It was unique and it won't be replicated again. It couldn't have been invented. It was a group of people who came together at the right time and it was amazing."

The families shared the same challenge and they circled the wagons against a common enemy. They tracked the success of their own loved one while cheering for the other patients and their families. If the counts for a patient began to rise, it meant the patient was starting to engraft, the first step toward survival. Patients who were healthy enough to exercise walked the perimeter of the floor and offered encouragement to other patients in passing.

The bonding was tempered, however, by the threat of becoming too close. "The Hutch was not a happy place," Doug said. "I think they would paint that picture, but I didn't feel it was. Too many people dying for me. We would walk the halls all the time. Aaron would have to do two trips around the floor so you went by every room and you got to know the people. Judy and I got to know the parents and everybody in the waiting rooms because you couldn't spend that much time in Aaron's room. It was more being of the room than in the room. There was a whole lot of awareness of what was going on. You'd see people come in; you'd see them after the transplant; you'd see them walking the halls; and then all of a sudden, they wouldn't be there. And you know they didn't go home. It was a hundred-day deal, so if you are missing on day thirty-three...that means the bad thing happened."

One hundred days was the targeted level of stay for a successful transplant patient to be discharged. If there was a medical determination that the patient was not going to make it, the family needed to be told. "They have to get ready for it," said Andrea. "The amount of time it takes varies from family to family, depending on how sick they really are. If they have been sick for a while they are probably used to the idea."

The cause was usually an infection that couldn't be controlled. The nurses would often be the ones to talk to the families—and the families were never ready to hear the news. "A lot of the family members needed time to accept that it was a failure," said Andrea. "That came into play before you pulled the plug on somebody because the family wasn't quite ready yet, so the chaplains were very active. People were dying.

"There were a couple of rocking chairs, and those were frequently used outside the rooms. I remember sitting with an elderly gentleman—his daughter was dying in the middle of the night—and hearing and appreciating for the first time that a parent should never have to see a child die first. It wasn't right. She was long past recovering, but he wasn't ready to watch her go. At that point we were waiting for him to be ready. Not until I had kids was I able to really appreciate that. I will always remember that.

"I can't tell you the number of times we knew patients were not going to survive; there was no hope for recovery, but there was yet another protocol they wanted to try. The families wouldn't ever give up hope, and it is a research institution. That is part of why the attendings (physician/researchers) rotated every month; they had to take care of these people every month. It got them out of their lab, where all they saw was data and the ideas for discovery. They rotated in so they could see the effects of their imaginations, their creativity, their ideas. It wasn't all just 'be back in the lab.' They would have to come out and see what their drugs were doing. They came from their bench and daily lab work to see the effects. That was supposed to be the ethical thing to do. It made them humble, but it still was always a research institute. It was really hard to see the family hold on longer and longer when the patient might be intubated and they might be on dialysis and when you knew the outcome wasn't going to change."

A lone chair just outside a patient's door was never a good sign. It was often the signal that a patient was near the end. Keith remembered how quickly things could change on the second floor. "When those blood counts were going up, you were cheering. Everybody was doing well and you were talking to all the families. I would leave and miss a day and then I'd come back. I would walk in and see a chair out in front of somebody's room. Sometimes there would be a nurse, but it meant somebody was in crisis. When that happened, a nurse would sit in that chair and be on full watch. You knew when you saw that chair there, or a nurse sitting in a chair outside somebody's room, that it was bad news, that they were probably not going to make it. When that happened, they were gone within a day or two."

"We wore masks in those days," said Nurse Pat. "To stay inside a room for ten hours without ever taking a mask off would be hard. That is why we had the chair. We couldn't leave the environment and we couldn't leave the room, but we could step outside the door to take the mask off, take a sip of water, and stuff like that. Yah, the chair was always a bad sign."

As Aaron's condition gradually improved, he began walking laps around the perimeter of the second floor for exercise. During one lap, he took an interest in Billy's room and noticed that Billy was very sick. The next day, after taking another lap around the floor, he noticed Billy's absence. "Billy is gone," he told Judy. Judy cried, but Aaron seemed to take the news in stride.

"He won't be at camp this summer," Aaron added. He walked back to his room and stopped to look in Billy's room along the way. Children perceive death in different ways, depending on their age. Aaron had been facing death since he was two years old and by age eleven, his concept of death was more like that of an adult. Billy's passing wasn't the first, nor would it be the last death Aaron witnessed on the second floor of The Hutch. Three days later, Judy told him of another child passing. "Teri died this morning, Aaron."

"It seems like everybody's dying," was his only response. The next day, after a long bout of vomiting and retching, Aaron told Keith, "I'm the next to go." After his mom arrived later in the day, he mentioned another child from the floor. "Sushil might die," he said. He was surprised the next day when Sushil was still alive. With so many children dying so quickly, Aaron saw death behind every door.

Chapter 15

A REAL BOY

lmo Zumwalt III checked into the LAF room next
door to Aaron on February 11, 1986. At thirty-nine, he
was older than most of the other transplant recipients.
Keith took note of the new resident, primarily because in
Vietnam, he had served under the chain of command of
Elmo III's father, Admiral Elmo Zumwalt II, Commander
of US Naval Forces.

Near the height of the Vietnam war, Admiral Zumwalt
ordered the spraying of an herbicide called Agent Orange
over North Vietnam. "Operation Ranch Hand" culminated
in more than eighteen-million gallons of Agent Orange
and other herbicides being sprayed over more than twenty
percent of North Vietnam. Ironically, the admiral issued the
orders to spray the defoliant knowing that his son, Elmo
III, was captain of swift boat PCF-35, which operated in the
area of the mass spraying.

In *My Father, My Son*, a book co-written by the father and
son, the senior Zumwalt wrote that his logistics people had
assured him that the spray represented no health threat to
humans. In the same book, the younger Elmo expressed his
belief that Agent Orange caused numerous medical problems
reported by Vietnam veterans: nervous disorders, cancer and
skin problems, and severe birth defects with their children.

Elmo III had more than a passing interest in the matter.
After returning from Vietnam, his first son was born with

learning difficulties. Shortly thereafter, Elmo III was diagnosed with two types of cancer, lymphoma and Hodgkin's Disease. When chemotherapy and radiation failed to arrest his cancer, doctors suggested a bone marrow transplant as his last viable option.

"I have never experienced so much physical agony," the younger Elmo wrote. "Vomiting when you have a bone marrow transplant becomes as routine as coughing when you have a cold. I coughed up blood of just about every color from cherry red to black. At times, my skin itched so badly that I scratched myself until I bled. Pain was the only constant."

Just prior to Elmo III's admission to the second floor, Aaron began to experience inexplicable high fevers and excruciating headaches. He was given regular doses of morphine for several weeks while they searched for the cause. One day, Judy called the nurse's attention to some blisters below and inside Aaron's right ear. The nurse exclaimed, "That's zoster!"

Herpes zoster, also known as shingles, is induced by the same virus that causes chicken pox. The virus goes into a dormant stage within the patient's body after chicken pox disappear. If the virus reactivates at a later time, it often causes severe pain before blisters appear. Zoster was a relatively common occurrence on the second floor of the Hutch and the nurses and the doctors were embarrassed for not suspecting the virus earlier. Dr. Donnall Thomas, the Nobel Laureate, came by Aaron's room and apologized to Judy and Aaron for the delay in diagnosis.

Aaron's shingles diagnosis contained a silver lining. The virus's high contagion rate presented a danger to the other transplant patients on the second floor, so they immediately transferred Aaron across the street to Swedish Hospital. He still remained in isolation—his immune system was still compromised—but his stay in the LAF room was over. He no longer needed to take the special powders and drugs associated with the sterile environment. More importantly, he could re-establish human contact. Judy could give him a hug.

After his recovery from zoster, Aaron returned to the second floor of the Hutch, but not to an LAF room. By leaving the segregated environment prematurely, he had broken the control standards of the clinical trial. Any data from his participation would be invalidated. It served as another reminder that behind every medical decision pertaining to Aaron's care, something was being measured, analyzed, and reported as part of the latest clinical trial.

Aaron's colorful drawings continued to incorporate battle scenes resembling those in *Star Wars* movies. Since early childhood, Aaron had used artwork to record the events of his life. His drawings often featured sailboats, animals, and other happy themes. The skies were always blue, his favorite color. His illustrations often reduced complicated events of the world into the simple view of a child. After Keith's mother died, the family attended a service where her remains were spread over a mountaintop. Aaron's black and white pencil sketch of the service showed a man pouring small particles over a cliff from what looked like a salt shaker. The caption read, "Went to Portland at large mountain. Dumped out Grandma Forman's ashes and then had a picnic."

His illustrated cookbooks combined his love of cooking with his passion for drawing. Maureen Miller, a neighbor who often took care of Heather, still has the cookbooks given to her by Aaron. "What he thought of you determined what kind of cookbooks you got," she said. "Some were colored, some were not. I have a whole cookbook and I have some coloring in mine!"

Aaron's depiction of the California Raisins Band, a fictional group of animated raisin musicians made popular by a television ad in the 1980s, remains my favorite. Aaron presented his drawing to Mary Lou and me during one of his visits to Eugene after his transplant, and we still display it in our home.

Judy tried to maintain some semblance of her regular life while spending the better part of four months with Aaron at The Hutch. She went home when she could. She maintained a regular running routine—it was the only thing besides her writing that helped her keep her sanity. Occasionally, the Bridge Girls brought their game, with dinner and wine, to The Hutch when Judy couldn't leave. They didn't have to work too hard to sneak in the wine, since the nurses reportedly shared an occasional bottle during shift change in the earlier, more casual days on the transplant floor.

Three days after Aaron returned to the Hutch after recovering from the zoster, he asked for something to eat. He had survived entirely on IV nutrients for six weeks since throwing up the popcorn and 7-Up he'd eaten the day before his transplant. For his first solid food in forty-one days, Aaron requested cereal and 7-Up. He took two bites and threw it up. Later, he took another stab at solid food, this time attempting a hot dog and raspberry yogurt. He ate three quarters of the hot dog before his stomach rejected it, but at least he was slowly regaining interest in food. "I want to eat," he said, "so I can get out of here!"

Aaron continued to take slow laps around the second floor, picking up stamina as the days went by. By March 6, he walked two and a half laps without resting. Two days later, his white cell counts recovered to the point they gave him a day-pass to go home for the afternoon. Eight-year-old Heather made a sign to welcome her brother home. She started to write "WELCOME," but changed it at the last minute to read, "We Love You, Aaron!" Her brother wasn't overly talkative to her, but he wasn't cranky. Heather celebrated Aaron's lack of acrimony. "Aaron's not grumpy to me!" she exclaimed as she sat down next to her brother to watch TV.

In thinking today about Aaron's life, I wonder what exactly he had to be happy about. When he looked in the mirror, he saw a bloated, unattractive version of himself. "I don't like the way I look," he would say or "I am the worst-looking person here." He didn't like being sick all the time and, more importantly, he disliked being so different from others. Aaron wanted to get well once and for all. He wanted to play with friends. He wanted to go to school. He was like the character Pinocchio, trapped in a wooden body and unable to do the things other boys could do. Aaron longed to be free of his cancerous body so he could be a "real boy."

It's difficult for two, let alone three parents, each with a different style, to coordinate their efforts to support, encourage, and discipline a child. Jointly parenting a child with a serious illness complicates things beyond measure. One evening, Doug arrived at the hospital for a visit with Aaron. He didn't like it when he saw how much help Judy was giving to her son. He became even more upset when he overheard Aaron refer to Judy as "Mommy."

"He wants him back to the tough Aaron," Judy wrote in her journal. On the surface, Doug's approach may have seemed insensitive. But it's a perfect illustration of the many dilemmas faced by parents of potentially dying children. If you're convinced your child is going to die, do you coddle them all the way to the end? Doug believed that Aaron needed to be tough to survive. It was their job as parents to steel him for the battles that lie ahead. Aaron needed to stay mentally strong and if he did survive, they wanted him to have the necessary life skills for his future. In Doug's mind, referring to Judy as "Mommy" represented a regression in mental toughness.

Keith took a more relaxed approach. He preferred to ask questions about Aaron's feelings and explore what was behind Aaron's actions. This proved to be the more challenging approach, since Aaron was generally a closed book. Nevertheless, Keith would likely have interpreted Aaron's reference to his "mommy" as an outreach for maternal support at a critical time. He was, after all, in a transplant ward with children dying all around him.

Judy was usually the final arbiter on which approach to take since she spent more time with Aaron than anyone. And she was his mother. Doug's insistence on toughness often led Judy to temper her motherly instincts to nurture. During one disastrous outing to Keith's place in Tacoma, Aaron threw up in the apartment and again in the car. "Not a pleasant trip back to Seattle," Judy wrote. "Fussed and cried a lot. I gave him more lectures about attitude and being tough—I think if we keep at him, he'll realize how important it is." Judy's parenting style always mixed pep talks with supportive hugs and "get tough" lectures. Oh, and admonishments for Aaron to be kind to Heather.

The perfect approach to handling all the demands and pressures of Aaron's situation did not exist. They were all trying to figure out how to survive. After their return to the hospital following one of Aaron's day passes, he decided he didn't want to take his pills anymore. "It was quite an unpleasant situation," Judy wrote. "He was flat refusing to take pills, and we were insisting," The situation exploded. Judy and Aaron went for a walk together down the hallway after things settled. She had a chance to unwind and Aaron had a chance to release. "He grabbed me and hugged me hard and sobbed. Not a fussy cry, just a good hard cry, saying, 'Oh, Mom, I'm just so tired of it all.'"

Their days became a mixture of small celebrations and reality checks. On March 30, they celebrated Easter by dyeing eggs in Aaron's hospital room. Three days later, Judy wrote two words at the top of her journal: "Sushil died." Over the following weekend, "Bri" died. Adam relapsed and made plans to go home to live out what time he had remaining. No further treatments were possible. Aaron's response: "I'm glad mine has decided to stay away."

By mid-April, Aaron was able to walk laps repeatedly around the floor. He carried a squirt gun with him and took shots at the doctors and nurses. He colored together peacefully with Heather, and then nailed her with the squirt guns, too. "It's the best he has been in his whole life!" Heather said. And most importantly, he began to eat. By late April, Aaron prepared to go home.

In a letter dated April 28, Dr. Storb officially turned Aaron's medical care back over to Aaron's regular physician:

Dear Dr. Niebrugge:

Enclosed find the final discharge summary of your patient, Aaron Forman with ALL in the fourth remission. As you know Aaron was given a bone marrow transplant from his HLA identical sister on January 23, 1986 following conditioning with high dose cyclophosphamide and 1400 rad of total body irradiation. Aaron had a prolonged hospital course because of chronic abdominal pain most likely related to acute graft-versus-host disease . . .

I discussed with the patient and mother the long-term outlook. The biggest hurdle to the ultimate success of bone marrow transplantation is recurrence of his underlying leukemia which can occur with an incidence of 40% between day 100 and 5 years after transplantation. The fact that he had acute GVHD which has now subsided is an additional good risk factor since it is generally accompanied by a lessened recurrence rate...Other complications are the patient's continued susceptibility to infections...Because of the risk for infections we recommend that Aaron stay away from crowds for another half year or so. This includes not going to summer camp this year. However, visits of movie houses and of Disneyland during day hours or out of season could certainly be contemplated.

For Dr. Dan's benefit, Dr. Storb listed the long-term side effects that could result from the transplant: sterility, impairment of growth and development, and cataract formation. He estimated the odds of Aaron developing additional cancers in the future at six times the general population. All of this assumed, of course, that Aaron survived the first year after transplantation.

Chapter 16

WHEN I WEAR MY MASK

J udy reigned in her enthusiasm as she drove to The Hutch to pick up Aaron the day of his release. "I was so excited driving up today!" she wrote. "I was also worried, afraid something might come up to delay his release." But when she walked by the nurses' station and saw balloons suspended from the television in Aaron's room, she knew the news was good.

Aaron walked out of the Hutch on April 28, 1986, a week shy of the ten-year anniversary of his initial diagnosis as a two-year-old boy. He had survived four relapses and was now entering his fifth remission. The longest interval Aaron had ever been in remission and off any sort of treatment had been fourteen months. Finally, they were rid of his leukemia. They had destroyed all of his original bone marrow and along with it all the deadly leukemic cells that had threatened his life for years. Heather's marrow had given him a new beginning, and while he expected to experience some residual damage due to the years of chemo and radiation, Aaron had a chance to begin life anew.

Aaron looked forward to being paroled from The Hutch, but he wasn't yet fully aware of the terms of his release. During the transplant process, the doctors had destroyed all Aaron's white cells and any immunities he had, including those from childhood vaccinations. His immune system was rebounding, but he no longer had protection from mumps, measles, rubella, polio, small pox, and yellow fever. He would be revaccinated in the future, but at a much later date. For now, he was susceptible to contracting any of those diseases.

He could not attend school for at least six months. Nor would he be able to attend Camp Goodtimes during the summer. Swimming pools, public or private, were forbidden. He had to wear his face mask for at least six months whenever he went to the clinic, the grocery store, or anywhere he may encounter other people. He had to avoid crowded places, people who are or have recently been ill, and children attending school. In other words, pretty much everyone. He could drop the mask only in an enclosed vehicle, outside in open space, or in his own home with family members. It was as if he had moved into a huge, modified LAF room.

Judy worked through her emotions at being discharged from The Hutch. The hospital had been their mothership for four months. She felt like they had been placed in a lifeboat and released into a stormy sea. "When we were first thinking of leaving The Hutch for home (over a month ago), I was afraid I was going to feel a sense of loss. I thought I might prefer staying in the (family) apartments, being around others who are going through the same thing. But, no, I prefer being away. I'm perfectly comfortable here at home with Aaron. I'm looking forward to being released to Dr. Niebrugge."

After leaving The Hutch, Aaron's cancer continued to weigh on his mind. "Don't you wish sometimes that you were something else?" he asked one day. "Like a bird—so you would never have cancer. I wish I was a piece of wood sometimes, so I would never die."

Judy insisted Aaron get busy with his schoolwork after his return home, even though he wouldn't be able to attend school until the next January, eight months away. He had missed much of fifth grade and would now miss the first half of his sixth-grade year. He had a lot of studying to do to catch up with his classmates at Sunset Elementary. Judy struggled constantly to get him to focus on schoolwork, but she refused to give up. Her battles with Aaron over schoolwork resulted in so many meltdowns that Judy eventually engaged Carolyn Mills, one of the fifth-grade teachers at Sunset Elementary, to tutor Aaron at their University Place home.

Aaron didn't work much harder with Carolyn than he did with Judy. "He didn't want to work on math," Carolyn said. "He just wanted to hang out." It's likely that Aaron's loss of cognitive function from the cranial radiation as a two-year-old had caused a decline in his interest and his ability to focus on things like math.

Aaron worked enthusiastically with Carolyn on outdoor projects, even if it was in ways his tutor may not have expected. "One of the things he had to do for class," Carolyn remembered, "had to do with geography or landforms. He was going to make a shadow box with a beach scene on it. He had to show different environments." Carolyn felt a little nervous when she went outside with Aaron. She knew he had just had a transplant and she wasn't certain of his health status.

"We walked down on the beach—just the two of us. He hadn't been home very long, and we were down there collecting shells. I would turn and say, 'Oh, here's a good one! And here's a good one! And what else do you think you need?' He was kind of following and following. Then, all of a sudden, I turned around and there's a crab right in my face and he goes, 'This is what I need!' I screamed and ran and he took off after me with this crab, trying to get me with it. I'm like, are you kidding me? Right now? We aren't supposed to be doing that. We're supposed to be calmly working on this shadow box and now you are chasing me with a crab? It was just so unexpected because here I am trying to be careful—'Oh, let me help you' and 'Would you like me to bend down and get that?'—and all of a sudden, he is chasing me with a crab!

"He had this sense of humor that was hysterical, but he wasn't out there with it like some other kid where you might say, 'That kid is really funny.' He was so optimistic. Aaron lived like he was going to live forever."

Shortly after Aaron returned home from The Hutch and two weeks after his twelfth birthday, a reporter from the Tacoma *News-Tribune* profiled Aaron and Judy in the Health section of the newspaper. "Ever since he was first diagnosed," Judy told her, "our goal was to make everything as normal as possible." Several large photographs alongside the article showed an inflated version of the child Aaron used to be. His wavy, brown hair had grown in darker and straighter this time, his wispy mustache and faint facial hair belied his twelve years, and his bloated face and waistline underscored the side effects from his continued steroid treatments. His body wouldn't recuperate completely until the doctors tapered him off of the drugs that caused the bloating.

Dr. Dan knew the remote chances of Aaron's survival,

but he focused on the positive when he was interviewed for the same article. "We're weaning him off his drugs now," he told the reporter. "By next September, he should be off most of them." If all went well, Dr. Dan would soon only need to see Aaron a couple of times a year. "He won't be limited at all," said Dr. Dan. "He can have a normal, routine life."

Aaron felt better physically and his energy rebounded. After the successful transplant, the family returned to their normal lives. Doug continued his work in the world of finance, Keith no longer needed to sleep three or four nights a week at The Hutch, and Judy spent more time with Heather. All three parents maintained their running regimens. Aaron and Heather returned to their old routine of spending every other weekend and each Wednesday evening with Keith.

By mid-summer, 1986, Aaron spent a lot of time inside movie theatres, one of the few places he could go in public where wearing a mask didn't make him feel self-conscious. In early July, he went to see *Top Gun*, the Tom Cruise action-thriller for the fifth time. Cruise's character, Maverick, exemplified the kind of daredevil courage and cocky attitude Aaron needed on his team. Aaron and his friends incorporated the film's action scenes into the choreography of their beach combat scenarios at Aaron's house. Aaron combined aerial dogfight scenes from *Top Gun* with those from *Star Wars* in his drawings. His intricate drawings could have come from either film. The theme song to *Top Gun*, Kenny Loggins' smash hit *Danger* Zone, became one of Aaron's battle anthems. One evening, Aaron received a call from Tom Skerritt, who played Tom Cruise's flight instructor, Viper, in *Top Gun*. One of Doug's friends who knew Skerritt, told him of Aaron's situation, and asked him to give the boy a call. Aaron talked to him for about half an hour and nearly had to be peeled off the ceiling after he hung up.

As a young child, Aaron had given little thought to the effects of the chemo drugs on his outward appearance. As a pre-teen, however, he became increasingly aware of how the world perceived him. In mid-July, he saw a picture of himself from the prior year, before his most recent weight gain. "I can't keep my eyes off of this!" he said. "I can't wait to look like this again!" He assumed that Mike Ditka, coach of the Super Bowl-winning Chicago Bears, had seen the article about him in the Tacoma *News-Tribune.* Concerned the photos in the newspaper had not done him justice given his recent physical improvements, Aaron wrote a letter to Ditka telling him among other things, "I look better now than in the newspaper."

Aaron didn't reveal his feelings very often. He developed coping skills to deal with looks or comments from others. Once when watching the movie *Mask* with Doug, Aaron cracked open the door just a bit. The 1985 film featured a boy with a disfiguring disease who was taunted by other kids at school as he struggling to be included. The boy ultimately used humor and intelligence to find acceptance. As they watched the movie, Doug mentioned to Aaron that people don't mean to be cruel and that the boy learned to deal with life the way he was. "Yah, like me," Aaron replied. "I've learned how to deal with it—when I wear my mask." Then he closed the door.

Aaron became more and more aware of the bad health hand he had been dealt and the basic unfairness of it all. On one occasion, after Judy informed him of yet another side effect or complication he had been diagnosed with, he asked Judy, "Have any of my friends had this?"

Perhaps the worst day of summer '86 was the Sunday in August that Doug, Judy, and Aaron drove Heather to Seattle to depart for Camp Goodtimes. Everyone knew Aaron was disappointed he couldn't attend. His suppressed immune system simply wouldn't allow it, but he didn't show any emotions at first. The camp had grown in importance to both Aaron and Heather as they got older, and each year their anticipation grew exponentially. A festival-like atmosphere engulfed the waterfront when the families showed up on Sunday morning to load their kids onto the *Spirit of Seattle,* a large ferry boat that would take them to Vashon Island. Most of the kids lived far apart and saw each other only once a year. There was always a buzz about who would be returning from last year and how they had changed. This was the only time of the year that the cancer kids and their siblings received all the positive attention they could handle. After enduring the effects of cancer for the entire year, they got to spend one week with others who viewed the world through the same lens.

Judy noticed Aaron's discomfort as departure time approached. "Kids were ready to get on the boat," she wrote. "Everyone in festive mood. Aaron said he wanted to leave—said he was tired. I knew he just wanted to be going. Someone mentioned it was nice Heather could go. Aaron disagreed." The day was a low point for Aaron, but in general things were beginning to look up for him.

The biggest indication of Aaron's improved health was the lack of entries in Judy's journal from July to October, 1986. Judy's writings were much more than a recording of daily events; they were a way for her to process her emotions. Blank pages generally indicated things were going well.

Her only writing of any significance was in reference to a letter she wrote to Bob Cleveland, the founder of Make-A-Wish Foundation, asking for financial assistance to take Aaron to Disneyland after he was given clearance to travel. She shared Aaron's ten-year journey through different radiation and chemo treatments, along with his four-month stay in The Hutch. "When he was at his lowest point," she wrote, "we promised him we would take him to Disneyland when he got better. Talk of that trip would always lift his spirits." Judy explained about Aaron's compromised immune system and his need to recover before he could travel. She included a donation with her letter and awaited a response.

Aaron re-engaged with his friends in late summer, hosting them for beach play and sleepovers at University Place. In October, Aaron went trick-or-treating with his buddies—his first time on his own with friends in a year. Judy worried. It was like inserting a player back into the starting lineup after he recovered from a serious injury. Could he keep up with teammates? Had his skills declined?

"I was a bit nervous letting him go," Judy wrote, "but I have to. I worried about him being warm enough, careful enough, etc. etc. He just wanted me to be quiet! He had a great time—came home at about 9:30 with a big bag of loot." Aaron was back in the game. The time for worries was over.

Aaron had continued with his regular monthly checkups through the year and on his November 10th checkup, his blood counts remained solid. "We don't have to come back until after the one-year checkup!" Judy noted. That was only a month away, but it seemed like a lifetime to Judy. "Longest we've been away from the doctor in a long time. The doctor was real pleased with the report. Relapse one year ago today."

Judy felt so good about Aaron's condition that she sat down in early December to write a letter of gratitude to her friends and family.

Dear Friends:

This past year again was full for all of us. Before I go into any detail, I will tell you our big news! Aaron is well and we are celebrating life this Christmas!

He spent nearly four months in the hospital at Fred Hutchinson Cancer Research Center through many ups and downs. We brought him home at the end of April and went through a few more tough weeks of regaining strength. He is now over taking medication and we are anticipating a return to school in January. A bone marrow transplant destroys the immune system and a period of one year is necessary to restore it to normal.

He has been feeling just great and looks completely back to normal. He is tested regularly and everything looks good. We are thankful to all of our friends who have been praying and thinking positively about Aaron this past year.

She sealed the letters, added a twenty-two-cent stamp, and put them in the mail. As Judy spread the good word about Aaron's health to her friends and family, Mary Lou and I were sending out birth notices for our second son, Chris, born December 6th of that year. Mary Lou's birth announcements and Judy's letters likely crossed in the mail. We were wrapped up in our own lives in Eugene.

There were no warnings as Judy drove Aaron to The

Hutch on Monday, December 15, for his first annual transplant checkup. All indications were for smooth sailing, but as she recapped the day's events in her journal that night before she retired, she recounted the abrupt turn of events.

"The day in Seattle went very well," she noted. "Aaron was real talkative; excited to be there; happy with everyone's comments on how good he looked. I think he looked better a month ago. I've been worried about his skinny look (droopy eyes, red gums).

"Pulmonary function went well. Then met with Dr., who said everything looked good. We were all high. Tough time when we did bone marrow, skin tests. Quite painful, but Aaron cheered up quickly after that. Walked to lunch, then to Swedish for x-rays, pills." Judy and Aaron wrapped up their day with a visit to The Hutch and drove home in great spirits.

They had returned home and were telling Doug about the whole day when the phone rang.

Chapter 17

I DON'T WANT TO DIE

D uring the year following his transplant, Aaron had shown all the signs of victory. His Hickman line was gone, his weight had dropped, and his bloated face had reduced to near normal size. He no longer took any medications, and in January his restored immune system would allow him to join his friends at Curtis Junior High School for the last half of his sixth-grade year. Christmas, Aaron's favorite holiday, was two weeks away. Which is why the news was so devastating when Judy answered the phone.

"It was the doctor with bad news. I just couldn't believe it was happening. Aaron knew something was wrong. He went upstairs crying. When I got off the phone, I had to tell him. The three of us cried together on the stairs. He was saying, 'I don't want to die. I don't want to go through a transplant again. It was a perfect match.'"

Judy was numb, and angry. Aaron had been so excited about going back to school, so proud of his progress. Keith came over right away, sat with Aaron and Heather for a while, and then took them to see a movie while Judy called her mom and dad.

Dr. Dan called. The doctors at The Hutch had filled him in. He would be in charge of Aaron's treatment from this point on, but Aaron still needed to meet with the transplant doctors at The Hutch in two days.

Judy, Keith, and Doug had known of Aaron's slim chance of survival for some time. The doctors had been transparent with them through each stage. Nevertheless, they were crushed when they heard Aaron had relapsed for the fourth time.

Judy closed out her journal notes in a predictable manner. "Doug and I both feel down, but we're convinced we must make the best of this…help Aaron keep his fighting spirit. Well, here we go again."

When they took Aaron to The Hutch two days later, Judy cried with one of the nurses, but she couldn't bring herself to go to the second floor. She couldn't face anyone. The week was supposed to be such a celebration.

It was rare to discover a relapse at the one-year checkup. The doctors couldn't guarantee anything from additional treatments, but Aaron had "a chance." Even if additional treatment worked, it would only do so "for a while." They couldn't say how long. The same drugs were not likely to be effective, since Aaron's cells had developed a resistance to them. Even if they could get Aaron's cancer in remission, the remissions would be shorter each time. "But if we don't try," Judy noted, "he won't get better."

Every parent wants to reassure their child in a crisis that everything is going to be okay. "It's not the end of the world," we tell them. "If you make it down this tough road, fight through these obstacles, things will be okay on the other end." But if your child is in the advanced stages of a fatal disease, things don't always end up "okay." If things go awry, and if you've assured your child that things are going to be fine, your child's faith in you diminishes. Sometimes it's best to say, "This is going to be difficult, and I don't know how things will work out, but I will be by your side every step of the way."

Aaron resisted Judy's attempts to discuss his situation. He had always declined to discuss his cancer on a deeper level and this time would be no exception. Instead, Judy gave him a pep talk about the importance of his attitude and his reasons for wanting to live. "We need to fight this with things other than chemo," she told him. She included in her pep talk a request that he cut back on his anger, at least as he targeted it toward Heather.

Judy met with Dr. Dan on December 18 to discuss Aaron's new treatment plan. Dr. Dan had consulted with the doctors at The Hutch. They agreed that the best approach would be to begin again with the basic induction phase they used when he was initially diagnosed ten years earlier. "He should regain remission," Judy wrote, "but the long-term outlook is pretty grim." They began the treatments and one month later, Aaron's blood counts showed that he was in remission yet again.

The doctors suggested that Aaron begin treatments with a new drug called 5-FU. Their recommendation made a statement in and of itself, since the drug was still under a Phase I clinical trial, a phase where doctors are still determining if a drug is safe to give to humans. Patients are generally ineligible to receive Phase I drugs unless all other known treatment protocols have failed. Doctors had no idea if the drug would work against Aaron's leukemia, and they could only guess at the appropriate dosage. Aaron had clearly stepped into the arena of experimental medicine. He would be participating in a trial for a drug that produced nasty side effects (diarrhea, mouth sores, pink eye, rashes, and headaches) with little upside. He would surely advance scientific knowledge, but any benefit to him was a long shot at best. Still, there was always a chance this could be his magic moment.

Few parents walk away when there is even the faintest hope that a new experimental drug or treatment will work for their child. Most parents cling to the slightest thread. What if they stop fighting and the wonder drug shows up tomorrow? Or next week? Or next month? How could they live with themselves if they gave up too early? None of us truly knows how we would react in the same situation.

The answer is not the same for everyone, according to Dr. Archie Bleyer, who spent more than five decades treating children and adolescents with leukemia. "We always leave it up to the family or the child, depending on their age. We rely on the parents if they are younger than eight or ten. Sometimes it's physician encouraged—I would occasionally encourage them, gently, to consider stopping.

"When the parents wanted to stop because they couldn't take it anymore, and they thought the child was suffering too much, more often than not we agreed. We brought in those services that provided comfort care, palliative care, for both the family and the patient. There are special child life specialists that do that. Social workers. Children's hospitals have the capability of accepting the end and working with the family, going through the care and legal issues that are involved."

On rare occasions, parents wanted to stop before all treatment options are exhausted. "When a parent wants to stop treatments before it should be done," said Dr. Bleyer, "it is just something that you have to deal with. Sometimes it comes down to the rights of the child, and whether or not the parents are able to understand the child has a right to live longer with the cure therapies and comfort measures available. It is far more common to have them want to go ahead than to have them want to stop. I think today it (stopping) probably should occur more often than it does. Families believe in social media so much they want to do more and more. There is always hope out there in the media to support a belief that they should continue no matter what, even if it may be more harmful, or more expensive than they can afford, and cause indelible injury to the family that survives."

In February, 1987, two months after Aaron's most recent relapse, our family took a vacation to Vancouver, B.C. On our way back to Eugene, we stopped in Tacoma to have lunch with Keith, Aaron, and Heather. The kids were staying with Keith since Doug and Judy had driven to Sun River, Oregon, for a well-deserved weekend break. Shortly after our arrival, we learned the tenuous nature of Aaron's health.

Keith had just pulled up to the restaurant when Aaron began to feel dizzy. His condition deteriorated rapidly to the point where Mary Lou and I took care of Heather while Keith rushed Aaron to the emergency room.

Within two hours, Aaron was in a coma. Keith called Judy and told them to come home immediately. He stayed with Aaron in his room all day, but he was unaccustomed to being the custodial parent at the time Aaron had a crisis. "I was feeling really lonely," Keith said. "I didn't realize how much. Later that evening, Doug's daughter, Kelley, showed up at the hospital. "When I saw her." Keith said, "it was like somebody was dying of thirst and you gave them a big glass of cold water. It felt so good to have somebody show up to give support."

As Doug drove the six hours home, Judy's ricocheted from anger ("Why can't the world just leave Aaron alone?) to worry ("What if he can't come out of this?) to prayer ("Please, St. Jude of miracles, we need another one here"). They drove directly to the hospital to find Aaron unconscious in a hospital room.

Aaron stayed in a coma for eight days. Dr. Dan attributed Aaron's condition to the cumulative effects of methotrexate and his previous radiation. He had a fever, his eyes were puffy, and he failed to respond to Judy's requests to squeeze her hand. Judy, Keith, and Doug bounced between hope and despair. The three of them cried around his bed as a priest came by to anoint him.

Finally, on day eight, Aaron came around. Keith and Judy had once again established their routine of alternating nights to stay with Aaron at the hospital. It was Keith's turn to be there. "A pediatric neurologist came in one morning," Keith said. "She looked at Aaron, and said something like, 'I'm kind of tired of this.' She grabbed his hands and his arms, pulled him up off the bed and shook him a little bit, like she was just trying to wake him up. He woke up. She ran him through a series of tests to see if he could hear her and respond. 'Touch your nose, touch your ears, blink your eyes.' He did everything she asked him to do."

At first, Aaron mumbled unintelligible words. The next day, he said, "Mommy, help me," and he asked about family members. He even asked to see Heather.

As Aaron lay in a coma, Dr. Dan continued discussions with the parents about which, if any chemo drugs to use for the next phase in addition to the 5-FU. They ruled out any more methotrexate. Two days after Aaron had emerged from his coma and had been released from the hospital, they began giving him prednisone again.

It was at that time, in February, 1987, that the three parents began to discuss their differences of opinion on how they should move forward. Keith voiced his concern to Dr. Niebrugge about continuing chemo. He thought a miracle had happened already. He wasn't opposed to maintenance drugs, but he didn't want Aaron to feel sick all the time because of the chemo. Judy didn't want Aaron to feel sick either, but she didn't feel good about discontinuing chemo altogether and relying solely on Aaron's immune system.

The parents agreed to continue the 5-FU treatments for as long as Aaron remained in remission. As the year progressed, Keith, Judy, and Doug continued to discuss how, or whether to move forward with Aaron's treatment. They always asked the same question: Without giving up, how could they give Aaron his best odds of survival without completing degrading his quality of life for the limited time he had remaining?

At the moment, Aaron's new drug regiment had induced yet another remission. Since his white cell count had risen to an acceptable level, he would be able to join his sixth-grade classmates in January as planned. Judy stopped by the school to share the news with Aaron's teachers, but in the end, his deteriorating physical health proved to be a stronger factor than his positive attitude.

Chapter 18

THE THOUGHT OF A MIRACLE

J
udy made plans for the future as if she didn't have a
care in the world. In late May, she bought invitations for
Aaron's thirteenth birthday party, coming up on June
16. "I can't believe we're planning his thirteenth birthday!"
she noted. "We had a few instances in the past few months
when we weren't sure he would make it to thirteen."

In January, she and Doug had taken Aaron to Maui to
fulfill a promise they had made while he was undergoing his
transplant. Soon after their arrival, Aaron began to experience severe abdominal pains. They evacuated him by air
ambulance to the main island, where he was diagnosed with
a bowel obstruction caused by some of his chemo drugs. By
the time he returned to Maui, Aaron had lost nearly half
his body weight and he was only able to wade for a short
time in the warm tropical waters. When asked later about
his trip to Hawaii, he told tales of surfing in the ocean and
never once brought up his hospital experience.

Two months later, the Make-A-Wish Foundation
arranged for Aaron, Judy, and Heather to visit Disneyland.
Eric Freitag and his mother, Margarete, joined them. The
night before their scheduled departure, Aaron came down
with a high fever. Judy called the doctor's office and the

nurse told her to go with her instincts. After a brief hesitation, she decided to go. 'We're not normal travelers. Aaron may not be pain and disease-free for some time. We can't wait until he feels great or we may never go."

During the trip, they visited the set of *Wheel of Fortune*, and met Pat Sajak and Vanna White. They took a ride with a California Highway Patrol officer in his black and white patrol car along the LA freeways, a high-speed trip they would never forget.

"There were times," Margarete said, "we couldn't leave or couldn't do what we wanted to do because Judy had to take care of Aaron. He didn't feel well pretty much that whole week we were down there." Aaron couldn't seem to get a break, but through nearly all of it, he kept a smile on his face and kept moving forward. He talked only of the good times after he returned from Disneyland.

On Easter Sunday, two weeks after his Make-A-Wish trip, Aaron was hospitalized in Intensive Care with pneumonia. Once again, Aaron asked his mom, "Have any of my friends had this?"

The end of the school year arrived and, though it's unclear how many days Aaron actually attended school that year, he walked across the stage on June 12 and graduated with his classmates from Sunset Elementary School. He tried to act casual, but Judy knew he was elated. "He couldn't hide it, even though he tried," she wrote.

Aaron's remissions were shorter and his relapses more frequent. His general health continued to decline in other ways. No matter where he went or what he did, he seemed to find himself in a medical crisis. Yet, he always rebounded.

Aaron attended Camp Goodtimes in August for the first time in two years. He stood alone on the top deck of the boat as it departed the dock. Judy worried about his welfare. "He's not the kind to go up to someone and say, 'remember me from two years ago?' But I think he'll find friends as they settle into their cabins. I think this camp can be a wonderful experience for him. Great for confidence boosting. I can't wait to find how things went!"

Judy worried needlessly. A boy named Jimmy recognized him from a prior camp and they became fast friends. He met a girl named Becky who had undergone a transplant the year before his—he danced with her at the punk dance. He returned from camp with stories of canoeing, horseback riding, swimming, and archery. The campers even traveled together to a Seattle Mariners baseball game in the middle of the week. Aaron told Judy it was the best week in camp ever. He looked the picture of health—smiling, tanned, a head full of hair, and happy.

On Monday morning, two days after Aaron's return from camp, Judy took him to see Dr. Niebrugge for a routine blood test and checkup. She could tell something was wrong the moment the doctor came in the room. Her throat tightened as she clinched her teeth and tried to breathe. The doctor told her that he had seen some suspicious looking cells, probably blast cells.

They came back out into hall to face a beaming Aaron. His smile turned to a glare when they shared the news. He cried quietly. Judy asked him if he wanted to go into a room to settle down and he said he just wanted to go home. As we walked out, he asked, "Why does everything always happen to me?"

On Monday, August 31, 1987, Judy noted "Relapse #5" at the top of the page in her journal. Judy knew the severity of Aaron's situation. She was thirty-nine years old and throughout her eleven-year battle against Aaron's leukemia her default position had always been to launch into battle, shoulder to shoulder with her son. She had fought and suffered alongside Aaron every step of the way, absorbing each painful procedure as if it were inflicted on herself. This time, however, a subtle change in tone infused her written prayers, showing an increased awareness that continuing the fight would take a heavier toll. "Please, God, give me the strength, and Aaron the strength, and understanding to get through this next phase in our lives. I just hope he won't have a lot of pain and discomfort, but I want to fight this as hard as we can, and that can cause some pain."

Dr. Dan told Judy they would probably try a regular induction regimen again, using the same chemo drugs they had used multiple times before: vincristine, methotrexate, prednisone, and L-asparaginase. If they could achieve a sixth remission, they could search out yet another maintenance program for Aaron. To say the doctors were grasping at straws would be an understatement, but they had no other answers. Many improvements in the treatment of acute lymphocytic leukemia had been discovered since Barbara Bush had been told to take her daughter, Robin, home and make her comfortable until she died. Aaron was fortunate to have lived for eleven years after his diagnosis, but now he, his parents, and his doctors faced the same choices that parents had faced since leukemia had been identified as a child-killer. ALL was taking another child's life, the doctors were out of known treatment options, and the child's mother was willing to do nearly anything to give her son a fighting chance.

Judy called Keith. For the second time, he expressed his concern over causing Aaron unnecessary pain while fighting the inevitable. Keith ultimately agreed to go ahead with another Induction phase, but he insisted that Aaron not suffer terribly from being given more drugs in a futile attempt to get better. One month after his most recent relapse, Aaron's cancer was declared in remission for the fifth time. As Judy sat in the doctor's reception area awaiting the official word, another mother came by with her five-year-old boy. The mother happily announced that she and her son were there for his last treatment. The little boy had been diagnosed when he was fourteen months old.

Judy reflected on memories of "last appointments" that had come and gone over the years. The young boy was approximately eight years younger than Aaron. Many of the clinical trials Aaron had participated in during the previous eight years led to incremental improvements in treatments for ALL, and most likely contributed to saving the little boy's life. Aaron was living his life's purpose without anyone realizing it.

Dr. Dan invited Judy and Aaron into his office and shared the latest bone marrow results. He had fewer than ten percent blasts in his cell count so he was technically in remission. They would once again consult with the doctors at The Hutch to determine which experimental drugs would give Aaron his best chance of survival.

On Monday, October 19, 1987, Black Monday hit stock markets around the world. The Dow Jones Industrial Average dropped nearly twenty-three percent in one day, the largest daily percentage decline in its history. The jolt in global financial markets stoked fears of another Great Depression. Doug worked as a senior executive in the world of finance. Yet there was no mention of it in Judy's journal. The family had much more serious things on their minds.

The holidays were approaching. Aaron loved Christmas more than any other holiday, and it seemed especially important this year that they take in special events when they could. On November 15, Judy and Doug took Aaron to a Seattle Seahawks NFL game against the Green Bay Packers at the Seattle Kingdome.

Aaron loved pro wrestling even more than football, so Doug purchased tickets to a WWF match at the Tacoma Dome. "You would have thought he won the lottery," Doug said. "He loved it. I'm there saying, 'this is so bad.' I'm grinning along with him and he's yelling, 'Yes!' They had a cage up there with maybe six or seven wrestling matches—the tag teams and the whole nine yards. He truly was in heaven. This was the best thing he had ever done and he couldn't wait to get home to tell Judy about it."

The weekend prior to Thanksgiving, Aaron's friend, Eric, visited him during one of his stays with Keith. They rough-housed as usual in the living room, pretending to be Hulk Hogan and King Kong Bundy, two of their favorite WWF wrestling heroes. When Aaron returned home to University Place that evening, Judy noticed some bruising on one of Aaron's hands and on his shoulder where he had bumped a table. As she tucked him in, he started crying, "I'm probably going to die from all these bruises! I'm going to get bruises all over." She held him close and tried to give him some encouragement.

Judy knew the excessive bruising was a sign Aaron's leukemia had returned. She and Aaron were back in Dr. Dan's office the next morning for another of the dreaded bone-marrow aspirations. "It was a very painful procedure," she wrote. "I had to grit my teeth to hold back my emotions. I knew at that point that the marrow was packed tight, indicating leukemia. I was trying not to think, just to comfort Aaron."

The marrow samples confirmed Judy's suspicions. Aaron's leukemia had returned for the sixth time. Aaron sat on the edge of the table, visibly slumped. Maybe he saw signs that the end game was near. Perhaps he was just exhausted from the roller coaster of relapses and remissions. As he sat with his head drooped, Judy read through a notebook with Dr. Dan and tried to identify other options for treatment. Any further treatment at this point would purely be in desperation. Time was short and the odds were long. There was nothing more he could offer.

Two days later, the day before Thanksgiving Day, Judy, Doug, Keith, and Aaron drove together to Seattle. The doctor spelled everything out for them. There were no guarantees. They couldn't say how long. But if they didn't try something, he wouldn't get better. Judy thought on the way home about what the doctor said. They had reached the stage where they needed to be realistic about what was happening. She understood fully the grim prognosis, and she pledged to live each day to the fullest. They would provide some good times for Aaron, but at the same time, keep the thought of a miracle in the back of their minds.

Chapter 19

WHAT DO WE DO IF THIS DOESN'T WORK?

"Have we asked Aaron what he thinks we should do?" asked Keith. He wanted his son to survive as much as anyone, but didn't necessarily share Judy's and Doug's perspective on how best to move forward. It was close to the end and the doctors had suggested another experimental drug. Keith thought they should add Aaron's voice to the discussion.

"No, absolutely not," Doug responded.

"Well, I think we should," Keith pressed.

"What if he says no" Doug asked. "What if he says he doesn't want the treatment? What if he says 'I want to die?' I can't let him do that."

Doug's argument prevailed, but Keith second-guessed himself later. "He made me see his point of view and I went along with it. I felt okay about it at the time, but in hindsight, I wish we would have let him die. I really think that is the choice Aaron would have made."

As the three parents negotiated their way toward a common strategy, Aaron weighed in on his own. On Thanksgiving Day, the young teenager approached his mom. "The doctor said they can't cure me. They just get a ten percent remission. What do we do if this doesn't work?" Judy held him close and told him they would just do the best they could. They went into the living room, where Doug joined them. As they took in the view of Puget Sound, Aaron told them, "I don't want to go through anything more. I'm tired of this. I don't want any more treatment."

Judy did her best to comfort him, to tell him she understood how he felt. She tried to pick up his spirits by telling him how strong and brave he was—how he had taught people to appreciate small wonders in life. It was clear at that point that he understood the seriousness of the situation. It was just as clear the parents weren't prepared to put the decision for more treatment in the hands of their thirteen-year-old son.

One week later, on December 2, doctors surgically inserted a new Hickman line into Aaron's chest so he could receive further, more intensive 5-FU treatments. Once again, ten-year-old Heather took an active role. Aaron's low platelet count demanded continual replenishment—everyone in the family donated whatever they could. Because of Heather's age, they had to make a one-hour round-trip drive to Seattle to access the special equipment needed to withdraw her platelets. She never complained.

Aaron marshalled his artistic talents to depict the ultimate battle between the "good" blue cells and the "bad" red cells. His most intricate drawing yet incorporated a large vat of blue liquid labeled "5-FU" from which friendly combatants withdrew the life-saving liquid and sprayed it in laser-like fashion at the attacking, and sometimes fleeing, red cells. A large machine labeled the "Rearanger" hovered over the aerial battle, sucking in evil red cells, converting them into the blue 5-FU cells, and shooting them out through a cannon to rejoin the battle. Aaron integrated emergency vehicles into the scene, their side panels decorated with red crosses to resemble ambulances with telescopic laser weapons on top.

Aaron had been sick for eleven-and-a-half years and his perception of death had changed as he got older. As a thirteen-year-old, his understanding of death closely resembled that of an adult. Occasionally, he would ask a question of a close family member about what happens after someone dies, but he still resisted any in-depth discussions on the subject.

"Grandma," he once asked Jeanne while sharing a milkshake with her, "would God let a boy take his teddy bear to heaven with him?" Another time, he asked her, "What would you do if I moved far, far away and never came back?"

From Jeanne's perspective, Judy didn't want Aaron to talk about his illness or to verbalize his feelings. Jeanne considered that to be more Keith's style, since he was a sociology professor and a counselor. Judy was a "make the trains run on time" kind of person. She had always borne the major burden of Aaron's care. Not only did she need to stay strong for her own sake, but she was the primary source of strength for Aaron. It wasn't that she didn't want Aaron to express his feelings—she had tried unsuccessfully many times to get him to share his thoughts. But it was not her default position to process emotions with him. Judy survived by providing structure, making a to-do list, holding the doctors accountable, and managing Aaron's meds. To spend any significant time processing her feelings may have cracked the fragile emotional structure she'd held together for more than a decade. She held things together for Aaron and for the family with a steely grit. During times of crisis, and there were many, she clinched her jaw and focused on shoring up Aaron. Then she went about ensuring the welfare of everyone else. She processed her feelings later by recording them in her journal. The few times she encouraged Aaron to discuss his feelings, he refused. Having been shut down by Aaron repeatedly, and understanding his reluctance to talk about his leukemia, she discouraged others from pursuing the subject with him.

Talking to a child who is dying of leukemia is complicated for myriad reasons. As medical researchers have worked toward finding better treatments for the disease over the years, others have tried to increase their understanding of the emotions that drive communication with dying children. In a 1965 paper entitled "Who's Afraid of Death on the Leukemia Ward?" the authors discussed the difficulty in creating an environment in which a child feels safe to ask questions and be confident of receiving an honest answer. At the time, children in the study did not receive open and honest answers about their condition out of fear of scaring them. When a child neared death, he would be moved to special room, leaving the other children wondering "what happened to Johnny?" They were told, "Johnny went home," "Johnny went to another hospital," or "Johnny went to the 13th floor." Over time, the children in the study came to mistakenly believe that the thirteenth floor was the place children were taken to die. One day, a nine-year-old boy was told he was being taken to the thirteenth floor simply because of capacity issues. He became unmanageable because he said he didn't want to die.

The children in the study had plenty of fears and anxieties over their illness, and since they couldn't trust the information being given to them by their caregivers, they turned inward with their emotions and were left to suffer alone. Following the episode with the thirteenth floor, the staff realized that to answer the question "What happened to Johnny" with anything but the truth prevented the development of any meaningful relationship between the child and the adult.

Talking to a child who is dying of cancer is an important if difficult conversation to have. But it is also important not to let the pressure of having such a conversation compel you into doing so if it doesn't feel appropriate. If the opportunity presents itself, however, it's important to be open and honest while sharing your memories. It's an opportunity to tell your child "I love you" and to say "Goodbye." Aaron increasingly understood his situation more clearly; he still didn't want to discuss it. If anything, as he neared the end of his life, he internalized even more of his feelings.

In *The Private Worlds of Dying Children,* Professor Myra Bluebond-Langner explored the reasons children with leukemia are often reluctant to discuss the deadly nature of their disease. She described a series of escalating changes in the children's self-concept as it relates to their leukemia: being well; being seriously ill; being seriously ill and will get better; always being ill and will get better; always being ill and will never get better; and dying. By the time Aaron was hospitalized in late 1987, his concept would likely have teetered between the last two stages. More than once while at The Hutch Aaron had mentioned he might be the next to die. So, if he suspected he might die from leukemia, why wasn't Aaron willing to talk about it more?

Professor Bluebond-Langner linked her study to the principles from another book entitled *Awareness of Dying.* According to the authors, terminally ill patients and those close to them proceed through a series of steps until they ultimately arrive at a "mutual pretense" phase, a point where each party knows the patient is dying, but silently agree to act as if he is going to live. Aaron knew he was going to die, his parents knew he was going to die, and the doctors and nurses knew he was going to die, but everyone acted as if he wasn't. The parties had arrived at this state of "mutual pretense" through their own words and actions. Each time a doctor took Judy or Keith aside to quietly discuss something urgent, like Aaron's potential death, a message was inadvertently sent to Aaron that the subject was off limits to discussion. Each time Aaron experienced a remission, the family's primary focus had been to re-group, summon a fighting spirit, and charge forward, avoiding any deep discussion with Aaron about the more likely outcome. For example, Doug's comments about Aaron being 100% of the thirty percent, while inspirational, didn't acknowledge with Aaron the grim reality of the numbers. It may have sent an inadvertent message to Aaron that the matter wasn't to be discussed. To talk about it made it real. The perfect world may be one in which children who are dying from leukemia and their parents are aware that the child is dying and talk openly about it. But Professor Bluebond-Langner's study concluded that "leukemic children, once they became aware of their prognosis…practiced mutual pretense to the end."

Doug knew that Aaron's awareness of death had changed. "Aaron was very aware that he may not live very long," he said. "There's a lot of information in the world about children who die from leukemia. Anyone who goes to cancer camp; they would have vigils and things for kids who have passed. He was very aware. But he didn't want to talk about it."

Keith also tried to get Aaron to discuss his feelings about death and dying. "I sat by his bed and I said, 'I want to talk to you about something and if you don't want to talk about it, just let me know.' I began to talk about death and all of a sudden, his hand landed on mine. I kept talking and it happened again. And I said, 'You don't want me to talk about this?' And he said, 'No, I don't want you to talk about it.' It was Elizabeth Kubler Ross stuff, near death experiences. I didn't want him to be afraid, and I was trying to say, 'You don't need to be.' I wish I would have said, 'You know, you are going to die. And I really love you and I am going to miss you.' I wish I would have said that and left it at that. Or I could have said, 'I'm going to miss you and I love you, and that's going to hurt.' I wish I would have addressed all those things and I never did, because it was like, if I do that he is going to give up."

Aaron spent the rest of December in and out of the hospital. Bleeding continued to be an issue and the family donated platelets in an effort to help. Any optimism Judy mustered was kept in check by the doctors. Dr. Niebrugge reminded Judy that this was not a miracle cure—in essence saying not to expect too much. Doug talked to her about the same thing, but it was hard not to hope for a miracle. "In Aaron's past treatments," Judy noted, "we always had a chance for a cure, so I am used to thinking that way. I don't know how I will react if the day comes when they say we can't do anymore."

In the midst of Aaron's hospitalizations, it didn't feel much like Christmas. While he was hospitalized, Aaron learned of an art contest sponsored by Children's Hospital for the cover design for their Christmas cards the following year. In his final artistic endeavor Aaron submitted a drawing of a snowman, complete with a corncob pipe, charcoal buttons, and a top hat adorned with holly.

Heather shared with Judy that she had gone to visit a school counselor. She was worried about Aaron and enjoyed the role of platelet donor, but she remained resentful that he was receiving all the attention. Judy took her to ice cream and talked to her about being grateful for her health, her friends, and her ability to attend school.

Aaron spent most of December in the hospital receiving massive doses of 5-FU. Christmas Eve, he was in the hospital again, waiting for his Hickman line to be changed. His face was bloated and his mouth was sore from the 5-FU; the drug had not worked as they hoped.

The day after Christmas, after a final trip to see Keith's sister in Longview, Washington, Aaron was hospitalized for the last time. Judy noticed Aaron's body was wasting away. "His legs are weak and sore. I try not to get upset looking at his body—thin legs hunched over his trunk, soft muscles. I couldn't help but flash back to two years old; Pat Origenes' comment about his beautiful little naked body. A perfect specimen it was!"

Dr. Dan brought Judy out of her trance, took her out into the hallway and told her, "You need to understand that he could get an overwhelming infection and could die in a week." Aaron was receiving platelets several times a day and Judy knew time was short. "These next few days may be very crucial for him," she concluded. "I hope he has some fight left in him."

Chapter 20

HE'S WITH ME

J udy sat in Aaron's hospital room, thinking about a future without her little boy. "At this time of year many people think about what the new year will bring. That's a thought I don't want to dwell on; I just want to think of the present and hope the next hour will be better than this one.

"Aaron is resting peacefully now—asleep with the effects of Demerol. They started giving him that last night for his pain, which was becoming quite unbearable. He really looks relaxed and peaceful right now. He really hasn't been too conversive, but I just like sitting here beside him. He just finished platelets and he's still bleeding. I feel so helpless."

Dr. Kimball, the on-call doctor sitting in for Dr. Dan, saw Aaron that evening and called Judy into the hall. He had a very serious look on his face.

"What has Dr. Niebrugge told you about Aaron's condition?" he asked.

"We don't expect the treatment to be a cure," Judy responded. "We know he is very prone to infection, could die from it, that he might have uncontrollable bleeding."

"Has he discussed with you your feelings about what to do for him in a crisis situation, if bleeding can't be stopped, or if Aaron needs to go on a respirator?"

The doctor needed to know how aggressive the parents wanted to be, knowing that Aaron can't live. He couldn't predict what might happen in the next day or two. He didn't demand answers right away, but since Dr. Dan was gone, he needed to know their thoughts. The doctor's words were very upsetting for Judy and Doug, even though they knew the grim prognosis. They kept hoping Aaron would heal. They wanted to put off his death to sometime in the future.

The next day, Eric came by with Margarete to see Aaron. "I remember visiting him in the hospital," said Eric. "We basically just sat and watched *Different Strokes* for a half hour and then left. I don't think we said more than five words to each other."

Ed and Jeanne drove up from Eugene shortly after Christmas to stay with Heather and help out the family. "We didn't know he might die soon," Jeanne said. "We knew he was in terrible shape and he was in pain."

Judy thought about Heather as Aaron languished. "I wonder if she realizes how serious this is," Judy queried. "She doesn't ask me much, but I think she listens carefully when I talk about Aaron to others."

"We knew it was going to be tomorrow or the next day or the next day," added Doug. "That was hard on Heather. But Heather was young. And when you're young, you're so resilient. She was very solemn, and very sad, but I think over the course of that last several months, Heather came to know that Aaron wasn't going to make it. Without even being told. This was worse than before."

Aaron's condition worsened until they admitted him to intensive care on January 3. Judy maintained her bedside vigil. "Sitting here by Aaron's bedside again. He really made a turn for the worse last night. Asks for Demerol all the time. It seems to help."

Judy didn't write for several days before re-engaging on January 7. It was Judy's turn to host the bridge girls that evening. She proceeded with her plans. Throughout Aaron's life, she had insisted on keeping a balance by maintaining their regular activities as much as possible. Keith and Judy had successfully taken turns for years spending the night with Aaron when he was hospitalized. It was Keith's turn so she proceeded to host the girls for dinner. The evening didn't go as planned.

Keith called the house just as the Bridge Girls sat down to dinner. The doctor had just been by. Aaron's counts were down, with probably fifty percent blasts. He would stop by in the morning to discuss options with them. The doctor said Aaron appeared different to him, ready to give up the fight.

"I went into bathroom to talk with Doug," Judy wrote. "We both cried. We thought we had prepared ourselves, but this seems so final. I cried my story to the girls, and Doug cried with Mom, Dad, and Heather. After I told them how bad I felt and what was happening, I said, 'OK, let's play bridge and put this out of our minds for a while.'"

Confident they were near the end, Judy returned to Aaron's bedside early the next day. Her only journal entry that day ended abruptly. "It's now 3 PM. We're up in Rm 692. A nice bright room. Aaron is sleeping, as he does most of the time. That's all he wants to do. Such an up-and-down day. Last night was such a low, low time. This morning when Dr. Dan called lab about the white count . . .

Judy didn't return to her writing until six days later.

"Aaron is gone. His breathing stopped and his heart stopped beating sometime between 6 and 6:30 Friday morning. We are still mourning greatly and will be for quite some time. His absence hurts very deeply. We're all having ups and downs throughout the days. It's easy to say, oh, he's better off now, he's out of pain, not suffering, at peace. That's all true, but we miss him terribly. He was such a vital part of all of our lives, so alive. So many memories have been rushing past these past few days. I want to get them down in this book. I want to keep writing about him, about us. To keep him alive in our minds."

A week after Aaron's death, during one of her runs, Judy ran into Marilyn Lewis, Aaron's home tutor for the last six months of his life. At first, they talked about Heather and the rest of the family. Then Marilyn told Judy about a talk she'd had with God.

When Marilyn tutored Aaron, they had evidently talked about God. Though no one else had been able to have the discussion, Marilyn had been able to make a connection. She assured Judy that Aaron was prepared for death. He wasn't scared or angry.

Marilyn, however, had been very angry with God. She had prayed for Aaron for a long time, and God had assured her that Aaron would be okay. After Aaron's death, she went to church, sat in the sanctuary, and had a real heart-to-heart with God. She told Him, "Wait a minute, this is not fair. You told me he would be okay. Did I tell him enough?

"He's okay," God responded, "He's with me."

In mid-January, Judy received a letter from Children's Hospital telling her that Aaron's drawing had won the Christmas art contest.

A month after Aaron's death, Judy sat down to write a letter to her son.

Dear Aaron,

I've been wanting to start my diary entries like this for a long time…Today I will. I'm sitting at the dining room table, all quiet here. Doug is sleeping on the couch. Heather is upstairs playing Nintendo.

Judy mentioned going through Aaron's room for the first time. She told him about all the teachers at Sunset Elementary. She concluded it as only a grieving mother could:

I thought I would feel better if I sat down to write to you. I think it has helped. I trust you are happy, thinking of us. I hope you don't feel alone. We're with you always.

                    Love, Mom & Doug, Heather

Keith struggled to understand the untimeliness of his son's death. "You know, he should have either died earlier, or survived. I think the least likely thing is for him to have died when he did. Most patients who died from leukemia at that time died earlier or they were cured. He had five or six relapses. There were some who went through the same process he did at that time and they got over it and they were all right, but to have gone that far and to have died was unusual."

I learned more details about Aaron's struggles after his death than I had known for the entire seven years I had been part of the family—his repeated relapses, his behavior toward Heather, his parents' emotional journey, and the endless suffering Aaron endured throughout his abbreviated life. Mary Lou and I were grateful that Aaron's torment had ended and we prayed that his family would find peace as they tried to move forward without him in their lives. Most importantly, we were extremely grateful that Aaron's trials were over and our family's involvement with childhood cancer had finally come to an end.

Little did we know.

Judy (top) and Mary Lou (bottom) were often confused for each other, even though their ages were eight years apart.

Even as adults, Judy (L) and Mary Lou (R)
are often mistaken for each other.

*In 2011, Judy and Mary Lou were invited back to
receive their O's from the UO Athletic Dept.*

*Judy and Keith met after he returned from Vietnam.
They discovered a shared passion for running.*

Mary Lou visited Aaron shortly after his leukemia diagnosis.

*Dr. Klaus Siebold reduced Aaron's pain and anxiety by
switching from Ketamine to nitrous oxide gas
for Aaron's cranial radiation treatments.*

Judy and Keith suspected contaminated soil near their house as a possible cause of Aaron's leukemia.

Judy used Aaron's courage as inspiration when she ran competitively.

Judy and Keith introduced Aaron and Heather to Tacoma's annual Sound to Narrows race.

After his leukemia diagnosis, Aaron incorporated medical instruments into his play routines.

Heather's arrival, one year into Aaron's chemotherapy treatments, brought an infusion of hope into the family.

Aaron enjoyed cooking. Favorite friends and relatives received copies of his cookbooks.

*Judy and Doug ran the Nike Marathon together in 1981,
qualifying them to run the 1982 Boston Marathon.*

*After Doug and Judy got married, Heather and
Aaron effectively had three parents.*

Affordable waterfront living on Puget Sound. Residents parked at the top of the hill, walked down a pathway, and crossed a double set of railroad tracks to reach their homes.

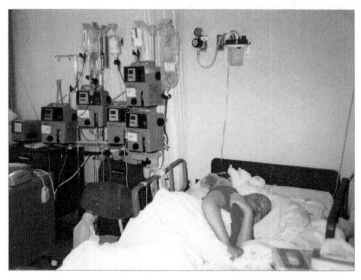

Aaron recovers from herpes zoster at Swedish Hospital after moving out of his LAF room at the Hutch.

197

Aaron and Judy walk the second floor
of the Hutch after his transplant.

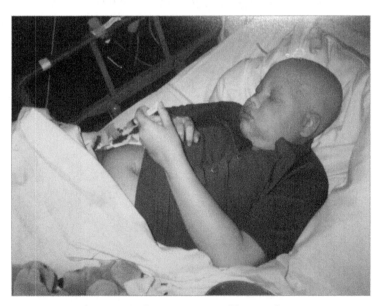

After years of treatments and hospital stays,
Aaron learned to flush his own intravenous lines.

Aaron and Heather loved each other
very much in spite of hard times.

Aaron, following his first relapse at age 6 ½.
He always wore a smile.

Heather and Aaron depart for
Camp Goodtimes in August, 1987.

Aaron celebrates his twelfth birthday at home in
1986 after being released from the Hutch.

Grandparents Jeanne and Ed Armstrong were always
a phone call away to support Aaron and Heather.

Four months after sharing the ring bearer duties at the
author's wedding, Aaron experienced his first relapse.

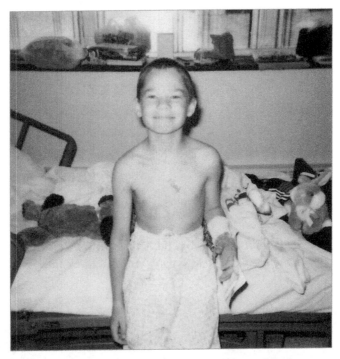

Chris at Doernbecher. "Port" was written on his chest to ensure the catheter was implanted in the right location.

Chris spent many long days on the blue sofa in the family room.

Chris and Matt enjoy a visit from Lizzie, a therapy dog, during Chris's stay at Doernbecher Children's Hospital.

Chris was amazed at how easily his hair fell out.

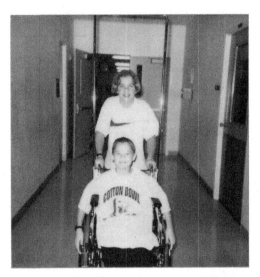

*Matt gave Chris a wheelchair ride the day Chris was released
from Doernbecher Children's Hospital.*

Matt and Chris are happy to be home from Doernbecher.

*Chris is comforted during a low point by his stuffed animal,
Elvis, and his new puppy, Griffey.*

*Chris's third-grade classmates surround
him on his return to school.*

*SF Giants catcher Steve Decker poses with
Chris before a game in Candlestick Park.*

*SF Giants third-baseman, Matt Williams,
signs a baseball for Chris in the dugout.*

Baseball became a metaphor for Chris's health status.
In his first game back, he stole home to score the winning run.

Every year since 1994, Mary Lou has placed a
luminary bag in memory of Aaron at the
American Cancer Society's Relay for Life.

*Luminaries honor Chris each year
at the Relay for Life in Eugene.*

*Children from Candlelighters are honored
each year at the Relay for Life.*

Alumni from Mary Lou's sorority, Delta Delta Delta, participate at the Relay for Life. Tri-Delta has raised more than $45 million to date for St. Jude Children's Research Hospital in support of childhood cancer research.

PART TWO

Chapter 21

TOO MUCH ALIKE

"The first time someone said I looked like Judy," Mary Lou said, "was when I was a student at Briggs Junior High School. A friend came up to me and said, 'Mary Lou, there's a student teacher here that looks just like you.' I said, 'I know, that's my sister.'" The friend didn't believe her, pointing out that her last name was different. "I know," Mary Lou told him. "She's married."

Briggs Middle School, as it later became known, would become Mary Lou's home for the better part of four decades after she graduated from college, earned her teaching certificate, and returned to the school as a physical education teacher. She spent her entire teaching career at Briggs except for two short stints at other schools early in her career. She worked at Briggs for so long that one day a student approached her and said, "Mrs. Bradley, you dated my dad in high school." She eventually worked at Briggs long enough to teach the grandkids of some of her former classmates. But she managed to retire before any of her students told her, "You dated my grandpa."

As an adult, the frequency with which Mary Lou was mistaken for Judy increased significantly. I've seen Judy's former high school or college classmates confuse Mary

Lou for Judy when they ran into Mary Lou in the grocery store or elsewhere around town. It has also happened when Mary Lou visited Judy in Washington, where Mary Lou knows very few people. "She would come visit," said Judy, "and people would say something like, 'Oh, my gosh! You guys look like twins!' It was comical. I would say, 'This is my sister,' and they would say, 'duh!'"

Each sister has the characteristic blonde-haired, blue-eyed look of their Swedish ancestors, though Mary Lou's eyes are more turquoise than blue. The two sisters stood at the same height—about five feet, four inches—and each has long legs, which contributed to their individual success as runners. They shared the work ethic and discipline passed on to them from their German ancestors on their father's side of the family.

Their mother, Jeanne, sees as many differences as similarities. "Their mouths are not alike, Judy's eyes are closer set, and their noses not alike. But still they look alike. Fascinating." In spite of Jeanne's comments about the contrasts in her two daughters, she often mistakes one for the other when looking at their childhood photos.

Both Judy and Mary Lou graduated from the University of Oregon, received degrees in physical education, and went on to become physical education teachers. "Since she was in the PE program at the same college," Mary Lou said, "we had some of the same professors and they often called me Judy. They knew it was me, but they would get confused, kind of like parents do."

Mary Lou and I often attend events at the University of Oregon and it is common for one of their professors to mistake one for the other, even after forty years. While in college, each sister competed for the Oregon track team,

Judy in the 880-yard dash and Mary Lou in the 400-meter hurdles. Both events are characterized by internal grit and toughness. Most people have neither the courage nor desire to run either race.

Sydney Russel, a former All-American track-and-field athlete, described the 400-meter dash as the most difficult running event in track and field. "You can't run all out and you can't run too slow. Coming off the last turn and down that last one hundred meters is the toughest thing to me. Your legs feel heavy. Your upper body gets tight. You feel like you are running in sand and carrying a piano. You have to fight through all of that and concentrate on your form. A lot of time you will see runners break form and just die and sputter to the line. It happens a lot. Even to the best of runners."

Russel was speaking of the 400-meter dash. Given that description, who would place ten hurdles in the path to make it even more difficult? Mary Lou would. She is tough.

Mary Lou competed on the Oregon Women's track team from 1974-1978. Unlike Judy, who competed in pre-Title IX days, when women athletes received little or no funding, Mary Lou began her college career two years after the landmark legislation passed. Nevertheless, Oregon didn't hand out scholarships to women track athletes until Mary Lou had nearly graduated. She recalled a time when a giant semi-truck pulled up to Historic Hayward Field and someone handed out a pair of spikes and a pair of running flats to each woman on the team. It was a big deal.

Thirty-two years after Mary Lou graduated from Oregon, the university invited Mary Lou and Judy to join other deserving women from yesteryear back to the University of Oregon for a special ceremony. They were awarded their athletic letters, or "O's," to commemorate their outstanding athletic achievements. Mary Lou is patient.

Like Judy, Mary Lou also likes to stay busy. She taught middle school full-time; she volunteered in both our boys' classrooms; she was president of the Parent Teacher Organization; she ran the concessions at the school's theatrical performances; she helped the boys with their homework every night; and she never missed one of the boys' sports events. In order to maintain her health and energy at the necessary level, she got out of bed every other day at five o'clock and ran three miles. Mary Lou is energetic.

Unlike Judy, who has never found her off button, Mary Lou does quiet her motor occasionally. Judy's parents couldn't get her to go to bed, but Mary Lou often approached her mom and dad to see if it was time to go to sleep yet.

As an adult, Mary Lou spends her down time watching movies on the Hallmark Movie Channel, watching the same plot play out over and over. Each love story turns out predictably, but Mary Lou often ends up in tears, as if the ending was somehow in doubt. Mary Lou likes a story with a happy ending.

While Mary Lou may have grown up with *Ozzie and Harriet*, her life was not without minor challenges. Her family tells a story about when Mary Lou, as a ten-year-old child, discovered that her pony, Mystery Boy, had broken into the barn on Christmas morning. He ate most of a bag of oats and scattered the rest around the barn. To the family's displeasure, Mary Lou insisted it all be cleaned up before the family could open their presents. Mary Lou could be demanding and inflexible.

As Mary Lou grew into adulthood, she changed from being Judy's pesky little sister to being her close friend and occasional running companion. Mary Lou was a junior at the University of Oregon when she learned of Aaron's leukemia diagnosis. She had just returned from competing at an out-of-town track meet when she walked into her Tri-Delta sorority house to find Bev Schull, an old family friend, waiting for her.

"When I saw Bev, I knew something terrible was going on. There would be no other reason for her to be waiting for me if she didn't have some bad news to tell me. Bev came right out and said, 'Aaron's been diagnosed with leukemia and your parents have gone up to Tacoma to be with Judy and Keith.'"

Mary Lou didn't know anything about leukemia, but she drove up to Gig Harbor as soon as she could to support Judy and her family. After that point, Mary Lou always made it a priority to see Judy and her family when they came to Eugene to visit Jeanne and Ed. After Mary Lou and I married and had children, she used her spring break and summer vacations to take our boys to University Place as often as possible.

Mary Lou and Judy didn't spend much time discussing their similarities. The subject usually came up only when the family got together or one of them was mistaken for the other. They didn't shy away from the comparisons, but each sister was confident in her own identity. But as events unfolded with their children, they would soon begin to wonder, "Is it possible for two sisters to be too much alike?"

Chapter 22

YOUR BEST-CASE SCENARIO

I don't know why I didn't feel more anxiety as I arrived at the annual board retreat for Serenity Lane, a non-profit drug and alcohol treatment center where I had been a patient ten years earlier. Prior to the start of the meeting, I mentioned to a physician and fellow board member that I might need to excuse myself for a phone call during the session, since our nine-year-old son had been experiencing a low-grade fever and leg pains for several weeks. Mary Lou would be calling me with the results after their visit to Chris's pediatrician. His response was brief, but telling.

"If your son is experiencing a fever and leg pains, why are you here?"

"You think it's something serious?" I responded. "I was told it was likely a soft-tissue injury."

"I'd say that would be your best-case scenario," he said. As we began our meeting, I no longer had the business agenda on my mind. I watched the door to the hallway nervously as I awaited the call.

When the door finally opened, I was out of my seat and walking toward the attendant before he spotted me. "Mr. Bradley?" he said. "I have an urgent call for you. You can take it on the house phone in the hallway."

As I picked up the receiver, I had no idea how my life was about to change. I heard Mary Lou take a deep breath before she blurted into the phone, "Chris has leukemia." She began sobbing. A cloud of horror and panic overwhelmed me. It was as if, instead of being called to the phone, I had been summoned to the window to witness an airplane crash. I grasped for some encouraging words to assure Mary Lou that things would be okay, but all I could do was stare at the burning fuselage and repeat, "I'm so sorry, I'm so sorry." Any lucid thoughts were immediately washed away by my tears. I've always regretted that I wasn't stronger for her, but in the terror of the moment, I was fighting off images of bald heads, puffy faces, chemotherapy, radiation, transplants, and relapses. I flashed back to the anguish I had witnessed with Judy and her family eight years earlier at Aaron's memorial service.

I finally composed myself and assured Mary Lou that everything was going to be all right. But even as I uttered the words, I doubted them myself. We agreed that Chris should be told right away and that Dr. Livermore could deliver the message with fewer emotions. I hung up as Mary Lou left to get Chris so they could meet with the doctor.

Chris's story had begun two weeks earlier when he awoke during the night complaining of severe aches in his legs. In those days, urgent care facilities didn't exist, so I took him to the emergency room at Sacred Heart Hospital in downtown Eugene.

The doctors examined Chris, took x-rays of his legs, and diagnosed a soft-tissue injury. "Likely a pulled muscle from either baseball or soccer," they said. Chris was a multi-sport athlete, so their conclusion seemed logical. The nurse gave him a dose of Tylenol with codeine and the pain disappeared.

I became less convinced of their diagnosis as Chris's pain lingered through the next week. A co-worker suggested Chris might be experiencing "growing pains," a common occurrence, according to my associate, where a child's muscle growth struggles to maintain pace with their rapidly growing skeletal structure.

When Jeanne, a child development professional, dismissed the concept as "an old wives' tale," we adopted the soft-tissue injury as the most credible explanation. We continued about our busy lives with the expectation the pains would soon subside.

When the pains returned two weeks later, they were accompanied by a low-grade fever. They reappeared at a most inopportune moment, the day before Mary Lou's parents' fiftieth anniversary party. Mary Lou and Judy had been planning the celebration for five months. Judy and Doug were scheduled to arrive on Friday from University Place. Judy and Mary Lou planned to meet at Silver Falls State Park on Saturday morning to finish decorating. Before running a few last-minute errands on Friday, Mary Lou had scheduled a late-morning appointment to see Dr. Doug Livermore, Chris's pediatrician. She told me later how it unfolded.

"Frankly," she said, "I don't know if I would have taken Chris to the doctor Friday if it had not been for mom and dad's anniversary party. My point was to get him to the doctor and get him some medicine so he would feel better by the party the next day." When Mary Lou took the morning off from her middle-school teaching job, she had no idea she wouldn't be returning to work for the rest of the school year.

"There's obviously something wrong," Dr. Livermore said after examining Chris's glands and thumping on his stomach. "His spleen is enlarged and he just doesn't look like the same old Chris."

The doctor gave Chris some Tylenol 3 to help with his fever and sent them across the street for an x-ray and a blood test. Mary Lou didn't notice at first that all the paperwork was marked "STAT." When she eventually saw it on the blood test—it was highlighted in yellow—she thought Dr. Livermore was helping them out, trying to get it done in a hurry because of her parents' party.

Dr. Livermore reviewed the test results alone in his office for a few moments before returning to the exam room. "Chris, I need to speak with your mom alone for a second," he said. Mary Lou sent Chris back to the waiting room so she could speak with the doctor.

Nothing could have prepared her for what he was about to say.

"Mary Lou, I'm sorry, but Chris has leukemia," the doctor said. Mary Lou's response was quick, defiant, and identical to Judy's response twenty years earlier.

"No, he doesn't," she said.

"Yes, he does," Dr. Livermore insisted. "It's pretty clear from the test results."

"How could that be?" Mary Lou persisted. The doctor expressed his shock when Mary Lou told him about what our family had already gone through with Aaron.

Doctor Livermore launched into an explanation about blood cell counts and other details of leukemia, but he had lost his audience.

"He told me what this was and what that was," said Mary Lou, "but I couldn't tell you one thing he said after that." She told Doctor Livermore she wanted to talk to me before she told Chris, but she worried about breaking the news to me over the phone.

Dr. Livermore guided Mary Lou down the hallway to his office, where she could use the phone on his desk to call me. "I remember walking down the hallway, crying," Mary Lou said, "Dr. Livermore was behind me. He put his hands on my shoulders and said, "I'm so sorry." Mary Lou picked up the phone and, maintaining her conservative fiscal habits even in a moment of crisis, warned Dr. Livermore that the call would be long distance.

On her way to the waiting room to get Chris after talking to me, Mary Lou ran into her mom in the hallway. Mary Lou had called Jeanne earlier that morning and told her that Chris wasn't feeling well. She shared her plans to take Chris to Dr. Livermore.

As with Judy twenty years earlier, Jeanne suspected something serious. "I don't know how, but I knew," she said. "Like I knew with Aaron. When we arrived, there was Chris, sitting in the waiting room with a comic book. I went over and sat down next to him and I asked, 'Where's your mom?'"

"She's talking to the doctor," Chris told his grandma.

Ed sat with Chris while Jeanne went in search of her daughter. "Right then," Jeanne said, "Mary Lou came out of his office. She saw me and she came over and just fell on me and started to cry. She said, 'He's got leukemia.' I wasn't surprised, but it was just awful." Lightning had struck our family twice.

In hindsight, I probably should have accepted one of my associates' offers to drive me over the mountain pass that afternoon. It took more than an hour to get out of the small town of Bend, partly because of my lack of street familiarity, but mainly because I couldn't see through my tears. It was tantamount to driving through a heavy rainstorm without turning on the windshield wipers. I knew Doctor Livermore was discussing Chris's diagnosis with my family as I drove, and I needed to get home.

The three-hour drive back to Eugene, along the scenic McKenzie River and through the spectacular Santiam mountain pass, is normally one of the most enjoyable trips imaginable. The panoramic views were lost on me that day as I raced home to be with my family. I called my mom and a few of my five siblings along the way, but limited cell coverage left me alone with my thoughts for most of the way.

I normally live a life of gratitude and optimism. I nearly always take the "glass is half full" approach to life. Mary Lou tells me that sometimes I am too quick in moments of adversity to "look for the blessing," that I am too eager to flip negative circumstances around to "look on a positive side." In their childhood, Matt and Chris often tired of my telling them to look for doors that are opening rather than focusing on their misfortunes. Chris once broke his arm in a baseball game and while we were in the hospital emergency room getting an x-ray, I began my optimistic banter. Chris interrupted me to say, "Yah, yah, Dad. I get it. Doors are opening everywhere. Not now, okay?"

Chris's leukemia diagnosis was a test I hadn't studied for. My only experience with childhood leukemia had been with Aaron. My mind took me to dark places. I imagined what the world would be like if cancer were to take my son's life. Our boys were the center of our universe. The thought of losing Chris to leukemia was more than I could bear. I didn't know the human body could produce so many tears.

As I raced down the highway, Mary Lou led Chris and her mom into the exam room. At first, Chris sat in a chair by himself before Mary Lou asked him to come over and sit on her lap, an invitation to provide comfort for her as much as for Chris.

Chris started to shake a little as the doctor explained the need to get him checked in to Sacred Heart Hospital as soon as possible, while arrangements were made for him to transfer to Doernbecher Children's Hospital two hours north in Portland. Mary Lou, still in denial about the urgency of Chris's situation, asked Dr. Livermore if we could attend her parents' wedding anniversary the next day before traveling on to Doernbecher. The doctor said no.

Though we had lost Aaron to leukemia, we knew very little about the specific characteristics of the disease. Chris' low white cell count meant his immune system was severely compromised. It represented a severe threat to his health and potentially his life. Dr. Livermore told Mary Lou to go home, pack a bag for Chris, and proceed to Sacred Heart as soon as I arrived home.

Chris maintained his composure until they got in the car. It's understandable how a nine-year-old boy would be puzzled. Aside from a few leg pains and low-grade fever, Chris felt completely normal. With a little pain medicine, he could have returned to his soccer and baseball teams that afternoon. However, as he listened to his mom and Dr. Livermore, he knew intuitively that he had reason to be concerned. He'd been barely a year old when Aaron died so he had no first-hand knowledge of leukemia. He knew only that it was a painful story with a bad ending.

"I don't get it," he told Mary Lou. "I don't feel sick." He began to cry at that point. It was a long, quiet ride home.

"My memory is sitting in Dr. Livermore's office," Chris said years later. "He was sitting there in his khaki safari shirt and Birkenstocks and in his regular calm manner making this announcement. Probably because of the atmosphere, it didn't seem so horrible to me. I was sitting there thinking, 'Oh, okay, so this is what it is. I'm glad we figured it out. Now we'll go fix it.' But I was also taking my cues from Mom. I looked over at her and she's just breaking up. By watching her I realized what I was getting into. He may have just called it acute lymphocytic leukemia. I'm sure he probably said cancer, too, but I definitely had no accurate sense of the scope or the seriousness of what that meant."

When they got home, Mary Lou sent Chris to his room to pack a bag for the hospital, much the same as Aaron had done for years. Our twelve-year-old son, Matt, sat at the computer desk with his back to the door in the corner of our family room, unaware of the news coming his way. Mary Lou walked over and sat on the upholstered arm of our light-blue sofa.

"Matt, Chris has leukemia," she said matter-of-factly.

"Oh, Geez," said Matt, as he put his face in his hands. Mary Lou couldn't tell if he was crying or not, but his face stayed in his hands.

"I'm sure at that point he was thinking of Aaron," Mary Lou said. "You know, the fact that he didn't survive. That's all he knew."

Matt had been four years old when Aaron died, old enough to have memories of playing with his cousin on the beach in front of the University Place house. He remembered visiting Judy and her family in the summertime and during spring breaks. Though he had a stronger memory of Aaron than Chris, Matt's experience was still that of a four-year-old boy. At Aaron's graveside service, for example, he had asked about the pile of dirt and why there was such a big hole dug in the ground. He lamented to his grandma Jeanne that we hadn't brought our shovels.

A fluorescent-orange, triangular-shaped quarantine sign hung outside Chris's door when we arrived at Sacred Heart Hospital, a signal that we had to don a protective mask before entering the room. Chris settled into his hospital bed, surrounded by an assortment of valves, gauges, and tubes extending from the wall. Family and friends came by to lend their support. Chris's head baseball coach, Casey, showed up with his son, Josh, and gave Chris a baseball autographed by Ken Griffey, Jr., one of Chris's major league baseball heroes. They also gave him a VHS copy of *Angels in the Outfield*, a 1994 movie in which an angel appears in answer to a boy's prayers to convert his favorite, but losing team, the California Angels, into a winner.

Our angels were our family, friends, and neighbors who immediately surrounded us with love and support. Ash Cope, a thirteen-year-old neighborhood boy, dug into his possessions and brought Chris a bag of Legos, a collection of comic books, and a Gameboy set with fifteen games. Our friends' outpouring of support laid a foundation of hope and, while we remained fragile, we knew we wouldn't have to fight this battle alone.

Dr. Livermore dropped by the hospital at about 9 p.m. to check on Chris. It had been a long day for him, too. I learned later that after Mary Lou and Chris left his office, Dr. Livermore sat at his desk, put his head in his hands, and cried. He had been Chris's doctor since birth and it could not have been easy for him.

"In my first rotation in pediatrics," Dr. Livermore told me later, "my first exposure to taking care of kids was in oncology. You go on a rotation, you pick up patients, you follow them for about six weeks, and then you pass them along to somebody else. You're not necessarily there all the time because as a medical student you have limited direct responsibility for them, but you spend quite a bit of time around them. There was a child who was roughly four, who had been diagnosed some time ago with neuroblastoma. It was advanced and she was clearly dying. We were at the limit of what could be done for her. I think everybody understood that. The people who understood it best were the mother and the little girl. The person who understood it the least was me. I gradually figured that out. The kid doesn't tell you stuff like that directly, but she knew. She somehow seemed at peace with it. Maybe she was just tired, tired of the things that had been done for her and to her. She finally did die. And the mother was consoling me. She'd had time to come to terms with it. And I hadn't. You never forget something like that. You never do."

Dr. Livermore's quick diagnosis of Chris's leukemia was remarkable in that it wasn't something he encountered very often—he personally diagnosed fewer than half a dozen such cases during his thirty-five-year career. His ability to discover Chris's cancer came from his intuitive powers and his observation skills. He drew an interesting parallel between working with pediatric patients and working in veterinary medicine. "Like animals, children are not always able to give you all the information you need and tell the story in a logical way," he said.

Doctor Livermore confirmed his suspicions by ordering the appropriate tests, something that may seem obvious on the surface. But Mary Lou and I know many children with cancer today whose parents were told repeatedly by their pediatrician that their child had a cold, the flu, or like in Chris's case, a soft tissue injury before they finally received a cancer diagnosis for their child. Two mothers I interviewed told how their child's pediatrician accused them of being "over-reactive first-time moms." Only after the moms insisted the doctors probe further did they discover the child's cancer.

Most mothers' initial instinct is to rely exclusively on their doctors, but many have learned that no matter how experienced and well-intentioned doctors are, they have a challenging job keeping up with high volumes of patients, myriad diseases, and all the current treatment protocols for every conceivable illness. They are human, after all, and if they suspected cancer every time a child showed up with a low-grade fever and body pains, they would burden the medical community with unnecessary tests. Nevertheless, the longer it takes to receive an accurate cancer diagnosis, the less likely you are to exclaim, "Thank god we caught it early!"

As Chris settled in that first night in the hospital, Mary Lou took out a new journal she had received as a gift at her fortieth birthday party several weeks earlier. Much like Judy, she processed her thoughts during challenging times by writing them down. "This book is very timely," she wrote, "because I will use it now to chronicle a new chapter in our lives." What a chapter it would turn out to be.

With Chris asleep and the visitors gone from his room, Mary Lou and I finally shared a quiet moment together. We lay together on what was supposed to be a fold-down bed, but felt more like an upholstered card table. We held each other quietly for a few moments until Mary Lou broke the silence. "I don't want Chris to die," she whispered. I tried to summon some comforting words to give her strength, but they wouldn't come. The truth is, she had spoken for both of us.

Chapter 23

YOU SCRAPE OFF A LITTLE BIT OF YOUR SOUL

D r. Jones didn't just come into Chris's room Monday morning—he made an entrance. "Hi, Gang!" he said, using the same two words he would use to greet us for the next three years. His nasally tone led me to mistakenly attribute his accent to Boston, but he was actually a native Oregonian, raised in the nearby Portland suburb of Beaverton. Both his grandfather and his father were doctors, and his dad, Dr. Richard Jones, has a science building named after him on the Oregon Health Sciences University (OHSU) campus.

"Dr. Jones was kind of the antithesis of Dr. Livermore," Chris recalled years later. "He was this portly sort of guy with a huge grin—the jolliest guy you're ever going to meet. It was like you're just coming to hang out and chat with good old Gary. He was a brilliant guy, but he was also a fun one." Doctor Jones' joyful and mischievous green eyes suited his personality perfectly. He was known to sing show tunes both while walking down the hallway and while doing his procedures. His light-hearted, but knowledgeable demeanor captured our confidence the moment he walked in the door. I began to feel hope for the first time since Chris's diagnosis.

When Dr. Jones saw the autographed Ken Griffey, Jr. baseball on Chris's nightstand, he said, "You know young man, as part of your treatment your doctor gets to have all of your autographed baseballs." Chris sat straight up in bed, eyed his baseball, and responded, "I don't think so."

"Well, then," said Dr. Jones, "Perhaps I could autograph it right under Ken Griffey, Jr.'s autograph?"

"Excuse me," replied Chris, "but do I know you?" Chris and Dr. Jones established a bond through their banter that reminded me of Humphrey Bogart's line at the end of the 1942 movie *Casablanca*: "Louis, I think this is the beginning of a beautiful friendship." This kind, unassuming doctor was going to save our son's life.

Mary Lou, Chris, and I had driven to Portland's Doernbecher Children's Hospital the day following Chris's diagnosis while Jeanne and Ed reluctantly proceeded with their party plans. It was too late to cancel the festivities, even if they'd wanted to. Many guests were coming from out of town—several had arrived already. They gathered up Matt and drove north to celebrate their golden wedding anniversary.

Jeanne knew she would need an explanation for Mary Lou's absence. She wasn't sure what to say, or even if she would be able to get the words out. The solution arrived on the back of a Honda CX500 motorcycle when Jeanne's unconventional Presbyterian minister, Rebecca Hazen, roared into Silver Falls' parking lot. Jeanne told her of Chris's cancer and Rebecca took charge. She went into the ladies' restroom and changed from her black leathers into a silky dress with pink and blue flowers on it. She called everyone together and prayed.

"Jeanne was having a hard time," Rebecca said. "It wasn't just that it was her grandchild; it was also that she had lost

Aaron as her first grandchild. I remember her thinking that, 'Oh, my god, the same thing is going to happen to Chris. And that's why she was so devastated. What I probably said was that it would be okay to pray for a miracle. And I assured them it was also okay to go ahead and celebrate Ed and Jeanne's fifty years together."

Driving to Portland that same day, Mary Lou and I passed the exit to Silver Falls. We lamented missing the party and we tried not to focus on the fact that the following day, Chris's Babe Ruth baseball team was scheduled to play their first game of the season. Chris had prepared all winter and spring to earn a starting position in the lineup and, at that moment, his missing the game was nearly as big an issue as his being hospitalized.

Doernbecher Children's Hospital is a nationally acclaimed biomedical research facility and Level I trauma center. For Oregonians living outside the Portland metro area, Doernbecher is the place you take your child when the situation is life-and-death or when all local options have been exhausted. News reports often combine the hospital's name with the phrases "life-flighted" or "air-lifted."

Entering the fourteenth-floor oncology ward for the first time was unsettling. It resembled a combination hospital ward-daycare facility. Children's voices echoed through the hallways. Picture the little children we've all seen on television—the little bald kids at the Ronald McDonald House. Those television images are sad, but we never think it will happen to us.

Little bald kids walked the hallways, their mom or dad pushing their IV poles alongside them. I stole glances into patients' rooms as we walked down the corridors. Babies, connected to IV lines, sat in metal cribs. Open doors offered a full view of families chatting casually around their child's bed. Children entertained themselves by coloring, reading, or playing cards and board games. Other rooms, their doors pulled to, were darker and discouraged intrusion.

Whatever brightness existed came from the nurses who scurried in and out of rooms, always with a shot of hand sanitizer from the wall dispenser. They smiled and addressed each child by name in a warm and friendly manner. The children responded in kind, as if the nurse was a favorite aunt or uncle. We breathed easier, both literally and figuratively, when we learned that facemasks were not required.

Like Aaron twenty years earlier, Chris's needed to undergo a bone marrow aspiration to confirm his leukemia diagnosis. Mary Lou and I stood in the corner of a small exam room as Dr. Jones began the procedure. I was intrigued by the process, but Mary Lou couldn't bear to watch. After he numbed the area on Chris's hip bone, Dr. Jones used a special needle, like a tree bore, to extract a marrow sample. He exerted more pressure than usual to draw an adequate sample into the syringe because the leukemic cells in Chris's marrow were so dense. Chris chatted through the entire procedure and afterwards, still rummy from the anesthesia, he asked to do it again.

Dr. Jones faced a full audience when he came by Chris's room to give us the bone marrow results Sunday afternoon. He brought promising news—Chris had acute lymphocytic leukemia (ALL), the "good" kind. While it had proven fatal for Aaron, ALL still offered a much better chance of long-term survival than all the other types of leukemia. He also shared with us that Chris fell into the "good" age category. Children over age two and under age ten stood a higher chance of survival. At age nine, Chris was on the cusp, but within the right range.

Some of the post-party participants had come to Doernbecher from Silver Falls to get an update and provide their support. Jeanne and Ed sat in the only two chairs in the room. One of Mary Lou's Tri-Delta Sorority sisters, Heidi, lived in Portland, and had rushed right over after hearing about Chris. My mom, Jean, had flown in earlier that day from Santa Rosa, California, and sat on the far edge of the bed. (Matt and Chris had two grandmothers named Jean: my mom, Jean, from California, and Mary Lou's mom, Jeanne, whom the boys referred to as Grandma "Eugene" to eliminate confusion) Matt sat at the foot of the bed with Judy, who had brought him along after the party.

Dr. Jones' experience had taught him the importance of bonding with young patients and their parents immediately. He enjoyed the process of connecting. "I used to live for you guys," he told me later. "The thing that turned me on the most was the new leukemia patient. With ALL, it is the worst thing that has ever happened in their lives, the worst thing ever. It was an opportunity to establish a relationship that hopefully allowed for communication both ways. It was important to get through some important things early on. What I was striving for was creating a relationship of working together in such a way that it doesn't matter what the outcome is, it is going to be okay."

Whether or not it turned out okay for the families, it often took a toll on the battle-tested doctors and nurses. Each new patient initiated a new emotional journey for them. "You have to scrape a little bit of your soul off each time," Dr. Jones said. "Sometimes, that pays back in dividends, like with you guys. And then sometimes, it doesn't.

Sometimes you are just scraping your soul." We had no idea at the time if ours would be a success story, but it was already grinding away at mine.

It had been eight years since Aaron's death. Judy, Doug, and Keith had managed to return to somewhat normal lives. But Judy had mixed feelings about joining us in Chris's room. "I felt like with Chris everything was so hopeful and good, but I didn't know if I wanted to be around because our outcome was not good. But things had changed so much by then and hopefully what Aaron went through would help Chris. I knew I could help out by telling Mary Lou some of the things that we went through, and not dwelling on the final outcome."

As Judy was worried about the effect of her presence in Chris's room, Mary Lou was thinking about the sisters' similarities and fretting that Judy may have to relive the worst parts of Aaron's journey. "Poor Judy, it hit her pretty hard," Mary Lou wrote. "Judy and I are just too much alike! It's pretty scary!"

Mary Lou and I would have understood completely had Judy decided not to come to the hospital, but we very much appreciated her support. She had been down this road before. Her fluency in the complicated language of chemotherapy was invaluable, especially when Dr. Jones explained Chris's three-year treatment protocol.

Dr. Jones went over all the drugs, their potential side effects, and how and when they would be administered. It was a lot to take in at one time—like he was reading to us from a medical dictionary. Judy listened along with the rest of us and asked a lot of questions that would not have occurred to the rest of us.

Dr. Jones listed the chemo drugs Chris would be taking initially—vincristine, 6-MP, prednisone, methotrexate, and others. Through Judy's questions, we learned that, though Chris would be receiving nearly all of the same drugs given to Aaron, the protocols had changed due to the clinical trials Aaron and others had endured. The most punishing phase, known as "Delayed Intensification," was not something we looked forward to experiencing. It had proven in trials to be effective in treating ALL and it was one of many effective therapies that had been unavailable to Aaron.

Judy's hopes that Aaron's experience would help Chris survive were well-founded. When Aaron first became sick in 1976, long-term survival rates for ALL were as low as fifteen percent, not much better than the odds given to Robin Bush in 1953. By the time Chris was diagnosed with the identical disease twenty years after Aaron's diagnosis, and eight years after his death, the survival rate for ALL was reported to be between seventy-five and eighty percent, provided the child completed three years of chemotherapy successfully.

When I asked Dr. Jones to confirm the numerical odds of Chris's survival, he side-stepped the question. "Chris is not going to survive seventy-five percent," he told me. "He will either survive one-hundred percent or he won't survive. The important thing is that we are going to do our best to give him the best treatment available." His response wasn't what I hoped for, but I understood his reluctance to provide an answer that could come back later to haunt all of us.

I remember Dr. Jones broaching the subject of clinical trials with us early on, but Mary Lou has no memory of any such conversation. I'm not sure how to explain that, except to perhaps attribute it to the "fog of war," a battlefield condition that causes confusion and loss of perspective in war conditions. My initial understanding of the trials was that they would give the most appropriate and effective treatment to all children, except for some randomly chosen ones who would receive a placebo. I was shocked they would consider such an approach and I rejected it out of hand. Dr. Jones clarified that, at a minimum, all children received the best-known treatment available. Trial participants were then randomized into groups to study the effectiveness of incremental changes in the treatment regimens.

We signed off on Chris's participation, but in retrospect, I remember assuming that any incremental changes would be in the positive direction. It didn't dawn on me that some of the trials might move the needle backward and that Chris's participation may have reduced his chance of survival. For example, the cranial radiation therapy administered to Aaron in 1976 was part of the standard protocol—it was considered to be the latest, most effective treatment to prevent relapse in the central nervous system. Further trials revealed that while radiation to the brain may have been effective in achieving remissions, the trade-offs in terms of the long-term cognitive damage done to children were unacceptable. Researchers eventually concluded that only under specific circumstances was it beneficial to subject the child to cranial radiation. They removed it from the standard treatment protocol for most ALL patients.

Still, subsets of ALL patients still received radiation or bone marrow transplants as part of their initial treatment protocol. The next step in Chris's journey would be to determine if he was in one of those subsets, specifically whether or not he had the "Philadelphia chromosome," a phenomenon that occurs in less than five percent of ALL cases, and carries a long-term survival rate of no more than twenty percent if treated with chemotherapy alone.

Mary, the seven-year-old daughter of our good friends, Pete and Joan (another of Mary Lou's Tri-Delta sisters), received an ALL diagnosis in 2001, five years after Chris. Doctor Jones initially prescribed the standard two-and-a-half-year chemotherapy protocol for young girls with leukemia. According to her parents, Dr. Jones generally confirmed an eighty-five percent chance Mary would survive. When further tests showed that Mary had the Philadelphia chromosome, the doctor referred them to the Hutch in Seattle, where they scheduled an immediate transplant. Two months after her diagnosis, Mary received the transplanted marrow of her twelve-year-old brother. The doctors told her parents that Mary was cured, but five months later, Mary's leukemia returned. She underwent a second transplant, but once again, the transplant failed. Mary died less than two years after her initial diagnosis, a cruel reminder of the random nature of childhood leukemia in choosing which child lives and which one dies.

Mary Lou and I trembled when we thought about subjecting Chris's brain to radiation or going through a transplant. The possibility of the cranial radiation, combined with the toxicity and long-term side effects from three years of chemotherapy, were almost more than we could bear. We had literally entered a house of horrors. Many parents said to us, "I could never do that," or "I don't know how you did that." My usual response was something like, "You take one step at a time, overcome one hurdle at a time, and keep moving ahead." A more direct answer was given to me by the mother of another leukemia child. "You just do it. What are you going to do, lay down on the floor and cry? You've got to take care of that child. And you've got to be strong for them. You don't get up with a menu of choices. You just have to do what you have to do."

The next day, results from Chris's spinal test would determine the presence or absence of the Philadelphia chromosome and any need for radiation. Mary Lou and I waited and prayed.

Chapter 24

SPINNING OUT OF CONTROL

C hris took two steps out the door toward the car before he stopped, bent over, and threw up on the driveway. Mary Lou looked at me, but said nothing. Chris, still doubled over, began to cry and shouted, "I told you I didn't feel like going!"

I stepped aside as Mary Lou helped Chris get back into the house, where he removed his baseball uniform and returned to the safety of the blue sofa in the baseball room. It wouldn't be the last time in this journey that Chris's leukemia led me to question my long-held assumptions about life.

I've always been a "mind-over-matter" person who believes that a positive attitude can make a big difference. Chris's Babe Ruth baseball team was scheduled to play the second game of the season that day. He had already missed the first game when he was diagnosed a week earlier. He wouldn't be able to play in this game, but I knew he missed being around his teammates. I felt like this might be a good time for Chris to learn the importance of resilience. He had told me all morning that he felt weak and nauseous and didn't want to go.

Mary Lou reminded me that he had only been home two days; that it had been only three days since his surgery;

and that he had been pumped full of toxins all week. Maybe this wasn't such a good idea, she suggested. I was convinced he would feel much better once he got to the ballpark. If he put on his uniform and showed up at the game, it would do him some good—a "get back on the horse" approach. It would also show his teammates and their parents his fighting spirit and let them see that he was going to beat his cancer. I insisted he give it a try. So, Chris reluctantly put on his brand-new red, white, and blue uniform and prepared to leave for the game. "We got this!" I thought to myself as we walked out the door, only to have him vomit.

We had received good news the day following our meeting with Dr. Jones. Chris's test results had found no evidence of the Philadelphia chromosome and eliminated any need for him to receive radiation or have a bone marrow transplant. After giving us the good news, Dr. Jones had surgically implanted a portacath, or "port" into Chris's chest just below his collar bone. Like the Hickman line Aaron used to facilitate his chemo treatments, the port eliminated the need for repeated needle sticks. It allowed blood to be drawn and medications to be given through the small device imbedded just under the skin's surface.

The Hickman had worked well for Aaron and thousands of other children over the years, but it had one potential drawback—it left a tube protruding from the skin. Though the tube could be taped to the skin or otherwise immobilized, the risk for active children was that the lines often got infected, tangled, or otherwise damaged over time. The more active the child, the higher the risk.

The port had no external tube sticking out from the skin. It was a small disc, about the size of a quarter, imbedded just under the skin's surface. After numbing the skin, a doctor or nurse injected a needle through the skin into the subdermal port and took blood or administered medications. Without the external tube associated with a Hickman, Chris's port would allow him to resume his normal athletic activities once we made it through the initial crisis.

The night following Chris's surgery had been our longest yet. Mary Lou and I alternated nights at the hospital, much the same as Judy and Keith had done, and it happened to be my turn. Chris moaned throughout the night, either from post-surgical pain or from his leukemia. I wasn't certain. At one point, he needed to use the bathroom—a challenge, given the tubes connecting his body to the frame of the IV pole. He got out of bed and became entangled in the tubing as he made his way to the toilet. The bathroom's tiny size did not allow adequate space for me to help him through the door while dragging along his IV pole and the attached line. He needed to pee urgently, but I was unaware of his nausea. The whole exercise culminated with his being entangled among the pole and the IV lines in the tiny bathroom, where he nearly peed and vomited simultaneously. I called for a nurse and did what I could to help, but this was definitely not in my wheelhouse. It was one of many times I felt like things were spinning way out of my control.

While Mary Lou and I focused on Chris during his hospital stay, Judy realized from her experience with Heather that Matt's needs may be neglected. She took him to a Portland Trailblazers NBA basketball game one evening to give him some special attention. Matt was twelve years old at the time, a budding socialite in the world of middle school. A week away from home with his younger brother at Doernbecher Children's Hospital was killing his social life. The ubiquitous world of social media did not exist at the time, but maintaining an active social life has always been part of a pre-teen's survival. The best we could do for him was to get the fax number from the nurses' station so he could share it with his friends at school. Nurses soon began delivering printed lifelines for Matt to Chris's room.

I followed Judy's lead and sat down for lunch one day with Matt in the hospital cafeteria to fill in him as best I could on our path ahead. I didn't know much more than he did at the moment about the exact direction we were going, but I assured him that his needs were as important as those of Chris. I explained how the urgency of Chris's illness and the nature of his treatments might create situations where Matt's needs were set aside temporarily. However, I asked him to raise his hand any time he felt that his priorities were not being considered. I promised to give equal attention to his needs as best I could, but looking back, I wish I done a better job fulfilling that promise. One of the things I learned about having a cancer diagnosis in the family is how little control I had in how things would play out on a daily basis.

By Thursday, Chris had responded so well to the initial doses of vincristine that Dr. Jones declared him in remission. This was quite a pleasant surprise, given that Dr. Jones' initial goal was to get Chris into remission within thirty days, the same standard that Dr. Origenes had used twenty years earlier with Aaron. Aaron had come in just under the wire, while Chris was in remission in less than a week. We took that to be an early sign for a more positive outcome for Chris. Dr. Jones said he would be discharging Chris that day!

The unexpected news initiated a flurry of activity, including a series of wheelchair races down the hallway by Matt and Chris. All week, we had deferred their repeated requests to go joyriding in the hospital's wheelchairs. It seems like a great way to celebrate our departure. Matt propelled his own chair while Mary Lou and I traded off providing the horsepower for Chris, whose body was already weakening, both from the leukemia and the battery of chemo drugs being injected into his system.

We returned home to Eugene on Friday, but I wondered if our lives would ever return to normal. In less than a week, cancer had contaminated every part of our lives. It scrambled our priorities, it infiltrated our conversations, it altered our schedules, and it factored into every decision, large or small.

"WELCOME HOME, CHRIS!" read two colorful banners draped across the front of the house, their message of merriment camouflaging what truly lay ahead. Chris hobbled into the house and retreated to the blue sofa in the family room, his refuge for the foreseeable future. From this strategic location, he could remotely control the fifty-five-inch television in the corner and the stereo system on the far wall. The family computer sat within reach on the nearby desk.

We generally referred to the family room as the "baseball room" because of its décor. Its walls and shelves displayed a vast array of team banners, collectible figurines, autographed baseballs, and framed photos of Major League Baseball players. A custom-designed, seven-foot long stained-glass window dominated the south wall of the room. A giant team poster of the 1986 World Series champion New York Mets, autographed by each player on the team, hung on the wall over the computer monitor. An eighteen-inch statue of Babe Ruth lorded over the fireplace mantle in the corner. Autographed bats from baseball greats Nolan

Ryan, Mike Schmidt, Pete Rose, Willie Mays, and others hung from a special wall display. A news reporter once did a story about our collection of baseball memorabilia and called the room a "Mini-Cooperstown" in reference to the home of Major League Baseball's Hall of Fame. Chris was a huge baseball fan and the room offered him a comfortable environment to convalesce.

Our first order of business after getting Chris settled was to come as close as possible to replicating the sterile environment of a hospital. The chemo drugs were killing off his cancer cells, but they were simultaneously compromising his immune system. We sanitized every hard surface—floors, walls, shelves, countertops, doors, fixtures, furniture, and knick-knacks. We replaced all cloth hand-towels in the kitchen and bathrooms with rolls of paper towels. We rid the house of bar soap and positioned germicidal hand-cleaner dispensers next to each wash basin.

Mary Lou and I marveled at the number of friends who reached out to us. "The phone just keeps ringing and ringing," Mary Lou noted in her journal. "We are so lucky to have friends and neighbors like we do!" Matt had a different perspective. Our phone line was tied up for hours by friends and family eager to receive updates and offer assistance. The busy phone line frustrated his efforts to re-establish his social lifeline after a week's absence. Consequently, we installed a direct phone line in his bedroom so he could get back in circulation.

We didn't cook a meal for at least six weeks after returning home. Our next-door neighbor, Jackie, surprised us with a barbecued chicken dinner the night we arrived home. The following day, another friend, Janet, brought that evening's dinner and a six-week meal schedule she'd put together among our friends. She provided a spreadsheet showing who would be bringing dinner each night and what they would be preparing.

My five siblings and their spouses showed up from far and wide to provide hope and assistance. They screened calls to keep us from having to repeatedly answer the same questions from well-meaning friends. My mom extended her visit indefinitely until we could get stabilized. There are advantages to coming from a large and loving family.

One of the biggest struggles we faced initially was getting Chris to take his chemo pills. In addition to the intravenous chemicals he was given during regular clinic visits, he took five different types of pills, most of which were the same ones prescribed for Aaron. Mary Lou copied Judy's approach and listed Chris's complex medication schedule on a three-by-five card. The system helped to manage the process, but it did not address the real challenge: Chris couldn't keep his pills down.

Chris had taken very few pills in his life prior to his cancer diagnosis, and this was a tough time to learn. Each attempt to swallow pills triggered his gag reflex and he threw them back up. Most of his pills were scheduled to be taken in the evening so this made for some very lengthy and emotional bedtime routines.

On any given night, Chris had as many as fourteen pills to take. He struggled for more than an hour to get ten or twelve of them down, one…at…a…time. Then, the last one or two pills triggered his gag reflex, ejecting all the pills into his "barf-bowl," a nine-inch stainless steel bowl with a ring attached to it that became his constant companion. We then started the process again.

We spent many nights with our heads in our hands. We were often tempted to just let it go for the evening and try again the next day, but we never seriously considered that to be an option. The pills were more than pills; they were the toxic keys to saving our son's life. We stayed at it each evening until he was able to keep them down.

Someone suggested we grind the pills into a fine powder and mix it with applesauce. The awful mixture came back up and we nearly ruined Chris's appetite for applesauce for life. We cut the pills up into smaller pieces, but the jagged edges of the fragments scraped against Chris's throat and made things worse. We refined our approach by smoothing the edges of each tiny piece with a fingernail file. The process took a lot of time and nearly quadrupled the number of pill segments Chris had to take, but it still didn't solve the problem.

Mary Lou mentioned our struggles to a pharmacist, who told her about a pill-cutting device. More importantly, a nurse told Mary Lou about the existence of empty gelatin capsules into which we could pack Chris's pills. By stuffing multiple pills into one smooth gel-cap, we reduced the total number of pills and made them much easier to swallow. Problem solved. We checked that box and moved on to the next challenge.

"I can tell the prednisone is taking effect," Mary Lou wrote. "Chris is hungry all the time. He really reminds me of Aaron when I see his face this puffy. The other thing that amazes me is how fast his muscles have atrophied. His legs are skinny now." Less than a month earlier, Chris had been one of the more athletic boys in his third-grade class. Now he struggled to walk thirty feet to the bathroom unassisted.

Chris's constant hunger from taking prednisone took no breaks at night. His food cravings made it difficult for him to fall asleep and when he finally dozed off, he re-awakened in the middle of the night with hunger pangs. When he called out to Mary Lou and me to bring him something to eat, it contributed further to everyone's loss of sleep and added to our already high levels of exhaustion and anxiety.

My mom came up with an ingenious solution. Each night at bedtime, we placed bite-sized chunks of watermelon in a medium-sized bowl and kept that bowl refrigerated by placing it into a larger bowl filled with ice. We covered the whole thing in plastic wrap, and set it on the nightstand next to Chris's bed. Next, we cued up a book on tape in his miniature cassette player and placed it, with his headphones, on the nightstand next to his lamp and the watermelon. When Chris awoke each night thereafter, he switched on his bedside lamp, chowed down the chilled melon, put on his headphones, and hit the play button on the cassette player. The next morning, we usually found him sound asleep next to an empty bowl, the headphones hanging from his ears.

After Chris's treatments began and we learned more about both the short-term and the long-term side effects of the drugs, I became less confident that we were on the right path. I wanted to know if any other effective therapies existed that exacted a smaller pound of flesh.

One friend suggested we have Chris drink green tea as a curative agent. Not only did Chris reject the tea after one attempt, but I felt like I lost some credibility in the process.

"Have Chris take shark cartilage," another friend suggested. "I know someone who used it and it saved his life after doctors told him he was incurable. The FDA won't approve it for use in the United States, but it is saving many lives in Mexico." The friend suggested the existence of a conspiracy between the FDA and drug manufacturers to ensure a market for the toxic chemo drugs being given to cancer patients. Could that be true? Absolutely. Were Mary Lou and I going to be the ones to defy conventional treatments and travel to Mexico with Chris? Not likely. There's no doubt these people had our best interest at heart, but their suggestions only served to foster doubt and confusion in an already chaotic situation.

No parent wants to sanction the poisoning of their child under any circumstances. We knew very little about the ongoing clinical trials other than a brief conversation with Dr. Jones. Mary Lou and I remembered the suffering Aaron had endured as a result of his treatments. And after eleven years of suffering, he hadn't survived. Should we blindly accept the recommendations of modern medicine? If less painful and less damaging alternatives existed, that would also provide a cure for Chris, we wanted to consider them. On the other hand, we didn't want to let our uninformed desperation drive us into seeking snake-oil solutions while ignoring the positive results achieved through decades of research. No solution was guaranteed, however, so each suggestion of an alternate approach opened the door to self-doubt.

Our decisions were also complicated by the fact that we had to make so many of them in such a short period of time. Less than a week earlier, we were told to get in the car and head to Doernbecher, where the doctors told us the chemo routine Chris would endure. Then we were told he would have surgery the next day, when they inserted is port. It wasn't until we arrived home and after the dust settled a bit, that we began to catch up with events and question whether or not we were on the right path. We didn't lack faith in the doctors, per se, but everything seemed so out of control. We wanted to feel like we had a voice, a choice in which direction we were taking our son.

In the end, our exhaustion from events up to that point left us no energy to pursue any other alternatives. We based our ultimate decision on our faith in Doctor Jones.

Chapter 25

HOUSTON, WE HAVE A PROBLEM

C hemotherapy treatments are never routine, but by the fourth week of driving the 200-mile round-trip to Portland, the process had at least become familiar. We stopped at the same rest area, one hour south of Portland on I-5 to apply EMLA, a numbing cream, to Chris's chest and lower back. The topical anesthetic took about an hour to numb Chris's skin and if we timed it right, we would arrive at the clinic prepared to go directly into the exam room for Chris's procedures. Timing was crucial. If the EMLA application was delayed, we would have to wait in the reception area until it numbed Chris's skin sufficiently. On the other hand, if we applied it too early, or if there was any delay on our arrival to the doctor's office, the numbing effects would wear off prematurely and the cream would need to be re-applied, initiating a new one-hour waiting period.

Chris removed his shirt and lay back in the back of the van while Mary Lou squeezed the small tube of the white cream over his port and covered it with a three-inch adhesive cellophane patch. She repeated the process on the lower part of his spine, the second area where he would receive an injection.

They were ready for us when we arrived at the outpatient clinic. Chris removed his shirt and climbed up on the exam table. Kaylee, our favorite nurse, probed the area around his port. Confident the EMLA had done its job, she inserted a needle. A small surgical tube with a threaded attachment now protruded from Chris's chest. Kaylee attached an empty syringe to the tube, drew a blood sample, and capped the vial to be sent to the lab right away for analysis. Next, she "pushed" a vial of saline solution through the tube to dilute the blood in Chris's veins and prepare for the next step. She replaced the empty saline vial with a syringe filled with vincristine, and checked again to ensure the vial was for Chris by reading his name and birth date on the label. She pushed the toxic chemical into Chris's port. How things had changed since Aaron's days, when they had to do a finger-stick to draw blood and inject vincristine through tiny veins in his hands.

Dr. Jones joined us in the exam room for the next step. "Hi, Gang!" He greeted us in his customarily cheerful manner as he began his physical exam of Chris's body. He always felt Chris's abdomen and checked the size of Chris's spleen. He probed around his testicles for signs of relapse. Mary Lou and I stood in the corner of the small room as Dr. Jones and Kaylee played the roles of two long-time acting partners who had their script memorized.

Kaylee began the second act by injecting a sedative called Versed into Chris's port. Versed was used at the time as a procedural anesthetic for children. "Vitamin V," as we came to know it, didn't render Chris completely unconscious, but it made make him loopy, like a drunken sailor. He slurred his words and babbled on throughout the procedure. The Versed also enhanced whatever mood

Chris was in at the moment he received the drug. If he was having a bad day when they gave him the injection, the Versed left us with a weepy drunk on our hands. If he was joyful when he went under, he joked throughout the procedure and emerged in a great mood, often asking for more Versed. The drug also causes memory loss, so Chris never remembered any of the procedure or the moments immediately afterward.

Chris began to read joke books on the drive to Portland to put his mind in a cheerful state. In the middle of one procedure, Dr. Jones mentioned quietly to Kaylee that he was having a challenge with the proper placement of the needle into Chris's spinal column. Chris suddenly blurted out, "Uh-oh. Houston, we have a problem." He referred to Dr. Jones by his first name, Gary, and playfully accused the doctor of being a playground bully as a child. Kaylee and Dr. Jones allowed themselves a slight smile, but remained focused on the task at hand.

Before giving Chris the spinal injection of methotrexate, Dr. Jones always gave us the same caution. "Methotrexate is yellow and if for some reason another doctor were to perform this procedure on Chris in my absence, you always want to make sure that the liquid is yellow." Vincristine and methotrexate were usually given to a patient during the same appointment. On more than one occasion, doctors had confused the two drugs and mistakenly injected vincristine into their patients' spinal cord. The result of such a mistake was complete paralysis and most likely death.

"Lay real still, Chris," Kaylee said as she rolled Chris into a quasi-fetal position, facing in her direction. She leaned over and enveloped his whole body with hers to ensure that he didn't move. She wrapped her right arm gently, but firmly over his shoulders. Her left arm gathered up his hips, ensuring that any slight movement by his legs would not extend to his spinal column.

Mary Lou and I had watched Dr. Jones do this procedure many times. As delicate as it was, he had always made it look so routine.

"Just a little sting, here," said Dr. Jones, as he inserted the first needle just under the skin to numb the area between Chris's third and fourth vertebrae. The skin around the injection site remained a light yellow from the antiseptic scrub Kaylee had given Chris earlier. No response from Chris. He was doing fine. Dr. Jones leaned over slowly and prepared to insert a second, much longer needle into Chris's spinal column.

We had seen him do this procedure enough times that I could project his next moves. He would inject the longer needle and hold a glass tube beneath it to catch the fluid draining from Chris's spinal column. The fluid would flow very slowly—drip, drip, drip—into the glass tube until Doctor Jones had collected the desired amount. After successfully retrieving the spinal fluid, Dr. Jones would unthread the full reservoir from the needle and hand the vial to Kaylee, who would then seal it, label it, and send to the lab for analysis along with Chris's blood sample. The final step would be to inject the methotrexate into Chris's spine.

Maybe it was because Dr. Jones had repeatedly made the procedure look so routine that Mary Lou and I were so traumatized when things went awry. The moment Dr. Jones stuck the needle in, Chris's began screaming. "Ow! Ow!" Chris yelled. "Make him stop!" Dr. Jones withdrew the needle, took a deep breath, and looked quizzically at

Kaylee. He tried once again, only to achieve the same result. Chris screamed repeatedly, "Make him stop!"

Dr. Jones excused himself from the room and returned with another doctor. Maybe Dr. Jones was having a bad day and the other doctor would have more success. The second doctor made an effort, only to produce more screams from Chris. Mary Lou and I stood by helplessly. The doctors couldn't come up with a reason why the procedure was not working that day, but they finally agreed to defer Chris's methotrexate injection until our next visit.

My sister, Sheron, who had joined us for the trip to Portland that day and who was waiting for us in the reception area, told me later she could hear Chris's screams in the outer office. I was beginning to learn more about what Dr. Jones meant when he said that treating kids with leukemia scrapes off a bit of your soul.

Today, doctors no longer use Versed to sedate children during bone marrow aspirations and spinal taps. An anesthesiologist puts the child to sleep using propofol, a general anesthesia. Kids call it "sleepy milk."

"And parents are no longer allowed to be in the room," Kaylee told me years later. "The change was really hard for some parents. But they've had a couple of times when the parents have passed out and injured themselves. The priority is the kid and his airway. We didn't need a parent in there crying and distracting anybody."

Back in Eugene that evening, Chris walked through the kitchen as Mary Lou and I were washing the dinner dishes. "Chris," Mary Lou began, "Dr. Jones felt pretty bad about how things went today."

"Why? What happened?" Chris responded. Mary Lou paused and looked at me. We simultaneously remembered the memory-suppressing properties of the Versed. "Oh, it wasn't a big deal," she finally answered. Chris continued on his way. The Versed had done its job. Chris had no memory of the excruciating pain he had experienced earlier that day. Mary Lou and I had a light-hearted discussion later about asking Dr. Jones if he would give each of us an injection of Versed before Chris's next procedure.

Chapter 26

ALL MUST DIE, AND SO THEY DO

Seven-year-old Anthony "Tony" Hays lived with his family in the tiny town of Brownsville, Oregon, about thirty miles north of Eugene. One week prior to Chris's leukemia diagnosis, our local newspaper published an article about Tony, who had been diagnosed with acute lymphocytic leukemia two years earlier. On learning of their son's cancer, Tony's parents, Loyd and Christina Hays, refused to take him to a doctor. As members of the Church of the First Born, they believed that prayer and their religious faith were sufficient to save their son's life. They and their fellow church members prayed fervently for the boy's recovery right up to the day he died. They watched their son die from what was by then a treatable disease.

Dr. Larry Fickenscher, the only pediatric oncologist in our town for more than thirty years, said that if Tony's parents had searched out a doctor when he was initially sick, there was an excellent chance the boy could have been cured.

Tony's grandfather, Ed Jensen, who was also the leader of the church, explained his beliefs when the family's story was chronicled by the television show *A Current Affair.* "The power of God hasn't changed. It's eternal, it's everlasting, it's almighty, and it works. In the sixteenth chapter of Mark,

Jesus says they shall lay hands on the sick and they shall recover. We believe these things because we've seen it. Our membership over the past one hundred years has survived rabies, tetanus, acute appendicitis, and cancer. But all must die, and so we do."

Prosecutors charged the boy's parents with manslaughter. The father cried on the witness stand as he described the final moments of his son's life. When asked whether or not his son had asked for a doctor, the father responded, "because of my beliefs and the admonitions of the Lord, I would have instructed him not to ask." The forty-four-year-old father was convicted of criminally negligent homicide and was sentenced to five years' probation. The mother was acquitted.

People often turn to faith in times of crisis. Or as a friend once told me, "There are no atheists in fox holes." For others, like nurse Kaylee, working through multiple crises had the opposite result. "Working with kids and cancer made me question my faith so many times because I saw so much suffering," she said. "There is just so much pain involved."

Kaylee saw a teenager die once under very challenging circumstances. "We were giving this kid so much Dilaudid (a powerful opioid pain reliever) and it wasn't working. The resident was very nervous about prescribing more medications. He kept saying, 'This should be working, but it's not.'

"The family was praying and saying he wasn't going to die, that God was going to use him as a witness to people here at Doernbecher. You don't want to say, 'Well, that's not going to happen.'"

The boy died and the family didn't accept it. For three days, they prayed and waited because they thought God was going to raise the boy from the dead. They were so sure that God had said he was going to heal him.

"I had a lot of talks with the dad," Kaylee said. "He was taking responsibility for his son's death. What does that mean? Does it mean he failed? That he didn't try hard enough? That he didn't confess a sin somewhere? If they believe that's how it works, what are they going to do now? They eventually came around to a different kind of belief that God could use it in another way."

Dr. Larry Fickenscher encountered other instances where a family's religious beliefs ran counter to getting them the most current medical treatment available for their child's leukemia. "I had one family that was really reluctant because they were Jehovah's witnesses. The Jehovah's Witnesses can't have blood or blood products. They had a four-year-old kid with leukemia, and the kid was going to die if he didn't get a transfusion, but it was against their religion."

Dr. Fickenscher sent the family to Doernbecher, where the hospital obtained a court order that made the child a ward of hospital for as long as it took to give the transfusion. After the transfusion, the court order expired and Doernbecher gave the child back to the parents. With this approach, the family hadn't transgressed. "That way," Dr. Fickenscher added, "I wouldn't be the bad guy, because I had to take care of this kid for three years and deal with his family."

Kathy, another mother of a leukemic child, combined her Catholic background with her Native American heritage to get spiritual help for her son. During one episode, when her son was in a post-operative coma after enduring a brain surgery to deal with a deadly infection, she tried out her healing skills when no one was looking. "I waved my hands over him and visualized the cancer. I physically pulled it out and made sure I threw it away from us. I always did it in sets of three."

During the same critical episode, some people visited her son's room and asked Kathy if they could pray over him. They lay their hands on her son. "Then things started happening," Kathy said. "Feet started twitching and things like that." Kathy considered them to be angels—she wasn't concerned about their origin or the minute details of their faith. It's not clear which of Kathy's efforts bore more fruit, but her son soon came out of his coma and is still alive twenty years later.

Kristina, a mother whose daughter was diagnosed with ALL in 1998, had been a devout Christian all her life. She described her transactional relationship with God. "I had always talked to God in my head. 'Lord, give us a parking spot. We would get a parking spot up close." When her daughter, Holly, was diagnosed with leukemia, her relationship with God changed. "I was mad at life; this was just so awful. I wasn't praying and I wasn't thinking Godly thoughts. All of a sudden, I saw a drop of water fall down into this smooth pool. All these rings went out. When I saw it, I knew God was telling me that we would be that drop of water and all those rings signified all the people we would touch."

If anyone had the right to be angry with God, it would be my mother in law, Jeanne. She remembered a conversation with her motorcycle minister, Rebecca, at her fiftieth anniversary party the day following Chris's diagnosis.

"I know you must be very angry with God," Rebecca told her.

"Rebecca, I don't understand that concept at all," replied Jeanne. "In the first place, I don't think God picks some kids to get sick. I don't think God helps some teams win a game. I don't think God likes this person better than that person. I just don't think that way, so I don't get angry at God. I never felt that, ever."

Mary Lou and I didn't raise our children in a religious household. I was raised by an evangelical Southern Baptist minister and as a result, I had rejected organized religion my entire life. However, Mary Lou and I both have a strong belief in God and we spent many nights praying for Chris to recover.

Chris shared his memories about asking for spiritual help when he was ill. "I wasn't raised Christian and I never went to church," he said. "There were times when I would pray. You do anything you can, whether it's appealing to modern medicine or to a higher power, to get better and to get through it. I don't think it really led me to any profound religious experience, but I had some pretty strong spiritual experiences. Seeing what it did to our family in a positive way, bringing everyone together, and having Grandma Jean come up and spend some time with us. It never pushed me to religion. It was more like, "Well, I don't know if I believe it, but it couldn't hurt, and there might be a God up there and I'd like to have him on my side.

"I think everybody is spiritual to some extent and expresses that in different ways. But everybody has to do something, because it takes more than methotrexate and prednisone to get through cancer treatment. I used what I knew and trusted that positive attitude that you always talked about. Maintaining an outlook where you think, 'Well, this is serious, but I'm not going die from it. I'm just going to keep going to bed at night, and coming back to sit on my blue couch."'

Had Chris ever been scared of the final outcome? "I think it's about not really letting that thought enter your mind," he said. "You're just going to get through it. If you need to turn elsewhere to find that strength, then you do. You take each individual incident as it comes. You get the shots in your leg and get through it; you get the spinal tap and get through that; but you don't really sit down and think, "Okay, well, I'm going to have to go do a dozen more of these leg shots and fifty more spinal taps. It gives an awful truth to the "one day at a time" thing. You just go out and make it through that day and then make it through the next day, and then eventually you're out the tunnel."

Chapter 27

HIS FIRST MOUNTAIN

"Chris Bradley, come on down! You're the next contestant on *The Price is Right!*" Rod Roddy, the timeless announcer with the distinctive voice on the long-running CBS game show, didn't actually call out Chris's name, but he and long-time host Bob Barker distracted Chris from his misery. He watched the show nearly every day during the summer of 1996. He got up at eight or nine and came upstairs to eat breakfast. He watched ESPN's *SportsCenter* for an hour or two and then *The Price is Right* was on from ten to eleven.

"The desire to do other things was there," Chris said, "but I really didn't have the energy. I was set up as well as I could have been on that blue sofa. I had all my immediate needs met, but there were some long days where I just sat down at the beginning and said to myself, 'Okay, I'm going to watch six movies today, listen to five episodes of *The Shadow*, and play video games for a while.'"

When Chris felt sick, he felt like he was always going to be sick. A lot of it was not knowing exactly how long it would be until he felt better. Stuck on the blue couch all day with his metal barf bowl, he became frustrated and angry. Boredom reigned when time stretched on. At times he was afraid of the next step in his treatment.

"I was probably a little bit frightened—there were a lot of pretty intense procedures for a nine-year-old. The needles they used on my legs for the L-asparaginase were huge and hurt like a mother. It was awful because they went so deep and right into the meat of my thighs with those big ole honkin' needles. They would stick the right thigh at the same time as the left thigh. It's like taking a big knife and sticking it into your thigh and taking it down to the bone. It was just the most intense pain. It created a knot in the muscle."

The L-asparaginase procedure Chris referred to had been a learning experience for all of us. It called for two nurses, one on each side of Chris, to simultaneously inject two large needles, one into each thigh, and then push the contents of the large syringes into his legs. It was painful under the best of circumstances. When things went smoothly, the two nurses emptied their syringes at approximately the same pace and time. The first time Chris was given the drug, however, one nurse noticed that she was falling behind the pace of her associate. She attempted to catch up by suddenly pushing harder on her syringe, creating a knot in Chris's muscle and nearly bringing him out of his chair. From that moment forward, anytime Chris's protocol called for the dual injections of L-asparaginase, I had a brief chat with the nurses ahead of time and reminded them that we were not in a hurry. I'm not sure they appreciated my intervention, but I learned that you can't advocate for your child too often.

Chris often lay motionless on the blue sofa in a state of nausea. "I was only able to eat certain things and anything else I might try would come back up into that bowl. I would go on these binges where I would pick something completely random and very specific, like a particular type of Bagel Bites. It was like I was pregnant. Maybe there was something about the medicine I was taking, but just one thing would sound really good for a long time, and that was all I could eat."

For several weeks, Chris would only eat grilled chicken wings from the deli counter at local Sonny's Market. Then, he ate exclusively Kraft Macaroni & Cheese. One day my mom made a batch of homemade mac & cheese with bread crumbs and four types of cheeses. Chris took one bite and rejected it. Another time, Chris developed an appetite for the chicken fingers that had been served in his school cafeteria prior to his illness. I contacted the school district, purchased a case of frozen chicken fingers from their wholesaler, and hoped his tastes wouldn't change before he ate them all.

Chris's mental attitude tracked closely with how he felt physically. Which is to say, he was often in a foul mood. Our empathy for him and our feelings of helplessness contributed to a gloomy atmosphere at home. Mary Lou quickly discovered that when Chris felt good, it had a direct relationship on how she felt.

We all struggled to find ways to improve Chris's mental outlook. In one attempt to lift his spirits, I brought home half a dozen VHS comedy tapes, including *The Three Stooges, Abbott and Costello's Who's on First,* episodes of *The I Love Lucy Show,* and a collection of skits from *The Carol Burnett Show.* I put the tapes in the recorder, confident that they would bring back the laughter from Chris that I missed so much. My heart ached to see my son smile again. But when the tapes began to play, Chris looked at me with a solemn face as if to say, "You really don't get it, do you?" That moment turned out to be one of the lowest for me as

I struggled to find a way to help get Chris, and the rest of our family, through this horrible experience.

Nine years later, I sat among 2,500 parents and students as Chris, president of his senior class, addressed his classmates at their high school graduation ceremony. As he looked back over his school years and the challenges he had overcome, he said, "My dad taught me years ago that humor is sometimes the best medicine." Only Chris and I knew the true meaning of those words as he spoke them. That one sentence took me back to the moment I walked through the door, videotapes in hand, and experienced crushing disappointment when they didn't have their desired effect. My eyes moistened as I realized that, though the impact of our actions is not always immediately apparent, it is crucial that we keep doing our best and have faith in the outcome.

As Chris's primary care provider, Mary Lou spent more time riding the emotional roller coaster with Chris than I did. "Chris has a lot of time where he doesn't feel real 'up,'" she wrote. "He gets pretty short and has snappy answers. We have tried to ignore them, but a couple of times I have asked him to stop being so rude. I don't think he likes the mood swings any more than we do. He told me he just sometimes wishes we would leave him alone. He doesn't like lot of questions."

Caregivers often feel the brunt of their loved ones' misery. But it doesn't take much to make up for the hard times. Mary Lou was sitting at the computer one afternoon typing an email. Chris looked up and said to her, "Mom, I couldn't go through this without you." That touched Mary Lou to her core. They gave each other a big hug. Times like that made up for the down times.

Chris smiled for the first time in a long time when Mary Lou suggested we get a puppy for him. One of her friends had a new litter of rat terrier puppies and she offered to let Chris have the pick of the litter. We drove to the friend's country home and watched Chris laugh and tumble around with the litter before he picked one out and brought it home. "Griffey" became Chris's couch companion for the next six months and stayed with our family for the next fifteen years.

Matt was also victimized by Chris's attitude and the demands of his care. As we struggled to deal with Chris's physical and emotional needs, we often failed to give Matt the attention he needed and deserved. Mary Lou and I committed to doing our best to keep Matt's interests and priorities in mind as we dealt with Chris's illness, but Matt still did not get the attention he needed.

Remarkably, Matt doesn't remember feeling neglected. "I was almost a teenager at the time," he said. "When you're thirteen years old, you're not consciously craving more attention from your parents. You're craving for them to back off. I think I was outwardly focused away from the family. What I really wanted to do was go spend time with my friends.

"I do recall feeling a sense of unfairness and frustration with the amount of leniency that Chris would get. That was the thing that often felt unfair. Chris was often rude and entitled and wouldn't get any consequences so it felt like there was a double standard in the household. Looking back on it, it's understandable that Chris would be in a bad mood, but I didn't feel so much empathy for that as a teenager."

Disciplining a child with cancer is a difficult proposition. Mary Lou and I struggled with it constantly. If we went easy on Chris when he needed to be disciplined, would he grow up being spoiled and entitled? On the other hand, it was difficult to discipline him for his poor behavior after seeing what he went through on a daily basis. We knew we would likely behave the same way under the same conditions.

Issues usually surfaced during a crisis. One evening, Matt was struggling with a complicated desktop publishing assignment that was due the following morning. He accidentally deleted the file and went into a meltdown. By the time he settled down, Matt shared his frustrations with Mary Lou. He told her that she never came in to say goodnight to him anymore. He said she was always with Chris and she never came into his room like she used to do. His comments hurt Mary Lou deeply. Perhaps because they were mostly true.

Mary Lou and I had plenty of excuses for falling short—I often worked long hours in order to earn the commissions necessary to pay our bills, while Mary Lou stayed home to care for Chris and manage the household. We collapsed into bed at the end of some very long days, but our physical and emotional exhaustion were no excuse for not spending more time with our older son. I still carry guilt for not being a stronger presence for Matt.

During his sickest days, Chris remained dependent on us for his most basic needs. When we weren't going to Portland, we were either emptying Chris's barf-bowl or otherwise monitoring his nausea. If we weren't occupied directly with medical providers, we were arguing with insurance companies, who systematically denied coverage on nearly every bill submitted to them. Dealing with the insurance companies turned into a part-time job and added a tremendous amount of stress to an emotionally overloaded situation.

Baseball became a barometer on Chris's health status and by extension how we were doing as a family. One afternoon on the way home from Chris's weekly trip to Doernbecher, Mary Lou dropped Matt off for his soccer match. Mary Lou stayed in the van with Chris. They were parked in front of some softball fields, where a team was practicing. Chris began to cry as he watched them. Mary Lou thought he was feeling sick from the chemo treatments. Then she realized it was because he wanted to be out there. He said he missed baseball so much. They left shortly afterward.

By leaving early, they did not stay to see the last of Matt's soccer match. It was another example of our focusing on Chris's physical and emotional needs while inadvertently neglecting Matt's need for attention. I'm not sure we could do it any better if given the chance to do it all over again. Ignoring Matt's needs was the not the result of a grand scheme to deprive him of attention; it was the cumulative result of making many small decisions as circumstances presented themselves.

Chris eventually decided he wanted to attend another Babe Ruth baseball game, albeit as a spectator. We took pizza to the game and parked near the field so Chris could watch from the car. He enjoyed the game at first—he analyzed all the plays. Then people began coming over to see us. Chris would have preferred to watch without all the commotion. He declined an invitation to go into the dugout. He didn't feel very connected to the team since they had formed just prior to his getting sick. He didn't know how to handle all the attention, and it was difficult for him to watch and not participate. We left before the game was over, but we hoped he would be willing to go again.

Chris wanted to return to his third-grade classroom at least once before the end of the school year. His teacher, Mrs. Bowker, was one of Chris's most ardent supporters. She delivered his schoolwork to him at home, along with scores of cards and a personalized videotape from his classmates. She worked with Mary Lou to make it happen.

The day for Chris's return to school came six weeks after his initial diagnosis. When the teacher announced an activity that called for the kids to work in groups of three, all the boys wanted to be in Chris's group. Chris used "rock, paper, scissors" to narrow it down to two boys. When Chris tried to keep up with the other boys at recess time, he fell and chipped a tooth. Some of the other boys commented to Mary Lou that they were surprised at his weakness. They mentioned that he had been one of the fastest and strongest boys in the class. It was a shock for some of them to see him with such diminished physical capabilities.

The day after Chris visited the school, we traveled to Doernbecher for his regularly scheduled chemotherapy. He received a vincristine injection in his port, a spinal injection of methotrexate, and underwent a bone marrow aspiration. By the time it was over, he headed back to the couch in the baseball room, where he stayed for the following week.

On Sunday, June 16th—Father's Day—we convinced Chris to get off the blue sofa and attend the last few innings of his team's baseball game. For the first time, he agreed to join them in the dugout.

"When the game was over, his spirits were pretty good," Mary Lou wrote. "He visited with several of his teammates and he was pretty upbeat. After the game, I looked over and saw Chris standing atop a pile of gravel. I asked him about it later and he said he used it as a test to see how his legs were doing. He wanted to see if he could get to the top of the pile without using his hands. And he made it. He climbed his first mountain."

Lest Chris get too comfortable atop the summit, it soon became time to begin the next phase of his treatment, Consolidation. After achieving his initial remission, the next step was designed to finish off any remaining cancer cells and prevent them from developing resistance to further treatment. During this phase, Chris would be taking nearly all of the same drugs he had been given to induce his initial remission, but in higher quantities. Many of them were identical to the ones given to Aaron during his Consolidation phase, with one major exception. Thankfully, radiation was no longer part of the equation.

We knew from our conversations with Dr. Jones that the real heavy stuff was further down the road during the Delayed Intensification phase, but we also knew we needed to take this one step at a time. This next phase would hopefully last only six weeks or so, leaving us time to pursue more normal summer activities in August and September.

In June, my brother George and his wife Patti contacted the San Francisco Giants and arranged for our family to attend a game against the San Diego Padres at Candlestick Park. Prior to the game, the Giants invited Chris to visit the team's dugout. He chatted with his favorite player, Matt Williams, and backup catcher Steve Decker before the game. Williams autographed a baseball and Decker autographed one of his game-used bats and gave it to Chris. The Giants went on to lose to the San Diego Padres, 7-4, but the day was a victory in its own right.

The following day, George and Patti took Matt on a special trip into San Francisco to visit the Hard Rock Café and to the Exploratorium, a museum of science, arts, and technology. Matt was thrilled. George and Patti helped us pull off one of those rare occasions where we put together a positive experience for Chris to offset his misery, and we balanced out the equation by giving Matt some well-deserved attention. We returned home with a little more bounce in our step.

Chapter 28

WHAT WERE YOU THINKING?

"**Y**ou can put your hands down, sir." The corrections officer's mocking tone reinforced my sudden bond with Chevy Chase's Clark Griswold from *National Lampoon's Vacation*. I'm not sure why I thought it was a good idea to give my family an unguided tour of Pelican Bay State Prison, home to more than 2,000 of the most violent inmates in the state of California. But here I was, my hands suspended over the steering wheel, hoping to be released for good behavior.

The prison, located north of Crescent City, California, and just south of the Oregon state line, housed the "worst of the worst" offenders in California's penal system, men who had shown a propensity for extreme violence both in and out of the prison system. One of the more notable residents at the time was Charles Manson, convicted murderer and leader of the cult known as the Manson Gang. My interest in the prison evolved from one of my childhood friend's involvement in its construction seven years earlier. I thought it would be interesting to drive by and take a look.

The story began several weeks earlier when I decided to buzz the hair off my head in a solidarity move with Chris.

Dr. Jones had predicted that Chris's hair would fall out from his next treatment episode.

"You can't be the only guy on the block without hair on his head," I told Chris as the barber accommodated my request. "The cool thing, Dad," Chris responded irreverently, "is that your face is already puffy!"—a reference to my genetically over-sized facial cheeks from my mother's side of the family.

Chris had not fully regained his strength, but Dr. Jones had temporarily reduced the intensity of Chris's treatments. We decided to meet George and Patti for a mid-summer camping trip in the redwood forests of Jedediah Smith State Park.

After several days walking through the redwoods and swimming in the Smith River, we drove our Dodge Caravan, with its bright white car-topper, into Crescent City to re-supply. On our return, I saw a sign indicating a turnoff from Highway 101 to Pelican Bay State Prison. "Hey, guys!" I announced. "Anyone want to see what a maximum-security prison looks like?" Without waiting for an answer, I took the turn.

I intended to do a quick "drive-by" before returning to camp, but I decided at the last minute to approach the front gate to ask a few questions. Surprisingly, I found the gate unoccupied. I saw none of the aggressive signage one might expect to see at the entrance to such a notorious prison, so I assumed it must be okay to drive on through.

Mary Lou sat in the front passenger seat. Matt and Chris occupied the rear captain's chairs and looked out the windows as we drove by a large administrative building on our left. "I'm surprised they let you get this close to the inmates," I wondered aloud as we passed an outdoor exercise area on the right. Small groups of prisoners milled around and lifted weights within the confines of an eight-foot cyclone fence. A few of them glanced in our direction, but they gave no indication that our presence was out of the ordinary.

I assumed we must still be in a public area since we had yet to encounter any official-looking personnel. "Let's see what's up here," I said, as we turned left and drove across a large, open parking lot. We had just exited the other side of the lot and turned onto a narrow two-lane road when I noticed a dark green sedan in the distance turning in our direction. Its tires kicked up dust as it accelerated around the corner. "I wonder where this guy is going like a bat out of hell," I muttered to Mary Lou.

It didn't take long to find out. When the sedan was within thirty to forty feet from of our vehicle, the driver turned abruptly at a forty-five-degree angle into our lane, locked up his brakes, and skidded to a stop in front of us. As we came to a sudden halt, a second, identical sedan executed the same maneuver in my rearview mirror. As I contemplated our predicament, I told Mary Lou and the boys to sit real still and for some reason, I thought it best to raise my hands above the steering wheel.

I followed the officer's instructions to lower my hands and complied with his demand for my driver's license. He asked a series of questions, each a different version of, "What were you thinking?" He pointed out that I was wearing the "uniform of the day," a reference to my collared, long-sleeved, blue-denim shirt, my denim jeans, and my buzzed head. Until that moment, I hadn't really put the whole picture together.

Our best evidence that we were misguided vacationers, and that my family members were innocent victims of my stupidity, was the white car-topper on the roof of the Dodge van. Had I not had my ID with me, the officer assured me, our family would have been held in custody for as long as it took to sort everything out. He told us that the inmates we had seen as we drove in were "weekend warriors," non-violent offenders serving time for drunk driving or similar offenses.

I answered a few more questions and, assured we were harmless, he decided against short-term incarceration. After a final shake of his head and roll of his eyes, he gave the "all-clear" to his fellow officers through his hand-held radio.

I turned our vehicle around and fell in between the two sedans. We formed a three-car convoy to the front gate, which I noticed was now attended by a guard. As we pulled away from the prison, I speculated that someone was going to pay a higher price than I did for our unannounced visit to Pelican Bay Prison.

Finding humor in a crisis is an important part of dealing with cancer. You don't always know where or when it will surface, but if our family had been unable to find some comic relief along our journey, the battle would have been much more challenging. Our experience at Pelican Bay provides fodder for laughter to this day.

Chapter 29

LET'S FIND SOME STICKS

---

hris continued to bounce back from the initial phases of his treatment as summer progressed. He entered the Interim Maintenance phase of his chemotherapy, a much lighter protocol than the Consolidation phase. We knew the dreaded Delayed Intensification phase still lie ahead, but we remained intent on participating in as many healthy activities as Chris could tolerate.

In July, we attended the American Cancer Society's Relay for Life at the University of Oregon's Historic Hayward Field. The annual event was the culmination of fundraising efforts by teams of volunteers, who gathered together for what has been described as "part celebration, part memorial, part campout, and part carnival." The term "Relay" was derived from each team's endeavor to keep at least one member of their team on the track for a twenty-four-hour period, transferring a baton as they took turns running or walking around the track.

When they weren't on the track, participants indulged themselves at the many food vendors and enjoyed musical performances by a variety of local entertainers. The ceremonies began at 12:00 noon on Friday and wrapped up at the same time Saturday.

Mary Lou had begun participating in the Relay two years earlier when she joined a team of her sorority sisters at Delta Delta Delta to raise funds in honor of Aaron. Childhood cancer was her sorority's national philanthropy and, coupled with Mary Lou's experience with Aaron, it seemed a perfect fit. Even before Chris's diagnosis, the event had become a highlight of the summer for Matt and Chris. How often do two nine and twelve-year-old brothers get to stay up all night eating, listening to music, and generally running around unsupervised, all with their parents' encouragement?

Following a brief opening ceremony, cancer survivors set a celebratory tone by taking a "Survivors Lap," cheered on by friends and family who gathered around the track in their honor. Anyone who had defeated cancer, or who was still battling the disease, wore a specially-designed purple t-shirt with "SURVIVOR" imprinted on the back. They wore their purple t-shirts with pride.

The most sobering part of the Relay for me came at 11 p.m. when the lights were dimmed and the music was muted for the luminaria ceremony. Small white paper bags, illuminated by votive candles and decorated with photos and tributes to loved ones, lined the interior of the track. Relay attendees walked around the track silently and absorbed the images of those who were fighting cancer, had survived cancer, or had succumbed to it. The ceremony lasted for an hour or more and was usually accompanied by a bag piper playing *Amazing Grace* in the distance.

The first two years we participated, Mary Lou labeled three luminaria "In Honor of Aaron" and decorated them with photos of our nephew at different stages of his life. After Chris's diagnosis, we added several luminaria with his photos and decorated them with phrases like "Knock cancer out of the Park, Chris!" or "You're our hero, Chris!" We always lined up the ones for both boys together along the track.

Mary Lou and I usually walked the track together during the luminaria ceremony. We stood together in the dark, taking in the images of Chris and Aaron on those simple white bags and thought about how much Chris had benefited from Aaron's sacrifices. Thanks to Aaron, Chris's journey with childhood cancer would be much less difficult and he stood a much better chance of survival. Although Chris had been only a year old when Aaron passed away, he had a bond with his cousin that would surpass that of most first cousins. This annual gathering at the Relay each year became a ritual that we still practice today.

The final big event of the summer, before beginning the Delayed Intensification phase of Chris's treatment, was to deliver the boys to Camp UKANDU, an American Cancer Society summer camp for cancer kids and their siblings. Neither Matt nor Chris were excited about going, but Mary Lou and I insisted they attend after nurse Kaylee promoted it energetically during each visit to Doernbecher.

After a three-and-a-half-hour drive to the camp, Chris refused to get out of the van. I understood his anxiety. This would be his first overnight camping experience without his parents, he didn't know anyone except possibly a few nurses and doctors, and he didn't adapt well to change.

Our van was parked among the other vehicles in the middle of a giant meadow-turned-parking-lot as parents and young campers arrived. Matt, always the explorer, ran off to check out the campground as soon as I applied the parking brake. Mary Lou soon became frustrated and went in search of the registration table. At least she could get the cabin assignments for the boys and begin the process of signing medical forms and liability waivers.

One of the tables was attended by doctors and nurses from Doernbecher, who collected and catalogued the children's medications so they could be dispensed throughout the week. They knew the needs of each child so there would be no decline in the children's medical care while they attended camp. For the most part, the only cancer kids who couldn't attend camp were those with depressed immune systems. Puffy-faced children with bald heads showed up with crutches, wheelchairs, and other signs they were receiving treatment for cancer.

UKANDU was the Oregon equivalent to Camp Good-times in Washington that Aaron and Heather had attended. It was located on the northern Oregon Coast near the town of Tillamook. A large lake flanked the east side of the camp and offered children a chance to boat, swim, and fish. The Pacific Ocean bordered the west side and provided the perfect venue for "beach day," a time when campers made sandcastles and dipped their toes in the fifty-degree tidewaters.

Mary Lou returned with the boys' cabin assignments, and we were preparing for another sales pitch to Chris when a man in his mid-fifties came bounding toward us.

Years later, Ray Beard, or "Toon" as he was known at camp, teared up as he recalled meeting Chris that day. He related it to meeting bewildered students on the first day of school during his thirty-year career teaching middle school. "Like sixth-graders, first-time campers come in—you've got to catch them at the door. They're like, 'What am I supposed to do here?'

"It was my first year at camp," Toon said. "I saw you and your wife, and I saw this little boy. I walked across the field and I said to Chris, 'I'm looking for Chris Bradley! Do you know Chris Bradley?' His eyes got big and he said, 'I'm Chris Bradley.' Ah, great! Let's go! He got out of the car and off we went across the field! I remember it distinctly and you guys were like, 'Whoa! This is going to work!'"

Toon's motto was, "if they're not having fun, we need to be doing something different!" He became known among campers and counselors alike for his tendency to stretch boundaries and pull shenanigans. One year, knowing there would be a big water fight to inaugurate camp festivities, and realizing the big recreational battlefield lacked adequate water resources, he mounted a plastic swimming pool on the back of his flatbed truck and filled it with water. "I had a portable gas engine and a pump so I drove the truck on to the field and we hosed everybody down. Our kids were up in the air so we had an advantage. There's probably a reason we shouldn't have done it, but I didn't ask." Toon was always more likely to beg for forgiveness than ask for permission.

"Our kids would go mess with other cabins at night. We snuck up on them through the trees in the dark with water balloons. The kids thought it was great! We tried to hide from Scamper (Toon's sister, and the camp enforcer). By all appearances, Toon kept Scamper busy. "If she found out we weren't where we were supposed to be, my sister would say, 'You're supposed to have those kids in bed by 8 o'clock! They need their rest!'"

If the schedule called for his boys to work with crafts two days in a row, he refused to go. "I realized that little boys want to walk in the woods with sticks and hit things. I'd say, 'Hey, let's go find some sticks and hit trees!'"

Toon always tempered his enthusiasm with an awareness of the children he supervised. "All that stuff is fun to talk about, but you have to be cognizant of these children and what they are dealing with. You have to figure out something you can do that is crazy, but not that crazy. We needed to be aware of the kids who had cancer and we frequently had to ask them, 'Have you had your meds today?'" At least twice daily, children undergoing chemo treatment walked to the medical cabin, where nurses dispensed methotrexate, 6-mp, prednisone, and other drugs.

Approximately one hundred campers were divided into groups by age and gender and assigned to ten cabins scattered throughout the forest. Each cabin had two or three counselors, with names like Thumper, Q-Tip, Pig Pen, Hoops, and Sequoia.

"It's a lot like the YMCA camps," Toon said, "but at the YMCA camp, you don't take kids to get their meds. There were always three or four nurses and two oncologists on call twenty-four-hours-a-day while they were there."

The activities were not limited to fishing, boating, and hiking. Many of the children's parents had treated them like fragile, porcelain dolls since their diagnosis. At UKANDU, the children played dodgeball, climbed ropes and rock walls, practiced archery, splashed in the surf, competed in an "Olympics" competition, and of course, attended the big dance! Nightly campfires included skits and singalongs.

"Every day was a blur of success," Toon said. "If the kids were happy and they weren't bored, that was a successful day. If they went to bed and fell asleep, that was even more of a successful day."

The cancer kids' siblings entered camp accustomed to taking a back seat to their sick brother or sister. The counselors, well aware of this dynamic, went out of their way to make the siblings feel special. Mary Lou and I saw early signs this would be a good week for Matt. As we departed, he had already found the twelve-year-old girls' cabin and was making new friends.

Mary Lou and I also stood to benefit from UKANDU. We hadn't had a chance to spend any quality time together since our lives had changed so abruptly three months earlier. We saw it as a chance to reconnect. We took in a movie that week, we went to dinner several times, we walked on the beach, we went to a baseball game, and most importantly, we talked to each other. We'd lived in the same house during the three months since Chris became ill. But due to the demands of taking care of Chris, doing what we could for Matt, and regularly driving four-hours round-trip to Doernbecher, we had been dealing separately with our own emotions. Or perhaps we hadn't been. Either way, it was good to connect again with my best friend.

The most indelible event at camp, the Memory Circle, was held after lunch on Tuesday afternoon. At the first campfire of the week, each camper brought a small container of soil from home. They combined the soil samples and used them at the Tuesday ceremony to plant a plant in memory of UKANDU children who had lost their battle during the previous year.

The week's activities culminated with a big hoopla in the main dining hall Friday night, where the kids watched a video production of the week's pandemonium. The camp's videographer went to great lengths throughout the week to ensure a clip of every camper made it into the video. Campers searched for their own image, bursting into laughter when they saw themselves or one of their friends.

As the campers were wrapped up in the presentation, several of the counselors snuck out early to light luminaries along the pathway to the final campfire. The luminaries, much like the ones from Relay for Life, were created by the campers during the last day of camp to honor not only fellow campers, but friends and family members who had lost their battle, or who were still fighting against the disease. As kids left the dining hall and headed down the hill toward the week's final campfire, they took in each message, each light.

Chris attended UKANDU four times as a camper and returned for many years as a counselor. Twenty-four years later, he reflected back on his experience.

"The goal for the week is to have outrageous fun, plain and simple, but it's treading a fine line between having fun and at the same time recognizing that everybody there has cancer, or their brother or sister has cancer. There's no overt mention of, 'Hey, we all have cancer,' but they don't sweep it under the rug. There's no way to, and it would be stupid to. It's such a significant part of everyone's life. You sort of forget about it and have fun, but still realize that's part of who you are, and that's what ties you to the rest of this family, whether it's the counselors or the other campers.

"It builds through the week as you get to know people more. For me, it really hit during that last campfire when the path to the campfire goes by all these luminaries that the campers made. You see the first one and it's made by a camper who has had cancer maybe, and the next one is in honor of somebody's grandma. After you've gotten to know these people for seven days at camp and then you see in succession everybody's life stories and everything they're going through, that was the most powerful moment for me at camp. It really hit me, because we're all there having fun, but each person has a story about their struggles and their battle with cancer. In just five minutes as you are walking to campfire, there are about 150-200 of them. You don't know who did all those bags, but you might know half of them. They just hit you one by one."

The final campfire on Friday night brought the week to an emotional conclusion. "First, there is hoopla and all kinds of silliness," Chris said. "At a certain point, things get toned down and all the skits and loud camp songs stop. The songs become more tranquil, more reflective. There's a spiritual element to it as well. We would have fun while recognizing what we're all going through. And sort of cling to that a little bit."

The final singalong concluded the campfire:

"I am one person singing this song, I am one person singing this song, I am one person singing this song, and I am not alone.

"We are two people singing this song, we are two people singing this song, we are two people singing this song, and we are not alone."

The progression continued until everybody stood together and sang, "We are not alone."

Chapter 30

ARE YOU WILLING TO BE A GUINEA PIG?

D uring the Vietnam war, Dr. Archie Bleyer was given the opportunity to fulfill his military service by working as an intern in the "Yellow Berets," a special program established under the auspices of the National Institutes of Health (NIH).

"They asked me what I wanted to do," he said. "I didn't know exactly what I wanted to be, but I wanted to study adverse drug reactions. They said, 'You want to learn something about adverse drug reactions? We're putting you on a pediatric leukemia service. You will learn about adverse drug reactions. You are going to see kids die.'

"I accepted that right away," he said. "In the pediatric oncology clinic, there was a room that had maybe twelve or fifteen beds in it. Sometimes, the beds had curtains that allowed you to do an exam in semi-private, but the curtains really couldn't hide what was happening. Deaths sometimes occurred because of acute reaction to a drug, like asparaginase. The other kids could see the trauma team and the code team coming in. The children could see the other children die in the outpatient clinic."

As Dr. Bleyer shared his memories of the clinic from the early 1970s, I was acutely aware that the drug they were testing, asparaginase, was one of the drugs given to both Aaron and Chris during their treatment. The drug's dosage and effectiveness had been determined by administering it to these children enrolled in clinical trials and who were likely to die, either with it or without it.

"It was being tested in patients who relapsed," Dr. Bleyer said. "And since everybody relapsed, we had many patients on whom we could test it. We gave it intravenously every day for twenty-eight days in a row, including Saturdays and Sundays. After fifteen to twenty days of injections, we had to find places to give the next injection."

Hickman lines and portacaths had yet to be developed in the early 1970s. Doctors often shaved the children's scalps to find more veins. A lot of kids had lost their hair already and it was easier to do. Doctors found veins in the feet, scalp, and abdomen to administer experimental drugs.

"These kids were already relapsed and they had previously been treated with three or four intravenous drugs," Dr. Bleyer said. "They were getting all these IV meds and transfusions so they had so few veins left."

"At the time I began my career in 1971," Dr. Bleyer recalled, "researchers had already been trying many of these drugs. By 1974, we were doing the asparaginase testing. There was no effective treatment available—it was all being developed. Certainly, Sidney Farber did his work in the late forties and fifties, but the real effort in terms of trying to figure out how to do all this started in the early seventies.

"I didn't want to go into pediatric cancer. I did it because I could learn how drugs could hurt people. But I also saw that they did good, so I stayed with it all these years. I'm glad I did because of what happened after that, the incredible turnaround. That is what your book is about—a miracle. The miracle."

From the late 1960s through the mid 1970s, there was general consensus among doctors internationally on how to achieve initial remission for children diagnosed with ALL. Remissions were achieved with most patients and were maintained for longer periods of time through various combinations of vincristine, methotrexate, 6-mercaptopurine (6-MP), prednisone, and asparaginase. But in spite of the extended remissions, most children eventually relapsed and died from their leukemia.

During the 1970s, a young German oncologist, Professor Hansjorg "Haig" Riehm, hypothesized that if, after patients achieved initial remission, they were given an even more intense battery of chemotherapy drugs, they might be able to lengthen their periods of remission. Most of his fellow scientists were skeptical. They suggested the intensified approach would surely kill his patients.

Dr. Riehm convinced three research centers, located in Berlin, Frankfurt, and Munster, to test the therapy. The BMF Trials, as they became known, proved to be one of the biggest success stories in finding a cure for childhood leukemia. He called the new phase Reinduction-Reconsolidation. In the US, it was later referred to as Delayed Intensification.

By this time in his career, Dr. Bleyer was in charge of ALL protocols throughout the United States for the Children's Cancer Group. He needed to confirm the German results himself. "I went to Germany and I brought it back to the United States. I got the Children's Cancer Group to agree to study it, to find out if it was as good as the Germans claimed it was."

The trials were "convincing as hell," according to Dr. Bleyer. "It was one of the most important trials that has ever been done. We called it Delayed Intensification."

The new protocol quickly became the worldwide standard for treating childhood leukemia. Overnight, the cure rate went from twenty percent to nearly seventy percent.

As the success rate treating leukemia patients continued to improve, doctors began to direct certain trials toward addressing some of the side effects patients experienced from their chemotherapy. Dr. Bleyer and his associates had studied patients over the long term who were now in their thirties. Patients were suffering long-term heart damage due to their being given Adriamycin. Trials were conducted whereby Adriamycin was replaced with daunomycin, a drug with much less toxicity. The new drug was just as effective against leukemia without the long-term cardiac damage.

Other trials weren't as successful. In one study, Dr. Bleyer and his associates attempted to reduce the level of long-term side effects by lowering the amount of vincristine and prednisone given to the patients. They chose a population of low-risk patients, children who were most likely to survive in the first place, and reduced the dosages given to them from a protocol that had achieved a very high cure rate. The trials were a disaster.

"I estimated how many dozens of kids we killed by trying to make it better for them," said Dr. Bleyer in explaining how clinical trials sometimes go awry. "Killing with kindness, in a way. They would have been far better off, those dozens—now I don't remember the number—if we let them have the long-term problems of vincristine and prednisone.

"We had to close that trial because we were killing the kids by letting the leukemia come back in," Dr. Bleyer said. This specific trial was being conducted during the same general time Chris was receiving treatment. The fact that doctors would risk children's lives for the purpose of reducing long-term side effects gives me pause. Had I known this was a possibility, that I might be risking my son's life to reduce the incidence of side effects twenty years down the road, I would have rejected it outright. But these have never been simple questions with simple answers.

Now that Chris has reached the age where the long-term side effects have become more of a possibility, such a study seems more reasonable. Today, sixty to ninety percent of childhood cancer survivors suffer from chronic health conditions. Thirty percent of those experience serious side effects, including heart disease, osteoporosis, and secondary cancers.

In another, more successful trial overseen by Dr. Bleyer, he hypothesized that large doses of methotrexate, given intravenously to patients in place of cranial-spinal radiation, would be just as effective, but without the horrible side effects.

Bleyer significantly increased the intravenous dosage of methotrexate given to his young patients. "I have the world record for the most methotrexate given to a human," he said. "The standard dose of methotrexate at the time was about twelve milligrams. When I stopped escalating the doses, we were giving 88,000 milligrams. At one point, we actually ran out of the drug."

The test was successful. The new regimen replaced spinal-cranial radiation and spinal injections. However, the new approach was harder to accomplish, since it required hospitalization over a four-to-five-day period. And the high-dose methotrexate brought its own set of horrors. Stacey, one of the mothers in a local support group shared her twelve-year-old daughter's experience with the high-dose methotrexate. "This was an evil, evil phase," she said.

"The first high-dose methotrexate she received peeled her feet to the point she couldn't walk. The skin just peeled off. They were raw. She was in so much pain she couldn't even get up to go to the bathroom some days without help. They did it four times in a two-month time span."

By the time Stacey's daughter was treated, the high-dose methotrexate was part of the established protocol. But the children who received the massive doses of methotrexate during the trials were generally those who had exhausted every other alternative. They would die unless a new drug was developed.

"There was no other option," said Dr. Bleyer. "We had nothing to lose. The parents wanted to keep going and we had nothing else to offer. It wasn't quite that straight-forward and simple, but these were patients who we knew weren't going to do well. It might help for a while, but it would be futile eventually. We had very reliable information that said we could benefit this patient for a while, but they are going to die.

"If you have a group that has a poor prognosis, you can start doing things before it's inevitable. Say you have a newly diagnosed patient with leukemia and they were going to die within a few weeks or months anyway. We knew that nothing was going to work with them. So, we tried something exceptional. You start with the most serious fatal situation. As soon as you have reason to believe the patient is not going to survive anyway, you can justify trying something new on them, rather than just spinning the wheels for a few weeks or months."

I asked Dr. Bleyer if he and his associates had crossed an ethical line, where the patient became merely the subject of an experiment? If patients had a chance to survive, they were treated with the standard protocol. But if they were anticipated to live for only another thirty to sixty days, they were identified as candidates for new drug experimentation.

"You mean a guinea pig?" said Dr. Bleyer. "The guinea pig issue is with us every single day in this world. Here's the problem: 'What we have ain't good, we'll do it because that's our standard, but are you willing to be a guinea pig?'"

Dr. Bleyer insisted that any such approach had to be approved by an Institutional Review Board (IRB). "This is extremely important. Has what I'm suggesting to you been approved in advance by the IRBs? The IRBs approve the idea of using something as if the patient is a guinea pig. The IRB has two primary roles. One is to ensure the procedure has a reasonable scientific basis—it's not just a rogue idea. And two, the patient's agreeing totally and in writing, with a full understanding—or the family if the patient is too young—and has signed legal informed consent. They've had every chance to ask any and all questions and research as far as they can or want to before they sign consent."

But what about the Hippocratic Oath, "First do no harm?" When they gave such high doses of toxic chemicals to dying children, weren't they potentially taking advantage of desperate parents, rationalizing their actions to make strides in the competitive world of medicine?

"It's hard to remember that we did so much to these kids," Dr. Bleyer said. "Talk about trauma. Of course, we had to do it—to learn how to treat them and to save some of them. It was justified that killing was worth it if we could save some of them. First, do no harm. Sometimes, that's not exactly a correct translation of that. I mean, that is what we always say, but it's not quite as dramatic as what that original Hippocratic Oath did say. Nevertheless, that's what we said.

And yet, in order to do any good, we had to harm. So, we violated that oath since the 50s in helping children with ALL. And if we hadn't violated the oath, as we now think about it anyway, I think we would still be where we were. So, first . . .do…some…*good.* We had to harm in order to do the good, including unfortunately death. The treatments were frequently so toxic that they killed, but they saved more lives by letting some kids die."

Chapter 31

HE DOUBLED BACK

"Hey, do you guys want to meet Bill Walton?" the nurse asked as she burst through the door to the exam room. "No," said Chris. "Who's Bill Walton?" Mary Lou and I contradicted him instantly and said, "Yes! Absolutely!"

I spun Chris's wheelchair around and followed the nurse out the door and down the hallway as we explained to him the phenomenon of Bill Walton. Walton's college basketball career began when he played for legendary coach John Wooden at UCLA, winning two national championships and named National College Player of the Year three times. The Portland Trailblazers chose Walton as the number-one overall pick in the 1974 NBA draft. His professional career included multiple MVP awards and championships with both the Trailblazers and the Boston Celtics. The NBA inducted Walton into their Hall of Fame in 1993. Walton is also known for his quirky personality and for being a lifelong fan of the Grateful Dead rock band.

We parked Chris's wheelchair in the hallway while Walton concluded his visit in a patient's room. When the door opened and Walton stepped out, he ducked his 6'11" frame to avoid hitting his head on the top of the doorframe.

Walton extended his hand to Chris, who had to bend his neck backward at nearly a right angle in order to speak with the basketball legend. Walton asked him who his favorite NBA team was, and Chris responded that he wasn't much of an NBA fan, an answer that only a nine-year-old would give to an icon like Walton. Noticing Chris's Seattle Mariners attire, Walton turned the conversation to Major League Baseball, stating his allegiance to the San Diego Padres. Chris, an expert on the subject, offered his opinion on the strengths and weaknesses of the Padre lineup and told Walton how his Padres wouldn't stand a chance against Chris's Mariners.

The two sports fans continued their banter uninterrupted for ten minutes until Walton was called to another child's room. Walton signed a basketball and gave it to Chris, along with his home phone number. Then he walked down the hallway to visit another child.

The chance encounter with Bill Walton turned things around on a day that hadn't been going well. The drugs from the Delayed Intensification phase were exacting a severe toll on Chris's health. He awoke that morning with severe stomach pains. We had learned from Kaylee that it was best not to ignore such symptoms so we called Doernbecher. We had planned to be in Portland that day anyway, so they suggested we stop by to see the on-call doctor. The examination had been tough. The doctor attributed Chris's symptoms to dexamethasone, one of the chemo drugs in his new regimen. The consultation was coming to a conclusion when the nurse came in. After our visit with Walton, we left the hospital and went to hang out in a bar, literally.

The Reel M Inn Tavern in Portland was an unlikely place for a nine-year-old boy and his family to spend a Saturday afternoon. Several months earlier, Bill Purdy, the fifty-four-year-old owner of the tavern, had added to the tavern's décor by hanging an umbrella upside down from one of the rafters. When one of his customers tossed several coins into it, he asked her what she was doing. She told him she was making a wish. That sparked an idea. Bill encouraged his other customers to toss money into the umbrella, too, with a goal of raising $3,000 to sponsor a Make-A-Wish trip for a sick child. Multiple fundraisers added to the pot and within six months, the bar patrons had met their goal.

When Bill informed Make-A-Wish Foundation of their success, he was given the names of two boys from which to choose: a four-year-old boy named Zach, who wanted to go to Disneyland, and Chris, who wanted to attend the 1996 World Series. When the tavern regulars struggled to choose between the two children, fearing that one boy might go without his wish being fulfilled, a generous patron solved the problem by writing a check for an additional $3,000. Both boys would receive their wish.

Mary Lou and I helped Chris transfer from the van to his wheelchair, aware of the balance between providing sufficient assistance and being overbearing. Chris wasn't shy about reminding us if we tipped the scale too far in either direction. He wore a navy-blue Seattle shirt and a matching baseball cap with "Griffey in '96" on the front panel. In a presidential election year where Ross Perot ran as a third-party option, Mariner fans thought their all-star centerfielder, Ken Griffey, Jr. might stand a chance, too.

Mary Lou rolled Chris through the front door. A crowd of eager patrons greeted the guest of honor with a buffet meal, a large cake, and lots of love and attention. Purdy fought to overcome his emotions as he described his motivations to a television reporter who showed up to cover the event. I was deeply touched that a man we had never met before had become so emotionally committed to helping our son and our family.

Make-A-Wish representatives spoke with the media and, thankfully, drew some attention away from Chris, who wore his game face in spite of the fact that his physical condition continued to decline. After a short time, we excused ourselves and made the two-hour drive home so Chris could retreat to his sanctuary on the blue sofa.

The next morning, Chris awoke with blood in his urine and doubled over with abdominal pains. We took him to the emergency room at Sacred Heart Hospital. We spent all day in the ER while the local doctors consulted with an oncologist at Doernbecher. They attributed the symptoms to dexamethasone, the high-dose steroid that had replaced prednisone during the Delayed Intensification phase. They sent us home with a suggestion to dial back the dosage until we returned to Doernbecher the following week.

At the time of Chris's diagnosis, Delayed Intensification was well-established as part of the standard ALL treatment protocol. It was one of the primary reasons so many children were surviving ALL. But that didn't mean it was easy. Chris had enjoyed a slight respite from the chemo during the mid-summer months. After his Camp UKANDU experience, he had almost begun to feel like a normal boy again. But the recovery didn't last long.

The powerful doses of chemo drugs brought back the nausea. The stainless-steel barf bowl became his constant companion once again. The high doses of dexamethasone devastated his body. Sleepless nights returned and brought with them around-the-clock hunger pangs. Once again, we placed a bowl of iced watermelon adjacent to his bed at night, and queued up books on tape.

Chris rarely ventured out of the house during this phase of his treatment. When he felt like doing so, we gathered the necessities for a successful outing—a blanket, snacks of his choosing, anti-nausea medications, and of course the barf-bowl. Most of the time, we aborted our plans when Chris abruptly threw up and retreated to the blue sofa.

We learned that things could have been much worse. Sydney, another mother of a cancer child, related her family's experience after her nine-year-old son began taking high doses of "Dex," a common named used by patients for dexamethasone. "For a year or so during the first year of his treatment, we had to remove the girls from our home and take them to my parents' house because my son was so violent and unpredictable. Within two months of starting treatment, he suddenly had this huge resentment towards the girls and me. He would try to kill us. We had to lock up all of the knives, scissors, shish kabob sticks, pencils, and pens. We put anything sharp in the cabinet with a chain and a lock. Any time I needed a knife, I would have to use a key. His self-harming was horrifying.

"The doctors said it was from the Dex. That made our days at Doernbecher doubly long. We would first do his chemo treatments and then we would meet with three mental health professionals. They worked with him for the first year and a half of his treatment to figure out all of this rage and how to handle it. After they reduced his chemo, his violent outbursts went away." We didn't feel good about hearing of other's problems, but it helped us to keep our misery in perspective.

As September approached, Mary Lou talked to Chris about returning to school part time. He loved school and had always been successful academically. However, he was becoming more self-conscious about his physical appearance and harbored doubts about his ability to participate in the all-important subject of "playground." Mary Lou also wanted to return to teaching her middle school classes. She looked forward to the day when her biggest problem was having forty students ignore her pleas to be quiet so she could take attendance.

Chris tried going to school one day, but he vomited before leaving the house and began to cry. "We talked," Mary Lou wrote, "and I found out that he really does not want to go to school until he feels good again, until he feels like he did this summer. He wants so badly to be a normal boy and not be different. Right now, he can't go back and play hard at recess and is never sure how long he'll feel like staying."

Chris's physical abilities declined rapidly from the Delayed Intensification. The initial rounds of chemo following his diagnosis had weakened his legs to the point he occasionally had to crawl to the bathroom. Under Delayed Intensification, he lost a third of his body weight, and he no longer had the strength in his legs to crawl. At bedtime, or when he needed to go to the bathroom during the day, one of us carried him. He lay on the blue sofa in the baseball room and returned to watching ESPN *SportsCenter, The Price is Right*, or movies.

We tried to lift his spirits in any way we could. Prior to his illness, we had always denied his requests to drive the electric cart around our local Fred Meyer (Kroger) store, insisting the carts were for people with physical limitations. We changed our tune and promised him he could drive them for as long as he wanted after his immune system allowed him to be around other people and he had the strength to get to the store.

During Chris's lowest moments, Ash Cope came to his rescue once again. Ash had been a casual friend of Chris for several years, but given the four-year difference in their ages, they formed the most unlikely of friendships. As Chris put it later, "Ash was a veteran of middle school by the time I entered third grade."

Not only had Ash been among the first to visit Chris in the hospital that first day; he was waiting for him when Chris returned home from Doernbecher, and he was there during the long summer days when Chris was anchored to the blue sofa.

"During those days," Chris wrote later, "I couldn't run around the neighborhood or go for bike rides with friends. Most days I couldn't even climb the stairs in my house. Ash came over every afternoon. We played video games, watched movies, or messed around on the computer. Generally, these were the same things I would have done by myself, or with Grandma around. Grandma was great, but she was not a good partner when playing *Mario*.

"I never sank quite as deeply into my baby-blue couch when Ash was there. A considerable age gap—more than a third of my nine-year-old life—separated us, but when he saw me falling behind the group, trapped inside when the rest of my friends were horsing around, he doubled back to make sure I was okay. He gave me hope when I needed it most, and my darkest months somehow came to be among those that I look upon most fondly."

Chris's Delayed Intensification phase turned out to be the lowest point of his cancer journey and epitomized the highs and lows of our roller coaster ride. Talking to NBA players one day; driving to the emergency room with uncontrollable diarrhea and bloody urine the next. His constant state of nausea and his barf bowl remained the only constants in his life. Acceptance and flexibility became necessities.

We had watched Chris suffer for months, but when his hair fell out, it underscored the toxicity of the poisons we were injecting into our child's body. "In a matter of two to three days, it was gone!" Mary Lou wrote. "It came out in clumps and with little effort. He had the softest, smoothest head you have ever felt! I just couldn't keep my hands off of it."

"I remember one night, lying in bed," Chris said years later, "and a bunch of it was on my pillow. I could just reach out and pull out tufts of hair. It's not like pulling grass, because when you reach down and grab a clump of grass, there's a resistance as you break the roots. It was like the roots dissolved and I could just pull out my hair, like pulling a cotton ball apart. It still hung on as long as you didn't touch it, but the slightest pressure and it came right out. "

We adjusted as additional side effects appeared. During one episode, Chris's legs began to ache, the same way they had done when he was initially diagnosed. It disturbed his sleep for weeks. Dr. Jones was at a loss to find the cause—this was not listed as a known side effect. Mary Lou and I were concerned that he had relapsed. To comfort Chris, Mary Lou slept on the floor next to Chris's bed for two weeks. The doctors eventually concluded that the pain came from the advanced state of atrophy in Chris's legs, once again caused by the dexamethasone.

As we dealt with the short-term effects of the chemicals, we postponed addressing any long-term damage they might be doing to his body: cataracts, bone thinning, heart issues, and secondary cancers, to name a few. We committed ourselves to doing the best we could for him in the moment. We would take it one day at a time and let tomorrow take care of itself, knowing that very little of this was within our control.

When Chris hit rock bottom in late September, he wrote a letter to the Seattle Mariners as he watched them on TV. He told them about his cancer. "I'm in the hardest part of my treatment right now and never feeling too good. I just lie there on the couch all day. I've been on the couch so long I'm getting tired of TV, but I look forward to watching you every day."

The Mariners were only two games out of first place and Chris wanted to see them in the World Series when his Make-A-Wish was fulfilled. He encouraged the team to do their best and he mentioned several of the Mariners' key players by name. He identified with their right-fielder, Jay "The Bone" Buhner, characterized by his shiny bald head and his full goatee. "Ken Griffey is my idol," he wrote, "but a couple of days ago, all my hair fell out so now I look just like Buhner. Since I am only nine, though, I am going to have to wait on the goatee."

Chapter 32

IT MAKES US STRONGER.

C hris sat upright in bed as Mary Lou gently pulled on the tape that held the six-inch tube against his upper left chest. The nurses had left Chris's port accessed the previous day during our visit to Doernbecher. I prepared to hand each item to her from the tray as she requested them.

We'd become accustomed to watching doctors and nurses inject caustic drugs into Chris's veins, but we initially balked when they suggested we do it at home, by ourselves. As part of Delayed Intensification, Chris was facing four consecutive days of vincristine injections for two successive weeks. Kaylee suggested that we could save multiple roundtrips to Doernbecher if we gave him his chemo shots at home. I was all in favor of saving time and gas money, but Mary Lou and I were both aware that if we spilled even one drop of vincristine on Chris's skin, it would burn him severely.

We briefly considered having Chris's pediatrician, Dr. Livermore, administer the injections in his local office, but the only time we had taken that path, it had been nerve-wracking for all of us. It was obvious from the beginning that Dr. Livermore and his nurse were taking extra precautions. He had Chris lie on an exam table and then covered his chest with a surgical drape that had a cutout through which he would access Chris's port. This represented a marked departure from what we were accustomed to at Doernbecher, where they just removed Chris's shirt, scrubbed the area with antiseptic soap, and inserted the needle. Dr. Livermore and his nurse worked so slowly and meticulously that Chris became nervous. His eyes searched out mine several times for reassurance that they knew what they were doing.

"They were all on pins and needles," Chris remembered, "and I'm just sitting there like, 'Okay, give me my shot now. Go ahead and stick the needle in. But they were so nervous because it's not something that they dealt with. Ever. I thought, 'What's the deal? You're a doctor, right? You know about this."

"He was so nervous about making a mistake," said Mary Lou. "He wore a light blue dress shirt and he had huge sweat marks around his armpits." As serious as chemo injections are, they had become routine for us after watching the procedure repeatedly. Having witnessed Dr. Livermore's anxiety the first time, we were a little reluctant to put him through it again.

With some trepidation, we decided to try giving Chris's chemo injections at home. "While we were in Portland," Mary Lou noted, "they accessed his port and left it connected so I could give Chris four nights of chemo treatments. It was scary at first, but I got the hang of it. They showed me what to do and how to do it. They gave me a bag of all the things I needed and I always had Larry there as my assistant. The clinic premeasured the drug. I had the tray all set up with clean swabs, syringes, needles, and flushing fluids."

The procedure called for Mary Lou to clean the opening with an alcohol swab, flush the line with saline, inject the chemo, flush with saline again, and then flush the line again with heparin to prevent clogging. Each time, she used a new needle and a new syringe. She cleaned everything thoroughly with alcohol swabs. I think what made her most nervous were the air bubbles in the syringes. I stood by to help her double-check for those.

"This was quite an experience," she wrote, "and it took me much longer than the nurses! Oh, the things I've learned since Chris was diagnosed! It's amazing the things I can do that I never thought I'd be able to do. This all makes us stronger, right?"

While Mary Lou perfected her nursing skills, I pondered our options, should Chris relapse. We knew that Aaron had relapsed many times, often after apparently being cured. If Chris relapsed, the probable next-step would be a bone marrow transplant. Judy had shared with me that there was only a one in four chance that an immediate family member would be a perfect match. Heather had been such a match for Aaron, but twenty-five percent didn't sound like favorable odds to me. I figured the best way to cover our bases with Chris was to get ahead of the game by testing Matt for marrow compatibility. If he wasn't a match, we could begin enlarging our family one baby at a time until we got a match. Mary Lou and I never discussed the idea in detail, but I wanted to consider all our options. I asked Dr. Jones if we should be testing Matt to see if he was a good marrow match for Chris. If he wasn't, should we begin thinking about having more children?

I didn't realize I was brushing up against a host of ethical issues. As it turns out, not only did some couples consider having additional children to get a donor match, but the advancement of genetic technology would soon provide an opportunity to guarantee the match through a controversial technology called Preimplantation Genetic Diagnosis (PGD). PGD is an invitro fertilization process that involves checking the fertilized egg's DNA makeup before transferring it to the uterus. This technology not only gives parents a chance to hand-pick the right genetic match for a transplant, but it also opens up the concept of "designer babies," where the parents could choose an embryo based on eye color, athletic potential, or a host of other traits.

I was unaware of the technology at the time. Thankfully, Dr. Jones didn't call me crazy; he just told me I was getting way ahead of myself. Chris was "eighty percent there." He was in the optimum age range, he had gone into remission early, he had experienced few of the common side effects experienced by other children, and he had accepted the chemo treatments well. He encouraged me to let things play out.

In late September, Dr. Jones tapered Chris off the dexamethasone and declared an end to his Delayed Intensification. It was time for Chris to begin the transition to the final phase of his treatment, "Maintenance." For the next two-and-a-half-years, Chris's chemotherapy protocol would include prednisone, 6-MP, monthly vincristine injections, and quarterly spinal taps. To anyone else, that may have sounded dreadful. But after what Chris had gone through, this sounded to us like a dream scenario. He would experience some lingering side effects of the Delayed Intensification so he would have to miss his Make-A-Wish trip to the World Series. Chris's white cell counts were still too low for him to travel. Moving among the large crowds at the World Series would put him at risk of getting an infection.

Chris's hair began to grow back in October, but it would be a month and a half before it grew in fully. He gradually began to regain his strength and by the second week of November, Dr. Jones told Chris he was no longer in danger of getting an infection by being around his classmates. It was finally time for him to go back to school.

Chapter 33

LIGHTENING THEIR LOAD

M ary Lou greeted the couple and their baby boy at our front door with a warm smile and a hug. Greg and Tanya Stolt had come by our home to introduce themselves and to share the story of their nine-month-old son, Andrew, who had recently been diagnosed with retinoblastoma, a rare form of eye cancer.

Tanya had been giving Andrew a bath several weeks earlier when she noticed a white spot in his left eye. She became more suspicious when the same spot turned up in photographs she took of Andrew. Greg and Tanya took him to see his pediatrician, who initiated a series of referrals, ultimately leading to Andrew's diagnosis.

The parents were given three options for treatment. They could have Andrew's eye surgically removed; they could have radiation administered to his eye, which would diminish his sight and deform the left side of his face; or they could enroll in a clinical trial that incorporated experimental laser treatments with chemotherapy. They chose to participate in the clinical trials.

The Stolts were one of many families who entered our world after Mary Lou joined a support group for families who had a child with cancer. It all began in November,

1996, six months after Chris's leukemia diagnosis. Chris had continued to rebound and we were becoming more optimistic about his future.

❦

SEVERAL WEEKS BEFORE CHRISTMAS, MARY LOU RECEIVED an invitation for our family to attend a Christmas party at the local Elks Lodge, sponsored by Candlelighters For Children with Cancer, a support group for families who have a child with cancer. The invitation was extended by Rae Ann and Jennifer, two moms who had kids with cancer, and who co-chaired the local chapter.

I recalled seeing photos of Rae Ann's daughter, Rachel, on donation cans in local grocery stores several years earlier in an effort to raise money for her bone marrow transplant. I had paid little attention to it at the time other than to donate a few dollars and ponder the horrors of what it must be like to have a child with cancer.

The Eugene Elks Lodge had sponsored the Candlelighters Christmas party for at least twenty years when we attended the first time. Each year, they provided a buffet meal and raffle prizes for the families. Children were entertained by clowns and face-painters while they awaited a visit by Santa, who brought gifts for all the cancer kids and their siblings.

Youngsters dressed in their holiday best scampered around a polished, hardwood dance floor. From nearby, I overheard several of them say, "He might come! He might come!" I assumed they were speaking of Santa, but I soon learned that they were referring to Dr. Larry Fickenscher, the only pediatric oncologist in our city for more than thirty years. "The kids loved Larry," said Janet Stimson, the manager from the Elks. "In a way, he outdid Santa." When Dr. Fickenscher walked in, the children gathered around him, eager to see their favorite doctor without having to receive an injection. Parents adored him even more, fully aware that he represented a lifeline to their child's survival.

Mary Lou and I were reminded at the Christmas party that it was okay to laugh and have a good time, something we had done sparingly in the recent past. We met at least two dozen families who had a child with cancer. They were dealing with the situation the same way we were, one day at a time. The party refreshed out spirits. As we left, Mary Lou made a prophetic comment about wanting to get more involved with the group.

Mary Lou attended the group's next function in January, a dinner for mothers who had a child with cancer. "Mom's Night Out" allowed the moms to escape for the evening from the difficulties related to having a child with cancer. "Five of us showed up," Mary Lou noted. "It was a nice, small group. We talked mostly of our families and our situations. That made for a lot to talk about!"

It hurt for Mary Lou to share some of her most painful memories, but it was nice to talk to others who could relate. After hearing the other mothers' stories, Mary Lou felt fortunate that Chris was doing so well. He had experienced few of the most severe side effects from his chemo treatments. Other moms talked of their children's suffering, primarily from the side effects of the chemotherapy.

Mary Lou became a regular at Mom's Night Out and began helping with the group's regular events. The monthly functions included an ice cream social, a movie day, an Easter Egg hunt, a barbeque, a horseback-riding day, a pumpkin patch wagon ride, and of course, the Christmas party. Each activity required sending invitations, managing RSVPs, reserving venues, arranging entertainment, and raising the necessary funds to pay for it all, since all the activities were provided at no cost to the families.

With each new story she heard at Mom's Night Out, Mary Lou became more engaged. With each event she helped coordinate, she witnessed the value of providing an outlet for families like ours who struggled with having a child with cancer. Chris was past the worst part of his treatment and had settled into the maintenance portion of his therapy. He hadn't recovered completely, and his journey was far from being easy, but we were blessed with broad support from friends and family. We both had health insurance. Chris certainly suffered, but he experienced fewer of the more serious side effects from his chemo than many of the other children.

Mary Lou shared our good blessings with the other families by doing whatever she could in a support role to lighten their load. When Jennifer and Rae Ann decided to step away from their co-director duties in mid-1998, I was not surprised when Mary Lou volunteered to take their place. It wasn't like she had a lot of free time on her schedule. She taught middle school full time, she coached track at another local middle school in the spring, she volunteered for all the boys' activities at school, she was president of the parent-teacher organization at Chris's school, and she had a child with cancer herself.

But each family and each child she met through Candlelighters found a place in her heart. She knew from our experience with Aaron and other children that all the stories wouldn't end well. She shared her blessings by doing as much as she could for all the other families in our area who found themselves in the same dire situation.

Mary Lou's taking on this new role meant that each child in our area who received a cancer diagnosis was referred to Mary Lou as a resource, usually as they were discharged from Doernbecher. We changed our phone message to, "You've reached the Bradleys and Candlelighters of Eugene. Please leave a message and we'll get right back to you." The message remains the same twenty-four years later.

In future years, the parents of Holly, Mitch, Stevie, Kelsea, Kayla, Jazmyn, Christos, McKenna, and scores of others called Mary Lou when they learned about Candlelighters. Mary Lou's fire was rekindled each time she met a new family. Their unique, but familiar stories reminded her of the despair we felt when we received Chris's diagnosis. She couldn't do anything clinically to help each child, but she could provide the families with comfort, inspiration, and hope.

On the occasion that one of the local Candlelighters children lost their battle with cancer, Mary Lou mourned as if she had lost a member of her immediate family. In many ways, she had. She attended each memorial service, not in an official capacity, but in the same spirit that a loved one would attend.

As more kids died from their cancer, Mary Lou compiled a list of "Angels," children whose lives ended way too soon. She mounted their photos on a large display board and she honors them each year at the Relay for Life.

Mary Lou's participation in Candlelighters is perhaps the most positive thing that has come from Chris's leukemia, second only to his survival. It is the door that opened wide when all the others were slamming closed. None of us had any idea at the time the impact her involvement would have on our family and others, and many families are grateful she chose to walk through the door when given the opportunity.

Chapter 34

THERE'S NO CRYING IN BASEBALL

T he score was tied and there were two outs in the bottom of the last inning. If Chris scored from third base, the game was over and we would win. As the batter stepped into the box, parents and players on both sides of the field screamed as only parents and players can. From my position as first-base coach, I watched across the infield as Casey, the third-base coach, conferred with Chris.

I knew what they were saying without the benefit of hearing their conversation. The opposing pitcher had lost some of his control over the past few innings. He had thrown several wild pitches that rolled twelve feet behind the catcher to the backstop. If it happened again, Chris needed to be ready to steal home. However, any attempt to score on a wild pitch was risky. There was always a chance the ball would hit the wooden backstop and bounce directly back to the catcher as it had done in an earlier inning. Should that happen again, Chris would be dead-on-arrival at home plate.

Chris's health had continued to rebound slowly since his leukemia diagnosis, but he still wouldn't be able to officially rejoin his Babe Ruth baseball team for another year. Casey Hogan, his head coach and presently our third base coach, had made every effort to keep him connected with the team. This particular game was an unofficial preseason game that lacked the rigid requirements associated with regular season games so Casey was able to temporarily add Chris to the roster. Though it was a "practice" game, the teams, the coaches, and the parents approached the contest as if it were a championship game. The game carried more importance to our family since this was Chris's first time on a ballfield since his cancer diagnosis. His hair had grown back and his face was not quite as puffy as before, but he had not yet regained his full strength. He continued to take daily chemo pills and he experienced a number of side effects, including a mild case of peripheral neuropathy, a temporary condition that affected the muscles and nerves in his feet. He couldn't run as fast as he had been able to prior to his cancer.

I feared that Chris wouldn't be able to make it home safely under the most favorable of circumstances. Prior to his leukemia, he had been one of the fastest runners on the team. His only frame of reference on the amount of time it would take him to sprint the sixty feet from third base to home plate was based on his memories from before his illness. I was worried that Casey would over-estimate Chris's current abilities and send him home for the third out. Under my breath, I whispered to Casey, "Don't send him, don't send him," somehow hoping that Casey would receive my message from across the diamond. I knew Chris would feel like he let his team down if he were called out, and I desperately wanted his first game back to be a success.

Casey and Chris finished their discussion and Chris took a step off third. The catcher squatted and gave his signal to the pitcher. Chris stretched his lead as the opposing pitcher went into his wind-up and hurled the ball toward the plate. As I both hoped and feared, the ball hit the dirt and skipped past the catcher and the umpire toward the backstop. The catcher spun and scrambled to retrieve the ball.

Casey had evidently not heard my pleas, since he began yelling to Chris, "Go! Go! Go!" Pandemonium reigned in the stands. The combined roar from the bleachers and both dugouts intensified the drama. Chris launched on command and sprinted toward home. My view from first base allowed me to compare Chris's speed and distance to that of the catcher as he grabbed the ball from the base of the backstop and pivoted toward an inevitable collision at home plate.

The two players plowed into each other and tumbled into a pile of limbs. Only the ump could see if the catcher applied the tag prior to Chris's sliding across home plate. The ump took a moment to add more suspense, as if that were possible, and extended his arms and elbows out to his sides in the universal "safe" sign. He probably called out his decision, too, but the deafening noise prevented me from hearing it.

Years later, Chris recalled what went through his mind as he looked down the third baseline. "I remember it being my first game experience in a while. I got over to third base. I didn't have the same speed that I used to or the strength, but I had the same instincts. I'm watching the ball, and I'm thinking, oh, that's by the catcher, that's far enough back there, so I took off. I've always been good at sports and fast so I still had that mental sports instinct. I remember sliding in there and knowing that I made it and then I looked up at the ump, waiting for the call.

"It really was one of those clichéd, story book endings— Hollywood movie-type thing—but beyond all the clichés, it really was symbolic of me coming back, playing baseball like I had before and scoring the winning run."

Chris's teammates bolted off the bench and sprinted toward home plate, where Chris was untangling himself from the catcher. They hoisted him onto their shoulders and carried him off the field as if he had single-handedly won the World Series.

In the 1992 movie *A League of Their Own*, Tom Hanks famously said, "There's no crying in baseball!" This day would be an exception. Mary Lou told me later that a number of mothers in the bleachers began crying when Chris scored. I stood at first base for longer than usual and allowed myself to recover emotionally before joining in the celebration. Casey told Chris's story to the coach of the opposing team. The coach approached me afterward and gave me a hug. A simple call by the umpire, safe or out, shone brightly as we looked for signs that life might someday return to normal. We were on our way back!

"As a little sidebar to that," added Chris. "That first summer we went down to see the Giants, and I went into the dugout and hung out with Matt Williams. Sometime later, I went to a Chamber of Commerce or Rotary meeting to talk about my cancer experience. I was up on the stage talking and a family friend who had known about my trip to see the Giants asked me to tell about my favorite baseball memory. I'm sure he expected me to talk about my trip down to see the Giants and see the major league players in the dugout. I started talking about this baseball game, my first time back, and how I ended up scoring the winning run, and being carried off the field. The person who asked the question was really surprised. At that moment, I remembered the trip to see the Giants and I thought, "Oh, that memory!"

Chapter 35

WHAT DO YOU THINK?

I can't believe three years are over and no more chemo for Chris!" wrote Mary Lou. "Yesterday, he had his last bone marrow and spinal—he breezed through it. This date seemed like so far away three years ago!" Chris received his final chemo treatment on July 28, 1999. Dr. Jones jokingly offered to continue Chris's chemo treatments if we were willing to make the 200-mile round-trip drive each week. Chris politely declined. He would still need to have a blood test once a month for the first year, an annual checkup for five years, and he would continue to take antibiotics for six months while his immune system recovered completely.

We suspected we weren't out of the woods entirely. Aaron had reached this point in his treatment several times, only to relapse at a later date. Dr. Jones told us that Chris had less than a twenty percent chance of relapse in his first year off treatment; ten percent during the second year; and if he remained cancer-free after two years, we could feel comfortable using the word "cure."

I often think of our leukemia experience in terms of a severe thunderstorm. When Chris was initially diagnosed, it was like being struck by lightning on a day when the forecast called for clear, blue skies. We had no forewarning and we were unprepared for the tempest that followed. Our family and friends quickly provided shelter, however, while Dr. Jones provided a weather forecast for the months and years ahead.

The storm took its initial toll, but within six months the darkest clouds had passed. Chris's two-and-a-half-year maintenance phase felt less like a severe storm and more like the continual rains we experience in the northwest. They can be depressing and make you wonder occasionally if the sun is ever going to come out again, but people generally go to work and function normally without the fear of being hit by lightning. It's a matter of hunkering down and awaiting the renewal of Spring. The longer Chris's cancer stayed away, the more feint the storm clouds became. But even on the sunniest days today, I sometimes view the horizon with suspicion, knowing the clouds could still exist just beyond my view.

Chris suffered from very few of the severe side effects from all the chemo drugs he was given over the three-year course of his treatment. He was never re-hospitalized; he didn't experience the terrible mouth ulcers suffered by so many children; and he rarely missed any treatments due to low white-cell counts.

Through Mary Lou's involvement with Candlelighters, however, we know many children whose experiences resemble back-to-back thunderstorms for the entire length of their treatment. They are in and out of the hospital regularly, they spike high fevers consistently, and they suffer from myriad physical ailments and behavioral side effects. Their parents are decimated financially and their family relationships are stretched beyond the breaking point.

In a moment of reflection, Mary Lou once told Judy how sad she was that Aaron's leukemia had taken his life.

She asked her sister if she ever resented the fact that Aaron died and Chris survived. Judy said the thought had never entered her mind. She was as joyful as we were that Chris did so well. There was no way she could live her life feeling angry and resentful about Chris's survival.

After Chris's final treatment, our family visited the Major League Baseball Hall of Fame in Cooperstown, New York, where we learned that the annual induction ceremonies were planned for the week following our scheduled return to Eugene. Some of the best players of all time, and several of Chris's baseball heroes, were to be inducted, including George Brett, Robin Yount, Nolan Ryan, and Orlando Cepeda. To witness such an event would be quite an experience for any baseball fan. If we extended our stay, however, we would miss the Relay for Life, scheduled at the same time at home.

Baseball has always been paramount in our lives. To see a Hall of Fame induction ceremony was a once-in-a-lifetime opportunity. But Chris's cancer experience had elevated the Relay to a high priority in his life. Mary Lou was fine with extending our stay in New York, as was Matt. When I approached Chris, I said, "It's up to you. What do you want to do?"

"What do you think?" he replied. I'll admit I had no idea. He was such a huge baseball fan, but his experience with cancer had altered his life and changed his perspective in many ways. I asked him once again.

"What you think?" he answered for a second time, with the impatience of someone who refused to state the obvious. He never did tell me his preference, but he didn't object when we packed our bags and headed to the airport to fly home on schedule.

Chapter 36

THAT MIXTURE OF HORROR AND SYMPATHY

"I don't even know where to start with Michael," Tracy said. "We were diagnosed with anaplastic large cell lymphoma when he was sixteen." Cancer moms always speak in the plural when discussing their child's diagnosis: "We were diagnosed;" "We were hospitalized."

Tracy had been coming to Mom's Night Out for about three years, making her a veteran in the eyes of the newcomers. "They said that I hadn't given the antibiotics enough time to work and they tried to send us home again. I said, 'He does not have an infection! He is dehydrated as hell and he needs some fluids. You need to put him in the hospital right now!' They asked me if I was a nurse and I told them, 'No, I am a mother and I know my son!'

"They finally did a biopsy. They called Monday morning and said we needed to get Mike to Doernbecher immediately. 'He has cancer,' she said. Those were her very words." Several of the mothers around the table nodded silently in response to Tracy's comments. Each mom could remember a specific incident when she learned to be her child's unwavering advocate.

The dinner gathering resembled an Alcoholics Anonymous meeting-turned-dinner-party. The dozen mothers around the table attended the monthly event to offer and receive support. The attendance was always a little larger in September, when Mary Lou scheduled the meeting at the Olive Garden restaurant because of their all-you-can-eat pasta special. Having a large group was not necessarily the goal. Mary Lou encouraged as much participation as possible, but newer participants sometimes felt more comfortable in the intimacy of a smaller gathering. They smiled tentatively, as if they needed to be taught again how to have a good time, and given permission to do so. It's not easy to enjoy dinner with friends when you have a child at home with cancer, no matter how well your child happens to be doing at the moment.

It was just as easy to spot the veteran mothers. Most of them had long ago given themselves permission to live and laugh again without feeling guilty. They chatted like sorority sisters, making it more of a gabfest than a cryfest. The seasoned moms had adopted the Candlelighters motto, "It is better to light a candle than to curse the darkness."

Two weeks after Chris received his last chemo treatment, Mary Lou received word that Jordan Thompson, the four-year-old son of a fellow baseball mom, Robyn, had been diagnosed with leukemia. Robyn joined Candlelighters and as soon as Jordan was stable, she volunteered to be co-director of the group alongside Mary Lou.

Mary Lou and Robyn had begun the informal dinner gathering in their normal manner by asking the moms to introduce themselves and say something about their child, and how they came to Candlelighters.

"I'm Anne," another mother began. My son, Ian, had Ewing's Sarcoma when he was nine," she said. The veteran mothers exchanged knowing glances. Some of them knew nearly as much about the other children's cancers as they did about their own child's illness. "Ian had a fist-sized lump in his leg," Anne said. "Lucky for us, Dr. Fickenscher was already our pediatrician." More glances. If cancer struck your child, you likely received a quicker diagnosis and a better long-term prognosis if Dr. Fickenscher was already your child's pediatrician.

"They shrank the tumor down using chemotherapy and then Ian had a bone transplant. One of the toughest things for Ian happened the morning of his surgery. Up to that day, he hadn't said much. He just listened to the doctors and did what he was told. I'd repeatedly told him that he needed to be more of a fighter and that he needed to fend for himself. But he never did. Then he woke up the morning of the surgery and he said, 'I don't know why I have to get my leg cut in half.' He refused to get out of bed.

"It took so much courage for him to finally put his foot down, but he chose the wrong time to do it. But today Ian is eighteen and he is doing okay." The veteran mothers recognized "okay" to mean "I am happy my child is alive, and we'll deal with anything else if and when it comes."

The mothers chuckled when the next mom, Janice, described how she told the doctor to "pull his head out of his ass" after he told her there was nothing wrong with her son, Matt, and accused her of being a paranoid first-time mom. She took Matt directly to the hospital, where he was diagnosed with two types of cancer. Janice's persistence likely saved her son's life.

Robin told the story of how she and her husband had decided not to have children, only to change their minds later on. She was still dealing with the irony and the injustice of having their only child, Kate, diagnosed with cancer.

Kallee's daughter, Kadence, had been diagnosed with tumors in her brain and in her spine. She praised her daughter's bright spirit and resilience after undergoing her ninth cranial surgery.

The mothers' stories became more incredulous as they made their way around the table. Mary Lou once told me, "Each family's story has a "wow factor.""

"We were diagnosed on May 10, 1999," the next mother said. She would never have said, "in early to mid-May" or "the second week of May" when referring to her child's diagnosis. For each mother, the diagnosis date for her child represented the end of normal life and the beginning of survival.

"I come here," a mother named Lori explained, "because I can talk about my son and his cancers and you don't look at me with that mixture of horror and sympathy."

Some of the mothers' stories were still in the early chapters. Laura, a forty-two-year-old nurse, whose two-year-old daughter had been diagnosed with an invasive brain tumor, was still coming to terms with her new life. "We used to make plans," she said. "We were going to buy some property and put animals on it. It was going to be sort of a bed and breakfast, a little farm where people come to visit the animals. Then right in the middle of it, McKenna got sick. Only recently have we started to think a little about the future again. Everything that seemed so important prior to the cancer now seems so small."

Stacey joined Candlelighters through the most unlikely of circumstances. "I was a front-end manager at Fred Meyer," she said. "Mary Lou and Robyn came in to do their shopping for the Christmas party. While I was ringing them, they told me about Candlelighters. I remember saying, 'God, I could not even imagine.' That was the second week in November and not two months later, my daughter got leukemia. That was the first interaction I had with Candle-lighters. I had no idea that I would be a part of it."

Each mom knew the what and the when of her child's cancer; none knew the how, nor the why. Their stories came together like pieces of a quilt. Each carried its own identity, but sewn together in a harmonious pattern with a common thread, they stitched together a cloak that comforted all of them. Today, the quilt unfortunately remains a work in progress, allowing for additional pieces to be added as new children are diagnosed with cancer.

"Most of you know our story," Mary Lou said, when the introductions came full circle. "I've been involved with Candlelighters since shortly after Chris was diagnosed in 1996. What you may not know is that my involvement with kids with cancer began more than forty years ago, with my sister and her two-year old son, Aaron. I was a twenty-year-old sophomore at the University of Oregon when I returned one day from running in a track meet to find one of our old family friends waiting for me at the Tri-Delta sorority house. She told me that she had some bad news to share with me."

EPILOGUE

More than thirty percent of the 16,000 new childhood cancer cases diagnosed this year in the US will be for acute lymphocytic leukemia. Ninety-five percent of children with ALL can be cured and more than eighty percent of children with other cancers will survive more than five years due primarily to the more than one hundred clinical trials open at any given time. Nearly all of the children of the Candlelighters moms I interviewed for this book have their child enrolled in at least one clinical trial.

Clinical trials have been part of the medical landscape for more than 250 years and will always play a major part in advancing scientific knowledge. The groundbreaking developments in the future are likely to be as controversial as the medical advances discussed in this book.

When Dr. E. Donnall Thomas explored the potential benefit of bone marrow transplants, he did so without the support of the broader medical community, who considered his methods to be reckless. When MD Anderson's Dr. Freireich suggested that patients be given heavy doses of drugs concurrently instead of sequentially, his peers thought he would be putting his patients at unnecessary levels of risk.

Sidney Farber, who developed aminopterin, or methotrexate, "was totally on his own," according to Dr. Archie Bleyer. "He had no support to do what he did. Nobody wanted to be with that guy. That's true of most of the innovators, pioneers. That's why they are pioneers."

One of the most promising, yet controversial areas of medical exploration today is the study of immunology, specifically CAR-T cells. "You'll hear that a lot during the next years," said Dr. Bleyer. "CAR-T, or Chimeric Antigen Receptor T cells. It's pretty exciting stuff, but it's like the early days of bone marrow transplants. It is either awful, ugly, deathly, or it's curative. If there's a Nobel Prize to be handed out in the leukemia world, it's going to be for CAR-T in ten or twenty years. But the danger of it is still so obvious that it's very experimental. I'll predict that it will replace bone marrow transplants."

Genetic testing has recently proved to be fertile ground in discovering genetic predispositions for contracting ALL. In a 2013 study published by Memorial Sloan Kettering Cancer Center, researchers claimed to have found a gene mutation tied to a heritable form of ALL. Scientists gathered data on every member of a family who had been touched by ALL over several generations. The gene, called PAX5, was carried by each person in the family. Further research is needed, but perhaps one day we will discover a genetic connection that explains why Judy and Mary Lou both had sons afflicted with the disease.

Children and their parents who receive a cancer diagnosis in the future will face the same choices of whether or not to participate in a clinical trial, one in which their participation may be more likely to contribute to research than it is to cure their child. The answers for them will be no less clear than they were for Judy, Mary Lou, or other families who predated them.

The development of future clinical trials will depend on the courage of researchers like Drs. Sydney Farber, E. Donnall Thomas, Emil J. Freireich, Jean Sanders, Hansjorg Riehm, and Archie Bleyer. Their willingness to risk their professional reputations and face their own personal trials may be crucial to unlocking the next scientific breakthrough.

Today, Chris's leukemia survival is an important part, but not the central focus of his life. As a young adult, he adopted the camp name, Styx, and returned to UKANDU as a counselor. When he can, he returns from Western Europe, where he lives with his wife and their young daughter, to attend the Relay for Life. It has been more than two decades since his diagnosis, so fewer people in his immediate circle know that he fought cancer as a child.

"With friends I've had for several months or a couple of years, I never know whether they know that I had cancer or not," he said. "It's not like you walk up to everyone and say, "Hi, I'm Chris and I had leukemia when I was nine years old. It might be six months down the line when I'm with a new friend and something about cancer comes on TV and an opportunity arises where I might share that I had cancer.

"I had a very serious illness and my cousin died from it. I feel lucky because we were in a situation where it strained us, but we got through it. What I went through was pretty crappy, but seeing what other kids were going through at Doernbecher at the time, it really changed my perspective. I feel lucky to have had the experience I did compared to the hundreds and thousands who weren't so lucky and had worse types of cancer."

Mary Lou retired from teaching in 2016, but she will likely never relinquish her volunteer duties with Candlelighters. She and Robyn are in their third decade of hosting

Mom's Night Out and organizing monthly family activities for children in our community diagnosed with cancer. Mary Lou continues to participate each year in the American Cancer Society's Relay for Life. She also works as a liaison between Candlelighters and her sorority, Delta Delta Delta.

Judy and Doug retired to upstate New York in 2005. Doug died in 2017 from complications after knee replacement surgery. Every year, Judy commemorates the dates of Aaron's birth and his passing. She travels often to visit with her family.

Keith and his wife, Terry, live in University Place, about a mile from where Aaron lived on the beach. Keith spends his time reading, walking his dog, and fly-fishing. He and Judy stay connected. He sees Heather and her family about once a year.

Heather lives with her husband and their three children in the Mountain West. Their youngest child is a son is named Aaron.

Matt lives in Eugene, Oregon, where he is co-founder and executive director of Whole Earth Nature School.

The author's mother, Jean, who supported Chris throughout his years of treatment, died in 2001 of a rare lung disease at age 66.

Jeanne completes the *NY Times* crossword puzzle daily, she works out at the YMCA three times a week, and she stays connected to the lives of her six grandchildren and five great grandchildren.

The author lives in Eugene, Oregon, where he is working on his next book.

ACKNOWLEDGMENTS

My sincere gratitude to the following:

To my wife, Mary Lou, for her endless love and support through a very long journey.

To my editor, Elizabeth Lyon, for your guidance through a very long process.

To Bob Welch for your great suggestions and your finishing touches.

To Mary Lou and Judy for sharing your private journals and your personal insights.

To Chris, Matt, Keith, Doug, Heather, and Jeanne for taking this journey with me.

To Drs. Archie Bleyer, Gary Jones, Larry Fickenscher, Douglas Livermore, Dan Niebrugge, Jean Sanders, Klaus Siebold, and Michael Soronen for sharing your medical experience and expertise.

To Nurses Kaylee Ray, Andrea York, Pat Groff, and all the other oncology nurses for your courage, your self-sacrifice, and your dedication.

To the many Candlelighters parents who shared their most personal stories.

To my readers, who improved this work beyond what I could have accomplished on my own: Tim and Carolyn Armstrong, Jeanne Armstrong, Sheron Bradley, and Shelley Morrison.

BIBLIOGRAPHY

"About Clinical Trials: Information from the National Cancer Institute." OHSU Health. Accessed 17 October 2008. http//www.ohsucancer.com/index. asp?fuseaction=trials.whatis.

"Advances in Patient Care and Research at Dana-Farber." Accessed 21 October 2009. https://www.dana-farber. org/abo/history/advances/default.html

"Albany parent convicted of manslaughter in faith-healing death of daughter with diabetes." *Oregonlive.com*. 11 November 2014. Accessed 17 April 2020. https:// www.oregonlive.com/pacific-northwest-news/2014/11/ albany_parents_convicted_of_ma.html

Anderson, Barbara. "Females Held Their Own on 7.6-Mile." *The News Tribune. 10 June 1973 Kitsup Sun.* 28 March 2001. Accessed 9 January 2020. https://products.kit-sapsun.com/archive/2001/03-28/0089_fred_hutchin-son_cancer_research_c.html

Bayefsky, Michelle. "Who Should Regulate Preimplantation Genetic Diagnosis in the United States?" *AMA Journal of Ethics.* Accessed 17 April 2020. https:// journalofethics.ama-assn.org/article/who-should-regulate-preimplantation-genetic-diagnosis-united-states/2018-12

Belson, Martin; Adrianne Holmes; and Beverley Kingsley. "Risk Factors for Acute Leukemia in Children: A Review." National Institute of Environmental Health Sciences. 19 March 2007 Accessed 31 March 2009. http://www.medscape.com/viewarticle/553132

Bluebond-Langner, Myra. "The Private Worlds of Dying Children." Princeton, New Jersey, Princeton University Press, 1978

Bradbury, Will. "An All-Out Assault on Leukemia." *Life* magazine. (November 1966):

Bush, Barbara. "Barbara Bush, A Memoir." Lisa Drew Books, Charles Scribner's Sons, 1994.

"Camp Goodtimes- A Summer Getaway Gives Youngsters A Break From Medical and Social Struggles of Cancer." *The Seattle Times.* Linda Keene. 27 June 1996. Accessed 3 June 2009. http://community.seattletimes.nwsource.com/archive/?date=19960627&slug=2336642

"Camp Goodtimes West: A place where kids can be kids." The American Cancer Society. Accessed 27 January 2009. http://www.cancer.org/docroot/COM/content/div_Northwest/COM_5_1x_Camp_Goodtimes.asp

"Cancer Reference Information: Clinical Trials." American Cancer Society. Accessed 11 April 2009. http://cancer.org/docroot/CRI/content/CRI_2_4_4X_Clinical_Trials_24.asp?rnav+cri.

"Childhood Cancer Facts." The National Children's Cancer Society. Accessed 20 April 2020. https://www.thenccs.org/cancerfacts

"Childhood Leukemia Was Practically Untreatable Until Dr. Don Pinkel and St. Jude Found a Cure." *Smithsonian* magazine. July 2016. Accessed 10 March 2020. https://www.smithsonianmag.com/innovation/childhood-leukemia-untreatable-dr-don-pinkel-st-jude-180959501/

"Children and Clinical Studies." Seattle Cancer Care Alliance. Accessed 16 September 2010. http://seattlecca.org/clinical-trials-children.cfm

Christ, Janet. "Wishing on a Parasol." *The Oregonian. 16 September 1996.*

"Chronological Listing of U.S. Milers Who Have Broken 4:00 In the Mile." *Track & Field News.* Accessed 19 June 2008 http://www.trackandfieldnews.com/archive.ussub4s.html

Cody, Mrs. James. "The Miracle at St. Jude." *Family Health/Today's Health.* (November, 1976):58-60.

Daniels, Penny and Terry Willesee. *A Current Affair.* 1986

Davison, Dave R. "Triumphant Trek." *Tacoma Weekly.* Accessed 21 February 2010. http://www.tacomaweekly.com/article/3228/

De Vries, Peter. "The Blood of the Lamb." Boston and Toronto: Little, Brown and Company, 1961. Burton, Natasha. "Divorce, Cancer Delinked: Child's Illness Doesn't Tear Up Marriage." *Huffington Post.*11 June 2012. Accessed 26 January 2019. http://www.huffpost.com/entry/divorce-cancer-child-illness-danish-study_b_1418122

Fertig, Angela R. "Healthy Baby, Healthy Marriage? The Effect of Children's Health on Divorce." Princeton University. June 2004.

"Five-Year Cancer Survival Rates 1962 vs. Present." St. Jude Children's Research Hospital. Accessed 6 November 2006. http://www.stjude.org/media/0.2561.453_2086_20345.00.html

Fleming, Alice and Tom Fleming. "Cancer in Children." *Cosmopolitan*. 155, No.2 (August, 1963):53-57

Foley, Genevieve and Marie McCarthy. "The Child With Leukemia, The disease and its treatment." *American Journal of Nursing*. 76, No. 7 (July, 1976): 1109-1114

Frei III, Emil; James F. Holland; O. Ross McIntyre; and Richard L. Schilsky. "A Concise History of the Cancer and Leukemia Group B." *American Association for Cancer Research Journals*. 1 June 2006. Accessed 15 October 2008. www.acrrjournals.org.

"Frontal Attack." *Time* magazine. Vol. LIII No. 26. 27 June 1949: 66-75

Glaser, Barney G. and Anselm L. Strauss. "Awareness of Dying." New Brunswick, New Jersey: Aldine Transaction, 2009.

Hill, Craig. "Sound to Narrows Strategy from two of its best runners." *The News Tribune*. Accessed 21 February 2010. http://blogs.thenewstribune.com/adventure/2008/06/12/p27175

"History of Relay for Life." American Cancer Society. Accessed 27 January 2009. http://www.cancer.org/doc-

root/PAR/Content/PAR_1_4_History_of_Relay_For_
Life.asp

Ipswitch, Elaine. "Scott Was Here." New York: Delacorte
Press, 1979.

"Kids like Rita: A doctor's drive to save children from deadly
blood cancers." *Fred Hutch News Service.* 2015. Accessed
12 February 2018. https://www.fredhutch.org/en/news/
center-news/2015/12/jean-sanders-saving-children.html

Karon, Myron and Joel Vernick. "Who's Afraid of Death on
a Leukemia Ward?" *Journal of the American Medical
Association Pediatrics.* May 1965. 393-397

Klein, Melissa. "The Legacy of the 'Yellow Berets.'" National
Institutes of Health. Bethesda, MD. 1998

Krueger, Gretchen. "Hope and Suffering: Children, Cancer,
and the Paradox of Experimental Medicine." Baltimore:
The John Hopkins University Press, 2008.

Kruse, Brandi. "Fred Hutch says farewell to beloved doctor."
MYNorthwest. 28 June 2012.

Kubler-Ross, Elizabeth MD. "On Children and Death: How
children and their parents can and do cope with death."
New York: Touchstone, 1983.

Kunkle, Dick. "Sound to Narrows: A Gathering Of A Few
Has Become A Happening." *The News Tribune.* 13
June 2009.

Lazlo, John MD. "The Cure of Childhood Leukemia: Into
the Age of Miracles." New Jersey: Rutgers University
Press, 1995.

"Lesson learned at Hutch helping dogs with lymphoma." *The Seattle Times.* 18 June 2014

"Man Describes Son's Death." *The Register Guard. 19 April 1996*

"Many Scientist Believe that the Dog Genome Holds a Wealth of Information that Will Benefit Human Health." Fred Hutchinson Cancer Center. Accessed 19 April 2020. https://www.fredhutch.org/en/news/releases/2004/05/doggenome.html

Martinson, Ida. "The Child with Leukemia, Parent help each other." *American Journal of Nursing.* 76, No. 7 (July, 1976): 1120-1122.

McGlauflin, Shannon; Jolene Munger; and Rebecca Nelson. "History of Leukemia." Accessed 11 April 2009. http://rebeccanelson.com/leukemia/history.html.

Moore, Kenny. "Bowerman and the Men of Oregon: The Story of Oregon's Legendary Coach and Nike's Cofounder." Emmaus, Pennsylvania. Rodale. 2006.

"Parents with sick children create siblings as tissue donors." *Medical News Today.* 6 May 2004.Accessed 12 April 2009. http://www.medicalnewstoday.com/articles/8001.php

Patterson, James T. "The Dread Disease." Cambridge, Massachusetts: Harvard University Press, 1987.

Perlmutter, Ellen. "What science has learned from treating leukemia patients like Jim Stewart gives Alex Myers a better chance." *Pittsburgh Post-Gazette.* 23 December 1997. Accessed 14 October 2009. http://www.post-gazette.com/pg/09168/977754-114.stm

Pinkel, Don. "Current issues in the management of children with acute lymphocytic leukemia." *Postgraduate Medical Journal.* (1985) 93-102.

Pochedly, Carl MD. "Cancer in Children: Reasons for HOPE. Port Washington, New York: Ashley Brooks, Inc., 1979.

Podolsky, M. Lawrence, MD. "Cures out of Chaos: How Unexpected Discoveries Led to Breakthroughs in Medicine and Health." Gordon and Breach, 1997.

Porterfield, Elaine. "Aaron Triumphs over the 'bad guys.'" *The News Tribune. 1 July 1986*

Ross, Walter. "The Official History of The American Cancer Society." New York: Arbor House, 1987.

Ross, Walter. "What Parents Should Know About Childhood Cancer." *The Reader's Digest.* (March, 1967): 83-87.

Sanders, Jean E. "Hematopoietic Cell Transplantation- How we got to where we are today."(2015)

Steelquist, Colleen. "Sanders Gives ALL Children Hope." Fred Hutchinson Cancer Center. 17 February 2005. Accessed 27 January 2009 http://www.fhcrc.org/about/pubs/center_news/2005/feb17/sart1.html

"Tacoma Narrows Bridge: Correcting the bounce too late." *Washington State Department of Transportation Connections.* Accessed 2 February 2019. https://www.wsdot.wa.gov/tnbhistory/connections/connections3.htm

"The Battle Over Faith Healing." *The Oregonian. Accessed 21 July 2008. http://blog.oregonlive.com/clackamas-county/2008/03/post/html*

"The Man Who Cured Leukemia." MD Anderson Cancer Center. Accessed 20 April 2020. https://www.mdanderson.org/publications/annual-report/annual-report-2015/the-man-who-helped-cure-childhood-leukemia.html

"20-20: By His Father's Hand: The Zumwalts." *ABC News*. Av Westin, Ena Riisna, John Laurence, Hugh Downs, Barbara Walters. 2 October 1986

"Understanding Clinical Trials." U.S. National Institutes of Health. Accessed 19 June 2008. http://clinicaltrials.gov/ct2/info/understand.

U.S. childhood cancer survival, 1973-1987. U.S. National Library of Medicine. Accessed 20 April 2020. https://www.ncbi.nlm.nih.gov/pubmed/7935174

"Who was Sydney Farber?" Dana Farber Cancer Institute. Accessed 21 October 2010. https://dana-farber.org/abo/history/who/.

Zumwalt, Admiral Elmo Zumwalt, Jr., Lieutenant Elmo Zumwalt III, and John Pekkanen. "My Father, My Son." New York: Macmillan, 1986.

ABOUT THE AUTHOR

In addition to being the father of a childhood cancer patient, Larry Bradley has volunteered for more than two decades with variety of cancer-support organizations, including the American Cancer Society's Relay for Life and Candlelighters for Children with Cancer.

Bradley retired in 2018 after a thirty-year career in sales and marketing. He and Mary Lou, his wife of forty years, live in Eugene, Oregon. They have two grown sons and two grandchildren.

Contact Information

Website: www.larrybradley.net
FB: The Author Larry Bradley
Twitter: @writerlarryb
Instagram: thelarrybradley
Email: le_bradley@comcast.net

Made in the USA
Middletown, DE
06 April 2021